The EFFECTIVE MINISTER of EDUCATION

A COMPREHENSIVE HANDBOOK

JERRY M. STUBBLEFIELD

BROADMAN
& HOLMAN
PUBLISHERS

Nashville, Tennessee

Scripture quotations marked (NASB) are from the *New American Standard Bible.* © The Lockman Foundation, 1960, 1962, 1963, 1968, 1971, 1972, 1973, 1975, 1977. Used by permission. References marked (NIV) are from the Holy Bible, *New International Version,* copyright © 1973, 1978, 1984 by International Bible Society. References marked (RSV) are from the *Revised Standard Version of the Bible,* copyrighted 1946, 1952, © 1971, 1973.

Library of Congress Cataloging-in-Publication Data

Stubblefield, Jerry M., 1936-
    The effective minister of education : the role of the minister of
education / Jerry M. Stubblefield.
        p.   cm.
    Includes bibliographical references and indexes.
    ISBN 0-8054-1062-7
    1. Christian education directors.   2. Christian education—
Philosophy.   I. Title.
BV1531.S683   1993
268—dc20   92-26105
                                                            CIP

Preface

In 1970 I became Minister of Education of the First Baptist Church, Greenville, South Carolina. I looked for books, articles, and pamphlets to help me understand the role of the educational minister. I had seminary training, earning the B.D., the M.R.E., and the Ed.D. degrees in Christian education. I found many books about staff relations, but none were directed specifically to my primary question: What does a minister of education do? The greatest help came from my professor and mentor, Ernest J. Loessner, a former minister of education and then seminary professor. His class notes and personal discussions proved very valuable to me.

In 1951, Findley Edge wrote this about the minister of education: "There is such a scarcity of material dealing with this field as a vocation that there is a great need for a complete book to be published that would serve as a guide for those who serve in this vocation."[1] There are several booklets that address various aspects of the work of the minister of education. I do not know of a single comprehensive volume to which the educational minister can turn.

Having taught a seminary course on the role of ministers of education for several years, I have had a difficult task selecting textbooks. This book is written for several reasons. First, I intend it to meet the need for a one volume book on the minister of education; it could be a textbook for college and seminary courses for potential ministers of education. A second purpose is that persons thinking about entering the ministry of education can measure their gifts, abilities, and skills against those needed by a minister of education. A third purpose is to clarify roles and duties ministers of education are expected to fulfill. Potentially a fourth is to assist pastors and church personnel committees. A pastor reading this book would have better knowledge of the work of the minister of education. By knowing what this staff member gives to the work and ministry of the church, the pastor is better qualified to provide adequate supervision. Church personnel committees could use this book to draw up job descriptions for ministers of education and clarify expectations and duties for them.

Who is a minister of education? Harry Munro stated:

> The director of religious education is a technically trained religious educator employed by the local church to have general charge of the educational aspects of its total program, and standing beside the minister as a professional member of the church staff.[2]

W. L. Howse, writing more than thirty years later, added, "A minister of education is a person called of God, adequately trained, and employed by a church to devote all or the major portion of his time to the educational work of the church."[3] Maria Harris identified the director of religious education as "a person who is a hired, salaried professional engaged by a parish to direct, organize and/or consolidate religious education programs within the parish."[4] In the Catholic church these directors are new, co-official, non-ordained staff members. She saw these persons as having skills in theology, education, and administration.[5] Donald Emler followed her pattern, saying the title "DRE" designates "the professional nonclergy person charged to lead the local church's educational ministry. The DRE has met the basic qualifications set by the denomination for educational certification at its highest professional level."[6]

My definition of a minister of education is this:

> A minister of education is a person called of God, trained as a Christian educator, called by a local church to provide leadership to the educational aspects of the church's total program, committed to devoting major time to the educational work of the church, and regarded as one who stands beside the senior minister as a professional member of the church staff.

For many years the director of religious or Christian education went by the initials "DRE" or "DCE." The minister of religious or Christian education has used "MRE" or "MCE." In part one, I use the titles appropriate to various periods of time. In the rest of the book, "ME" is used to mean the minister of education. This ministry is open to men and women, so both masculine and feminine pronouns are used throughout the book.

This book is written experientially. While there are many references cited it was not my intent to write from a research viewpoint.

I have tried to share my insights and some of my struggles. I have slanted this book toward the practical work of the minister of education.

The book is arranged in four major divisions answering four questions:

- Who is the minister of education?
- What does he/she do (competency skills needed)?
- What are his/her important relationships?
- How does one get started as a minister of education?

Readers also will find the book can be read sequentially, or it can be consulted for major sections or an individual chapter. Each chapter stands alone but references may be made to other portions of the book as appropriate.

Many persons contributed to my awareness of the work of the minister of education. I am grateful to my religious education professors at the Southern Baptist Theological Seminary: Ernest J. Loessner, Findley B. Edge, Robert A. Proctor, Sabin P. Landry, William R. Cromer, Jr., and Allen W. Graves. They opened my eyes to the potential ministry of Christian education in the local church by showing me how the church could reach its maximum potential through the educational process. Not only were they good role models, but they were also encouragers and friends. My colleague at Golden Gate Baptist Theological Seminary, J. Roger Skelton, shared many insights and a deep love for the church and its educational ministry with me.

For more than thirty years I have associated with ministers of education. I have learned much from them. I have been enriched by their professionalism and their great love for Christ and the church. Their friendships have greatly enriched my life and my ministry. I served two churches as Minister of Education: the First Baptist Church, Greenville, South Carolina, where I served for five years, and the Tiburon Baptist Church, Tiburon, California, where I served part-time for three years. The Greenville Church called a novice to serve a church rich in educational history and tradition. It was in this church that I learned theory could be translated into practice. Tiburon kept my teaching at the seminary honest as I translated theory into practice. Both churches reinforced my convictions about the competency of the people of God to carry out the teaching ministry of the church.

Many persons contributed to the completion of this project. I am grateful to my wife, Joanne, for her help in putting the book into a

better stylistic form. She has been supportive and encouraging, not
only for this project, but throughout my ministry. Several persons
read the manuscript and offered helpful suggestions that strengthened
the work. Those who read the complete manuscript were Ernest J.
Loessner, J. Roger Skelton, Michael Harton, and Mancil Ezell.
Daniel Aleshire was helpful on the chapter, "Theologian"; Barry
Stricker also read it and made many perceptive suggestions. Terry
Swift read the chapter on "Personal and Family Relations." A
special word of appreciation is expressed to my classes on "The
Minister of Education." Much of this material was presented to
them. They provided helpful suggestions and clarified and strengthen
the ideas. Barbara Gross, my secretary, helped with the computer
diskettes and the printing of the manuscript. She also helped put
the figures into good form. Each person's contribution is greatly
appreciated. If there are flaws in the book, I am responsible for
them.

I am grateful to the administration of Golden Gate Baptist
Theological Seminary for a semester sabbatical that permitted me
to complete the manuscript and for their continued encouragement
and supportive spirits.

Notes

1. Findley B. Edge, *Does God Want You as a Minister of Education?* (Nashville,
Broadman Press, 1951), Preface.
2. Harry C. Munro, *The Director of Religious Education* (Philadelphia: The
Westminster Press, 1930), 16.
3. W. L. Howse, *The Minister of Education* (Nashville: Convention Press, n.d.),
11.
4. Maria Harris, *The D.R.E. Book: Questions and Strategies for Parish Personnel*
(New York: Paulist Press, 1976), 2. Her book is written for directors of religious
education functioning in the Catholic church.
5. Ibid., 3.
6. Donald G. Emler, *Revisioning the DRE* (Birmingham: Religious Education
Press, 1989), 4. Emler was a faculty member at Centenary College when he wrote
this book.

CONTENTS

Part III
What Are the ME's Relationships?

Part IV
How to Get Started as an ME

Part I

Who Is the
Minister of Education?

Part I seeks to answer the question: Who is the minister of education? It is crucial that MEs accept who they are if they are to work effectively in this ministry.

Chapter 1 describes the biblical idea of calling, various spiritual gifts, different New Testament ministry functions, and the work of ministry. This chapter establishes a biblical basis for the person and work of the ME.

A historical survey of the ME profession is made in chapter 2. The functions common to MEs are traced from biblical times; then more modern antecedents are recounted. The ME is a phenomenon of the twentieth century. Attention focuses on the beginning of the ME role to its maturing in the early 1990s.

Chapter 3 delineates the special attributes needed by MEs to serve effectively in their educational and personal leadership roles. Unique personal traits needed by the ME are reviewed.

Professional aspects are explored in chapter 4. Areas considered include education and professional training, being a church-centered person, commitment to evangelism, the issue of ordination, plus competency skills essential for the ME.

Part I concludes with an experiential reporting of thoughts MEs shared with me about their joys in educational ministries.

1

One Calling—
Varieties of Expression

The New Testament identifies a variety of ministers—pastors, evangelists, and teachers. The pastoral ministry has existed since New Testament days. Teachers functioning as ministers also served alongside pastors during the Early Church era. They recognized a variety of ministerial expressions. The New Testament emphasizes that a pastor should be "able to teach" (1 Tim. 3:2, NIV). All ministers have a teaching function to fulfill. One purpose of this chapter is to illustrate the biblical antecedents of the ME's position.

While the New Testament church had no problem receiving a teaching minister, the twentieth-century church sometimes has a different perspective. This is seen in the way church members view the calling of a minister. In the congregational tradition, when a church needs a pastor or senior minister, they appoint a pastor search committee (also called a pulpit committee). They gather resumes on potential candidates, screen them, and recommend the person they feel the Holy Spirit is leading them to call as their minister. The church then issues a "call" to this person to become pastor or senior minister.

When a church seeks an ME (or other staff member), the personnel or other appropriate church committee has the responsibility. This committee follows the same procedures and processes as the pastor search committee. Rather than "call" the candidate, the church often votes to "employ" or "hire" the staff person.

These examples illustrate different attitudes church members and churches have about the various ministers and ministries within the church. This raises the following questions to examine and answer:

- What does the Bible teach about ministerial calling?
- Is there a hierarchy of Christian callings?

- Should a church "call" a pastor and "employ" or "hire" other staff ministers?
  - What is the work of ministry?
  - Is the ministry of education a valid ministry?

This chapter seeks to answer these and other pertinent questions and issues.

A Practical Concern

Before discussing these questions and issues, a practical concern must be considered. For most of my ministry I worked in a support or secondary position. I taught both at the college and seminary level. I served as one of several professors in the department of religion and religious education and was responsible to the dean. I served as an ME under the supervision of the senior minister. I worked on a large, metropolitan associational (group of churches) staff with the director of missions as my immediate supervisor. Every organization, including the church, must have a recognized and identifiable leader. In the local church that person is the pastor or senior minister. I have no problem accepting the pastor as the chief administrator of the church. The pastor should be perceived as the first among equals. Westing notes, "There is diversity of function among equals. The headship, or role of leader, does not destroy equality."[1] This is the leader of the congregation and of the church staff. Though the church is the source of authority and of final appeal, the pastor has the authority to lead and oversee the staff. This issue is discussed under the question of hierarchy of calling.

The Meaning of Calling

The word *calling* has several different meanings. The dictionary defines it in three distinct ways. First, it is a business, a profession, an occupation, or a trade. Second, calling is "an invitation; command; summons." Third, it is "a spiritual or divine summons to a special service or office."[2] Calling is synonymous with vocation, career, work, or trade. This view holds "calling" as no more than one's occupation or career. My use of the term "calling" is the third dictionary meaning. Calling is the response of a person to the leadership of God to accept a special ministry. In most denominational traditions the idea of calling is understood as a church related position rather than a Christian in secular work. This tendency equates calling with being engaged in Christian service or vocation full time.

I feel uncomfortable with this idea because it distinguishes between Christians—the idea of clergy and laity—which is not a New Testament teaching. I like the idea expressed on the barn of a watermelon farmer in southwest Georgia: "Christianity is our business, we farm only to pay expenses." He is correct: a Christian's primary task is to engage in the business of Christianity, regardless of how he or she earns a livelihood. Being a Christian servant of God is the principal function of every believer.

Every Christian first responds to God's call to receive Christ as personal Lord and Savior. By responding to this summons we expect to engage in some ministry or service for God. Thus every Christian is a minister and has a ministry to render. Clowney states, "Every Christian has his/her own calling, a calling as a child of God and a servant of God."[3] A person can and does serve God as a business person, homemaker, laborer, store clerk, or professional person. Responding to God's gracious call in Christ means submitting one's entire life to God's will. Barnette notes, "Calling is a symbol of the experience of the act of being drawn into a redemptive relation to Christ and commissioned to serve in the kingdom of God...the redeemed are sent forth as ministers of reconciliation, as witnesses to the whole world, of the saving grace of God."[4] This is the call of God to all who embrace Jesus as Lord and Savior, not just those who enter a Christian vocation.

Calling in the New Testament

In the New Testament the term "call" (*klēsis*) is a theological term referring to God's call to salvation.[5] The call is to serve God in the world through the church by building up the church (the body of Christ) with personal ministry.

> Within the "general calling" to be ministers, there are particular callings to a variety of ministers differentiated by a variety of gifts. Each Christian has one's own gift or gifts from God to exercise in the upbuilding of the church for the common good (1 Corinthians 12:4-6). The nature of one's ministry is determined by one's gift through which the life and work of the church moves forward.[6]

Clowney adds, "Since the scope of a man's ministry is determined by the riches of his spiritual gifts, the recognition of a man's field of service is dependent on the recognition of the gifts granted him by the spirit for that area of ministry."[7] Thus, a person's ministry relates to one's spiritual gifts.

Spiritual Gifts

The concept of "calling" describes various ministry functions listed in passages on spiritual gifts. An examination of the functions of spiritual gifts is crucial to properly understand calling. Ephesians 4:11-13 reads:

> It was he who gave some to be apostles, some to be prophets, some to be evangelists, and some to be pastors and teachers, to prepare God's people for works of service, so that the body of Christ may be built up until we all reach unity in the faith and in the knowledge of the Son of God and become mature, attaining to the whole measure of the fullness of Christ (NIV).

It is not the purview of this book to exegete the various functions listed, but to focus only on the last one mentioned—pastor and teacher.

Although some separate the terms pastor and teacher, the commentaries unanimously agree it should read pastor/teacher. The terms are complementary. The sentence structure shows they describe the same person fulfilling two functions. The other functions are introduced by the word "some." If Paul had intended two separate functions, he would have introduced both pastor and teacher by the word "some." Both the pastoral and the teaching functions were necessary for the church to be what it needed to be.

Bruce writes, "The Church can never dispense with men who preach the gospel and bring men and women to the knowledge of the truth, nor yet with men who can teach and guide in the way of truth those who have been evangelized and converted."[8] Thus, he notes the need for ministers to do a variety of ministries: "They are the men who tend the flock of God and care for its well being, showing other Christians by precept and example alike the path of Christian faith and life."[9] Carver's rationale of the pastor/teacher's role is this: "When the gospel was preached in any place, divine guidance and direction in the new fellowship, its organization, its discipline and its functioning in its community would be necessary."[10] The use of the term "pastor and teacher" suggests this person provides leadership for the flock and instructs them in doctrinal matters. The emphasis is on the functions of the office rather than on the officeholders. Some interpreters feel the apostles and prophets refer to leaders in a general sense, describing how the gospel began in each community.[11]

Discussing teachers in 1 Corinthians 12:28, Barrett concludes, "Presumably they were mature Christians who instructed others in the meaning and moral implications of the Christian faith."[12] Barclay concludes the same:

> They were teachers. In one sense they had the most important task in the whole church; they were not wanderers; they were settled and permanent in the work of one congregation. They had a triple function.
> (a) It was their function to know and to pass on the story of the life of Jesus. It is to them that the story of Jesus came down in the church. (b) Therefore these teachers had to teach and open out the Christian faith to the converts who came into the Church from the heathen world. They had to teach and to explain the great doctrines of the Christian faith. It was in their hands that the purity of doctrine lay. It is to them that we owe it that the Christian faith remained pure and was not distorted as it was handed down. (c) These teachers were also pastors. . . . And the duty of the pastor was to shepherd his flock and to keep them safe. . . . The shepherd of the flock of God is the man who bears God's people on his heart, who feeds them with the truth, who seeks them when they go astray, and who defends them from all that would hurt or destroy or distort their faith. And this is no official office; it is the duty that is laid on every Christian that he should be a shepherd to all his brethren.[13]

The pastor/teacher is gifted so that one can be responsible for the day-to-day building up of the church. Foulkes comments, "Every pastor must be 'apt to teach' (1 Timothy 3:2; Titus 1:9), though it is evident that some have preeminently the gift of teaching, and may be said to form a particular division of ministry within the church."[14] This establishes teaching as a unique ministry exercised in the church context. Many churches call their minister, "pastor," and call the ME, "educational pastor." This is consistent with the idea of the pastor/teacher in Ephesians 4:11.

Another passage describing spiritual gifts is 1 Corinthians 12:28-30. Paul began by listing the various offices or functions in the church and closed with a series of questions about who has the gifts necessary for each office.

> And in the church God has appointed first of all apostles, second prophets, third teachers, then workers of miracles, also those having gifts of healing, those able to help others, those with gifts of administration, and those speaking in different kinds of tongues. Are all apostles? Are all prophets? Are all teachers? Do all work miracles? Do all have gifts of healing? Do all speak in tongues? Do all interpret? (NIV).

This list omits evangelists, and teachers have a separate function from that of pastor/teacher in Ephesians 4:11. The office of teacher evidently existed in the first century churches in both Corinth and Ephesus. Paul's questions suggest that no one had all the spiritual gifts nor could all have the various gifts. Each was to use God-given gifts to strengthen and build up the church.

The third passage that deals with spiritual gifts is Romans 12:6-8:

> We have different gifts, according to the grace given us. If a man's gift is prophesying, let him use it in the proportion to his faith. If it is serving, let him serve; if it is teaching, let him teach. If it is encouraging, let him encourage; if it is contributing to the needs of others, let him give generously; if it is leadership, let him govern diligently; if it is showing mercy, let him do it cheerfully (NIV).

Again, teachers are a part of the ministry team of the New Testament. Acts 13:1 and 15:35 also identified teachers alongside prophets and preachers. God gave the gift of the teacher as He gave the other gifts—apostles, prophets, evangelists, and pastors. Therefore, the various God-given gifts are exercised in keeping with the purpose for which each was given. This benefits the entire church and simplifies the church's ministry.

The Work of Ministry

Ephesians 4:12-13 explains the purpose for the various God-given gifts:

> To prepare God's people for works of service, so that the body of Christ may be built up until we all reach unity in the faith and in the knowledge of the Son of God and become mature, attaining to the whole measure of the fullness of Christ (NIV).

Foulkes summarizes this verse: "The Church is increased and built up, and its members edified, as each member uses his particular gifts as the Lord of the Church ordains, and thus gives spiritual service to his fellow-members and to the Head."[15] These gifted persons equip God's people for ministering work, for Christian service. The purpose is that the church be built up or strengthened as lost persons are saved, added to the membership, and nurtured to Christian maturity.[16] The minister's aim is that members of the Church are fully equipped for service to Christ. Barclay concludes, "It is the function of the office-bearers of the church to see that the members of the church are so educated, so helped, so guided, so cared for, so sought out when they go astray, that they become what they ought to be."[17] The idea of building up or equipping suggests an educational or instructional work that must be done. The minister's aim is not to do all the work of the ministry but to see that others engage in this service. Barclay contends that the work of the church consists as much in practical service rendered as in preaching and teaching. These three tasks—to equip the people for ministry, to build up the church, and to unify members in the faith—are the minister's immediate, day-to-day aims. The purpose of ministry goes beyond the activities of the church. These are greater eternal purposes. Paul stated that the final aim is that the members would experience unity and exemplify maturity. Barclay maintains that church members should be examples of impeccable Christian manhood and womanhood. The final aim is greatest, that the members should reach a stature that can be measured only by the fullness of Christ.[18]

William Hull notes the significance of the equipping task:

> Ephesians 4:12 gives the biblical foundation for a theological idea of "equipping" that is crucial to the vitality of the church. It defines the primary work of various specialized ministries. They are completely "outfitting" all Christians so that they can fulfill the service that makes the church grow in unity and strength.[19]

Accomplishing these goals requires that individual Christians are thoroughly trained and equipped to engage successfully in acts of ministry. The minister adopts the role of an equipper or enabler. His or her task is not to do all the church's work. It is the equipping role of ministry that insures the work done is greatly expanded, involving more people. Some may resist this approach for fear of losing their jobs, but educational ministers are equippers by calling. By the nature of calling they can never work themselves out of the equipping ministry. Problems occur when ministers feel they are the only ones who can fulfill specific, ministerial duties. Hull observes that "anytime a minister attempts to do all the work of a church, no matter how small it may be, his efforts are doomed to failure."[20] When ministers are preoccupied with carrying out a multitude of duties, they rob themselves of time and energy to focus on what they were especially called and trained to do. The minister who becomes a competent equipper and enabler multiplies ministry through the work of those prepared for service. As more persons are equipped for ministry, the ministry done by the members and by the church also multiplies.

Biblical Antecedents

The position and function of the ME has biblical antecedents. In the early church the teaching ministry was well-established, meeting the need to provide instruction for new converts. Whether they were paid ministers or mature Christians in the congregation did not negate the necessary function they served in the life of the church. Those given the spiritual gift to serve as teachers were encouraged to exercise the gift to the fullest without any reservation.

The New Testament church recognized the validity and the necessity of the teaching ministry. Today's educational minister can proudly point back to biblical models for the ministry that God and the church have called them to do. Scripture does not prove that the ME existed in the New Testament, but the work of educational ministry has biblical foundations and roots.

Hierarchy or Servanthood?

If one takes the position that the order in which the various gifts are listed places them in priority order, then a case is built for the idea of a hierarchy of calling or of ministry functions. Scriptural evidence supports the idea that there is a common purpose for all the spiritual gifts. It is to equip and enable the people of God to do the work of ministry, which is to build up the church. Instead of a hierarchy of calling, the biblical model is that of servant leadership. Each gift is commended and needed for the church to be all God intended it to be. Some believe a pastor or a foreign missionary has a superior calling to other church staff members.

The hierarchy theory is perpetuated mainly because of an administrative principle that every organization must have a key or dominate leader. This is true. The church charges the pastor to be the chief administrative officer. The pastor is responsible for leading in the accomplishment of the total work of the church, including the work of each church staff member. This position is occupied by virtue of being called to be the pastor of the church. However, one also should earn the right to be the chief administrator by the way one leads and functions. Ideally, one fills this post by status and function. Each staff member is a minister. As a minister, each is a servant of God and the church. The pastor is the chief servant in the work of the church. The pastor should be perceived as the *lead* servant who provides direction to a servant membership.

While Ephesians 4:11-13 describes the specific purpose or function of spiritual gifts, none is placed in a hierarchy over another. First Corinthians 12:28-30 questions whether anyone has all the spiritual gifts. The nature of the questions suggests no one does. The emphasis of Romans 12:6-8 is that the person who holds a gift should use it for the building up of the church and for the glory of God.

Each minister receives the same calling—first to become a Christian and then to serve Christ as led by the Holy Spirit. The New Testament witness is that God called, appointed, or gave certain persons spiritual gifts to carry out a variety of ministries needed by the church and for Christian witness to the world in which the church dwells.

Called or Hired?

This issue—understanding calling and gifts—is complicated by the church that "calls" a pastor and "hires" a ME, music minister, youth minister, or other professional staff person. Some churches use the term hire because they give the senior minister the authority to hire or fire other staff members. My denomination practices congregational polity in which, ideally, the congregation—not a pastor, committee, or board—calls all staff persons including the pastor. It seems paradoxical that one church will both "call" one minister and yet "hire" another. If a church needs various ministers to provide leadership for several ministries they feel God wants them to do, then each minister should be as carefully considered as the senior minister.

Notes

1. Harold J. Westing, *Multiple Church Staff Handbook* (Grand Rapids: Kregal Publications, 1985), 25.

2. Clarence L. Barnhart, ed. *The World Book Dictionary*, Vol. One (Chicago: Field Enterprises Educational Corporation, 1974), 287.

3. Edmund P. Clowney, *Called to the Ministry* (Phillipsburg, N.J.: Presbyterian and Reformed Publishing Company, 1976), v.

4. Henlee H. Barnette, *Christian Calling and Vocation* (Grand Rapids: Baker Book House, 1965), 12.

5. Ibid., 17-18.

6. Ibid., 22.

7. Clowney, *Called to the Ministry*, 51.

8. F. F. Bruce, *The Epistle to the Ephesians* (London: Fleming H. Revell, 1961), 85.

9. Ibid., 85.

10. W. O. Carver, *The Glory of God in the Christian Calling* (Nashville: Broadman Press, 1949), 149.

11. Ibid., 148-49.

12. C. K. Barrett, *The First Epistle to the Corinthians* (New York: Harper & Row, Publishers, 1968), 295.

13. William Barclay, *The Letters to the Galatians and Ephesians* (Philadelphia: The Westminster Press, 1958), 174-75.

14. Frances Foulkes, *The Epistle of Paul to the Ephesians* (Grand Rapids: Wm. B. Eerdmans Publishing Company, 1963), 119-20.

15. Ibid., 121.

16. Kenneth S. Wuest, *Ephesians and Colossians in the Greek New Testament* (Grand Rapids: Wm. B. Eerdmans Publishing Company, 1953), 101.

17. Barclay, *The Letters to the Galatians and Ephesians,* 176.

18. Ibid., 176-77.

19. William E. Hull, "Equipping: A Concept of Leadership," *Church Administration* (January 1972): 6.

20. Ibid., 7.

2

From Whence We've Come

The professional ME is a happening of the twentieth century. It began with the Religious Education Association and the Hartford School of Religious Education in 1903. The Chair of Sunday School Pedagogy at The Southern Baptist Theological Seminary in Louisville, Kentucky was established in 1906. As early as 1907 several persons served as paid Sunday School Superintendents in local churches. They were the forerunners of the educational minister. Southwestern Baptist Theological Seminary, Fort Worth, Texas began a School of Religious Education in 1915.

Antecedents for the work of educational ministry date back to early days in the Old Testament. Parents were advised to teach religion to their children. Deuteronomy 6:4-9 says:

> Hear, O Israel! The Lord our God, the Lord is one! And you shall love the Lord your God with all your heart and with all your soul and with all your might. And these words, which I am commanding you today, shall be on your heart; and you shall teach them diligently to your sons and shall talk of them when you sit in your house and when you walk by the way and when you lie down and when you rise up. And you shall bind them as a sign on your hand and they shall be as frontals on your forehead. And you shall write them on the doorposts of your house and on your gates (NASB).

Parents were their children's teachers about God and His ways. Someone also provided religious instruction to the parents so they were skilled in teaching religion to their children; one function of the priest was to be an instructor or teacher of the Law.

Biblical Antecedents

The Old Testament term *Torah* also means divine instruction. The Torah was the instruction to the priests about the oracles of God and the requirements of God. These teachings were transmitted to the people. Priests were the agents of instruction. The adults, particularly the fathers, conveyed these ideas of God to the family, including the children. During early Old Testament times, the priest was more an organ of revelation, giving counsel in the ordinary affairs of life. "The teaching function of the priesthood seems to have taken precedence over the sacrificial."[1] Deuteronomy 33:10 lists both, but teaching is first: "They shall teach Thine ordinances to Jacob and Thy law to Israel" (NASB). The priest was variously the teacher, the administrator of justice, and a worship leader.[2]

After the exile another class of teachers arose—the scribes. These men were professional exponents and teachers of the law. Ezra serves as an example of the scribe who was an interpreter and teacher of the law. There also arose the position of the rabbi, who was well versed in the law and charged with teaching the law. The title "rabbi" was one of respect given to a layperson as contrasted to the priests and scribes. The rabbi was a model similar to that of the early educational minister of the twentieth century who began as a layperson and then became a minister. Some educational ministers choose to remain laypersons rather than become ordained ministers.

The Need for the Professional Religious Educator

With the founding of the Sunday School in 1780 and its development in the 120 plus years that followed, the need for an educational minister began to be felt. With the enhancement of the Sunday School came the normal school whose function was to train teachers to teach in the school systems of that day. By 1900 the public school was on the way to being established and functioning in most of the states in the United States. Before teacher training became popular for public school teachers, Sunday School teachers compared favorably with public school teachers. The Sunday School began as a lay movement and has remained so. As large numbers of persons began preparing for a teaching career, they received training in psychology, methodology, and principles of teaching. This called attention to a need for similar preparation of those teaching in our churches. Two men, John Dewey and George Albert Coe, had a significant influence on the development of religious education. Furnish states:

> These men, together with others, injected into education the
> notion that there is a scientific way to solve problems—not only
> the technological problems of industry but the problems of
> learning, character building, and institutional organization.[3]

These scientific discoveries invalidated the old, transmissive teaching approaches encouraged by the *Uniform Lesson Series*. Furnish
describes the challenge:

> Instead of attempting to pour pre-selected content into the
> minds of pupils, teachers were challenged to discover subjects of
> interest to students, help them engage in activities related to
> that interest, and then guide them as they reflected on their
> experiences. Pupils were led in stating problems, positing alter-
> native solutions, testing opinions, evaluating and drawing
> conclusions.[4]

With each advance in the training of teachers for public education,
the Sunday School was disadvantaged.

Public schools were neither designed nor intended to provide
training in religion, ethics, and morality. The church was, therefore,
compelled to strengthen and further develop what it was doing in
religious education. Large numbers of lay volunteers were already
leading religious education activities, such as Sunday School and
youth programs. The great challenge before the church was to har-
ness and prepare these volunteers to be more effectual in what they
were already doing.

Other issues were important in the development of the professional educational ministry. There was a growing belief that the
educational ministry of the church had to be more comprehensive
than simply holding Sunday Bible study classes. Another issue was
that churches were offering an increasing number of educational
activities and opportunities for different congregational groups.
With increased activities, the necessity grew for someone in a full-
time leadership position to coordinate, supervise, and plan a comprehensive well-balanced program. Also influencing the beginning
of the profession was the increase in pastoral responsibilities as
churches grew. Pastors found it difficult to give the time and energy
needed to provide leadership for the educational program which was
now a major segment of the church's life.[5]

Several facts helped set the stage for the entrance into the church
of a specially trained person to provide leadership to the church's
religious education program. As the Sunday School grew and
developed, it continued to rely on volunteer lay leaders. The university and normal schools prepared persons to serve as public school

educators using modern psychology and scientific methods. Churches felt it important that the church school be as strong as the public school. The remainder of this chapter describes the developments within the church that led to the beginning of the ME and the growth of the profession.[6]

The Progress of the ME Profession[7]

A Professional Is Born

Various reasons have been given for the need of the ME. Many pastors were active in helping their churches grow. Their churches grew beyond what one minister could handle adequately. These ministers and churches began to look for help with educational activities. Since seminaries of those days were not training ministers in religious education, the pastor and the church had to look within the church, often toward their Sunday School superintendents. Trying to provide help to the educational program of the church, pastors and church leaders began to hire paid Sunday School superintendents for their administrative skills and their leadership in outreach activities. These persons lacked training in educational psychology, pedagogy, and curriculum planning, but they met the need for administrating the Sunday School program. Occasionally these persons were professionally trained public school teachers and administrators. They functioned alongside the pastor serving more as a layperson than as a minister. Women were also used in this capacity, usually with the title "Educational Secretary."

Paid Sunday School superintendents did not provide the total leadership needs of a Christian education program; they were, however, helping the churches grow through their proven ability to lead the Sunday School, their spiritual maturity, and their belief that the Sunday School was an evangelistic tool of the church.

As early as 1907 the *Religious Education Journal* reported that there were persons serving as paid Sunday School superintendents in local churches. By 1908, William H. Boocock was carrying the title "Director of Religious Education" at the First Presbyterian Church in Buffalo, New York. Furnish identifies eight persons who began serving churches through religious education before 1910. None of them began with the title of director of religious education but were granted the title during their ministry in local churches. One of the eight was a woman who served in the Church of the Disciples. Others joining the trend were Methodist, Baptist, Presbyterian, and Congregational churches.[8]

The Future is Ours (1910–1930)

In 1910 the Religious Education Association sponsored the first meeting for directors of religious education. Their records revealed ten persons serving as directors of religious education (DREs). They held a conclave as part of the meeting of the Religious Education Association. There are no records of who attended the meeting or how many persons identified themselves in the new profession. It is significant that the leaders of the Religious Education Association felt there was a need for such a meeting and took the initiative in calling it.[10] Out of this and later meetings came the Association of Directors and Ministers of Religious Education.

In 1915 educational directors were represented in several denominations including Congregational, Baptist, Unitarian, Presbyterian, German Evangelical, Methodist, Episcopal, and Disciples. The major evangelical denominations in America saw the need for the DRE and secured such persons to serve their churches.[11]

Some believe the profession was generally for women but records do not support this view. Furnish reports, "In 1910, there were no women listed as charter members of the REA [Religious Education Association] who related to local church programs in a professional way."[12] During its early years, few women are identified as members. This early trend changed and young women were considered as possible candidates for the profession. By 1926 Paul Vieth reports the profession was almost equally divided between men and women, 203 and 192 respectively. Although it was dominated by men initially, it has always been open to both men and women.

During this period the profession wrestled with issues of definition and standardization. Attempts were made to define the functions and duties of the DRE. Consideration was also given to how the DRE related to groups within the local church. Much discussion was held about the qualifications needed to serve as a DRE.

Until 1922, DREs were encouraged, supported, and promoted by the Religious Education Association. In 1922 the Sunday School Council of Evangelical Denominations and the International Sunday School Association merged to form the International Council of Religious Education. This new organization was the result of cooperation between Protestant denominational bodies, while the Religious Education Association had individual members. The Association of Directors and Ministers of Religious Education existed as part of the Religious Education Association until 1928. Then a new organization began, the Association of Professional Educators in Local Churches.[13]

Bingham and Loessner describe this early period:

> The vocation had an insignificant beginning and was slow in establishing itself in the thinking of pastors and church leaders. In those earlier years some larger churches employed "paid Sunday School superintendents" whose primary task was to "run" the Sunday School. These early educational leaders were mostly young businessmen with excellent ability to organize people and promote a strong program of visitation and enlargement for the Sunday School. Most of them lacked in theological education or basic training and frequently were without college background. They were more promoters and organizers than educators. The pastors "hired" them to grow larger Sunday Schools. Their primary interest, therefore, was not in the teaching-learning processes but in organization and reaching people.[9]

These were truly pioneers who enriched the evangelistic and outreach ministries of the churches. Their work as organizers and promoters may have hindered future educational ministers.

These two decades were times of prosperity and great optimism in America. If sheer numbers are evidence of the success and popularity of the position, then the DRE had arrived. The profession had grown from ten in 1910 to eight hundred by 1926.[14]

Disillusionment and Despair (1930–1945)

This prosperity was not to last. With the economic crash of 1929, churches faced the same financial difficulties as other areas of life. They felt the severe effects of the depression years and of World War II as did the religious education profession.

It is naive and unfair to attribute the decline the religious education profession experienced totally to the economic and social conditions. Also appearing on the scene was a new orthodoxy in religion. There was the realization that religious education could not cure all the world's wrongs (as some believed and espoused).

Also contributing to its decline was a lack of understanding about this vocation, especially in the churches that radically separated the work of the pastor and the work of the religious educator. On the other hand many church leaders lacked a clear view of the work of religious education. They expected the director to be involved in areas of the church that did not relate to educational training or specialization. Potential church staff conflicts magnified the problems encountered by religious educators as jealousies and other issues arose. Some religious educators added to the problem through arrogant attitudes. Some churches had been too hasty in adding religious educators to the church staff, only to find they were inadequately trained or prepared for their work.

Furnish provides further significant insight into the problem when she writes:

> Ironically, those who were best trained brought another problem to the profession, a kind of "professionalism." They were long on theoretical and technical training, but short on the ability to get along with others or without practical experience necessary to undergird the theories.[15]

An excellent example of the problems of professionalism is a book written during this period by Professor W. A. Harper of Vanderbilt University, *The Minister of Education.* It is the mythical story of a church that needs an ME. The pastor convinces the proper church bodies and leaves to interview potential candidates at three seminaries. Two of the seminaries are not appreciative of the educational ministry so the pastor goes to the third. There he finds a suitable candidate who is completing doctoral studies. In due time the young man arrives at the church. Meetings with the lay leadership of the church always end in the educational minister giving spontaneous talks on various educational subjects. These talks discuss curriculum, organization, and teaching methodology. Each presentation is enthusiastically approved and carried out by the people. My impression was these were Harper's class lectures put into the mouth of the young educational minister. For every problem encountered by the church, the young ME has a ready answer. It is accepted without question by the congregation, the senior minister, and church school superintendent (also a public-school superintendent). It reads more like a fairy tale than a handbook for an ME functioning in a local church setting.[16]

Of the many difficulties contributing to this dismal period for the DRE, undoubtedly the most negative was the depression of the 1930s. Many churches found they could not afford to have a staff member other than the pastor. It was a time of mere financial survival for both people and institutions. Not all educational directors vanished, but it was a period when not many persons chose to enter the profession. At this point more women than men were in the profession with women comprising 75 percent of religious educators.

The educational minister has always struggled with being required or assigned duties other than education. The increase of women as directors of religious education along with the dire economic conditions added to this problem. Many were assigned secretarial tasks not only for their work but also for the church and were sometimes called the "Educational Secretary." Other combinations of work were popular such as education and music, or education and youth. Once additional duties were added to the educational duties, it became almost impossible to escape from them, even after the financial crisis was over. Furnish provides a good summary for the period: "The retreat of men from the profession, the necessity for combination jobs, and the lack of job opportunities all whittled away at the status of the profession."[17]

Bingham and Loessner emphasize two other significant issues. First, the depression forced many churches to fire their educational staff due to the lack of funds. Second, "many of the churches found the depression a good excuse to let some of them go also because their promotional tactics had caused tension and misunderstanding within the life of the church."[18]

In spite of hardships, significant change occurred during this period that helped give the profession a new image. Various titles had been used, the most popular one being director of religious education. Suddenly, both the words "director" and "religious" were questioned. The term director was descriptive of coldness and professionalism. Director also conveyed the impression of being dictatorial or too directive. The term religious was objectionable since it was not specific enough and lacked depth. The issue was not completely settled, but the two terms, director of religious education (DRE) and director of Christian education (DCE), endured.

Recovery and Growth (1945–1965)

With the end of World War II, a new sense of hope and a growing economy helped the church to focus again on the importance of Christian nurture. Immediately after the war, church membership increased significantly. As the Sunday School grew, the need for training more teachers was often an overwhelming task facing volunteer Sunday School superintendents. This forced many churches to seek professional leadership for their religious education program.

Church buildings that had not been completed due to the economic depression were now completed. This church building boom called for leadership from professional religious educators. Innovations in teaching methodologies altered public school education. Church school teachers needed training in these latest approaches. The need for religious educators in the church became more intense. Many denominations began to develop new curriculum. These new materials, requiring new skills and approaches, were educationally sound but not easy to use. Again, DCEs were needed to plan these new curriculum materials, to promote their use, and to train persons in their use. Although some religious educators had little to do with planning new curriculum materials, they were expected to use whatever their denomination provided. Much of their time was spent in training Sunday School leaders and leaders of other church organizations to use the material produced.

While the previous period saw few persons enter the profession, these two decades saw the numbers greatly increase. Even though there were more than 11,000 persons serving as religious educators, there were not enough persons trained to meet the needs. Many denominations began to establish standards for the educational training of persons desiring to enter the field of religious education. Those denominations lifted the position of the DRE to a higher professional level and showed denominational support for their work. The need for denominational certification caused those entering the profession to seek adequate initial preparation and to further their professional growth through continuing education programs.[19]

Religious educators were now perceived differently. Bingham and Loessner observe:

> It was not until after World War II that the churches began to see in the educational staff members more than promoters, organizers, and business managers. The term "minister of education" became acceptable to the churches, and all educational workers in the churches were accorded higher status in the thinking of the people.[20]

The question of title seemed to be resolved during this period. Three titles became sanctioned. The "director of Christian education" was for those who lacked theological, professional training; these were often laypersons. The "minister of Christian education" described one who had theological training. For some denominations this indicated the person was ordained and served full time.[21] "Educational assistant" designated those who had not met the standards of the profession. This title was also for a person assigned to work with an age group, or who lacked experience. In my denomination, educational background was not related to a person's title. It has been much slower than other evangelicals in setting educational standards although some attempts were made. Often the title accepted was one the pastor designated.

Clarification and Advancement (1965–Present)

I have been a student, participant, and observer of the profession during this period. No one has attempted to assess or describe what happened to the profession after 1965. Having served in a ministry of Christian education during these years, I cannot be totally objective, but I can identify some trends and patterns I have observed.

As churches peaked during the mid to late 1960s, the demand for Christian education leaders in the churches was more than could be supplied by the graduates of seminaries and divinity schools. Not only was there a great need for ministers of education but also churches were adding age group staff members—preschool, children, youth, and adult ministers. In the late 1960s several major denominations cooperatively produced new curriculum designs with each denomination producing its own material.[22] My denomination made major changes in curriculum and developed a new grouping and grading plan. This intensified the need for the professional Christian educator.

Church growth tapered off with drastic declines setting in by the latter part of the 1960s and continuing into the 1990s. Most major evangelical denominations experienced continuous decline for more than three decades. In some ways the period from 1965 into the 1980s was similar to that occurring after the depression as one of disillusionment and decline. Staff positions were eliminated or were forced into combination roles. Many churches were unable to support multiple staff ministries. Interestingly, this period also witnessed the growth of many churches into very large congregations. While some positions declined, the number of educational ministers grew.

Again during the 1980s enrollment in programs to train professional Christian educators increased. Optional tracks of studies were expanding. Theological or divinity students could choose to pursue the following degrees: Master of Christian Education, Master of Religious Education, Master of Arts in Christian Education, Master of Divinity in Christian Education, or Master of Divinity with a Christian Education major.

As churches increased in size, the need for more specialization in Christian education multiplied. One California church has twenty-two ministers on staff with a minister for each major age group in the church and ministers to meet special needs such as single and senior adults. This pattern is repeated in other geographical areas, leading to new titles for the ME. Many function as program director, program coordinator, executive minister, program minister, and program consultant. They seek to coordinate, direct, and supervise the church's educational ministry and program.

Part of the profession's advancement has been the setting of standards and certification criteria in many denominations. Some require candidates to complete degree programs in Christian education or to major in Christian education for divinity degrees. Denominations which have certification standards for ministers of education include: United Church of Christ; The Lutheran Church—Missouri Synod; The Church of God—Anderson, Indiana; The United Methodist Church; and the Roman Catholic Church.[23] Several denominations are attempting to establish or revise their standards of certification for the educational minister.

Professional Organizations

With the increase in the number of educational ministers, the need for professional organizations also arose. On the interdenominational level two organizations provide support and professional help for the ME. First, some sections of the biannual meeting of the Religious Education Association are for the practitioner in Christian education. The other organization is the Professional Association of Christian Educators, formerly called the National Association of Directors of Christian Education.

Many denominations have Christian education organizations. National bodies include the Christian Educators Fellowship (United Methodist Church), the Association of Presbyterian Christian Educators, the Association of Christian Church Educators (Disciples of Christ), the Southern Baptist Religious Education Association, the Association of United Church Educators (United Church of Christ), Association of Christian Educators (Church of Christ), and the Community of Religious Directors (Roman Catholic). In addition there are many local, state, and regional organizations.

Trying to discover the number of persons now serving local churches as educational ministers proved an impossible task. The national religious education associations are the only sources for this information. I will summarize the data received from the various denominations. It is not the complete picture.

In 1975 there were 5,128 persons functioning as ministers of education. These persons were from seven denominations and members of the National Association of Directors of Christian Education. The denominations represented were Southern Baptist, United Methodist Church, American Baptist, Disciples of Christ, Unitarian-Universalist, Presbyterian Church, U.S., and the United Church of Christ. The one new group is the Catholic Church.

In the late 1980s there were approximately 12,700 persons serving as MEs. Many who function as educators have titles that do not reflect their educational assignments, i.e., associate pastor. Among those serving as MEs, the largest number are Southern Baptists or Roman Catholics. Information about the number of persons ordained was not available.

Notes

1. George A. Buttrick, ed. *The Interpreter's Dictionary of the Bible,* Vol. K-Q (Nashville: Abingdon Press, 1962), 881.

2. Ibid.

3. Dorothy Jean Furnish, *DRE/DCE—The History of a Profession* (Nashville: Christian Educators Fellowship of The United Methodist Church, 1976), 17.

4. Ibid., 17.

5. Louise McComb, *DCE: A Challenging Career in Christian Education* (Richmond: John Knox Press, 1963), 11-12.

6. Harry C. Munro, *The Director of Religious Education* (Philadelphia: Westminster Press, 1930), 1-18.

7. For the years 1903–1965 I will follow Furnish's outline. This is the only book I have discovered that describes the growth of the ME historically.

8. Furnish, *DRE/DCE—The History of a Profession,* 22-23.

9. Robert E. Bingham and Ernest Loessner, *Serving with the Saints* (Nashville: Broadman Press, 1970), 112.

10. Furnish, *DRE/DCE—The History of a Profession,* 22.

11. Ibid., 29.

12. Ibid.

13. Ibid., 33.

14. Ibid., 29. These numbers are estimates by Henry F. Cope and Paul H. Vieth who were leaders in the religious education movement at the time.

15. Ibid., 38.

16. W. A. Harper, *The Minister of Education* (Ashland, Ohio: University Post Publishing Company, 1939).

17. Furnish, *DRE/DCE—The History of a Profession,* 40.

18. Bingham and Loessner, *Serving With the Saints,* 113.

19. My own denomination, Southern Baptist, operates with congregational polity; thus the local church sets the standards and in essence certifies each ministerial candidate. While operating six theological seminaries, enrolling about 20% of those enrolled in such schools in America and Canada, the denomination has not established standards of certification or professional training.

20. Bingham and Loessner, *Serving With the Saints,* 113.

21. Some Baptists use the title "minister of education" without trying to indicate one is ordained. It is used generically to describe the person who functions as a minister of education.

22. *The Church's Educational Ministry: A Curriculum Plan* (St. Louis: The Bethany Press, 1966).

23. There are other denominations who have established standards for certification for MEs. These responded to a letter of inquiry.

3

Personal Characteristics

Ultimate success for the ME is heavily dependent upon the ability to incarnate the gospel message and the personhood of Jesus Christ. Louise McComb feels that "the most important qualification of all is vital Christian experience. Only a person whose own character is genuinely Christian can hope to lead others in a growing Christian experience."[1] Harris suggests a personal characteristic needed by educational ministers is "an inner kind of time, characterized not by the passage of minutes, but by the quality of the present in which we live, and by the intensity of awareness we bring to this present."[2] Personal characteristics that enhance the educational ministry include: integrity, good people skills, Christian growth, love for people, a healthy self-image, ability to teach, intellect, enthusiasm, being a Christian model, and steadfastness of purpose. This chapter analyzes those characteristics as they relate to educational ministers.

Integrity

When pastors talk about qualities they look for in a ME, they describe educational skills. They want someone to grow a Sunday School, train leaders, and administer the educational program. They often add, "I want a person of integrity." Part of personal integrity is being honest in one's personal and professional life. This involves paying debts, being honest in speech, and doing what one says one will do.

Integrity includes single-mindedness—knowing where you are going and using ethical means to get there. This means not being easily side-tracked, even when it appears plans are not succeeding.

At such times, the ME with integrity will listen to others, heed their counsel, and continue to attempt the goals that lie before him.

One of the hardest things any person has to do is admit making a mistake. It is tempting to blame someone else for problems and mistakes. A leader cannot be right 100 percent of the time. Integrity means owning one's mistakes and weaknesses.

Integrity involves being responsible for one's actions. It also means being accountable for one's areas of work. I once had a secretary who felt that she was totally responsible for everything that came out of her office. That is a heavy burden to bear. Her job was educational secretary, but she assumed responsibilities the church had assigned to me. MEs must take responsibility for what happens in the church's educational ministry. President Harry S. Truman had a famous saying on his desk: "The buck stops here." Educational ministers must not be afraid to take responsibility for the people with whom they work and for the educational program they direct.

Good People Skills

MEs should have good human relation skills accompanied by professional competency in Christian education. While all ministers should have these skills, they are particularly important for educational ministers. Good people skills include:

• **Sensitivity to the needs of people.** MEs are aware of the feelings, needs, and motivating facts that affect the persons with whom they work. They have a sincere, genuine interest in people. They avoid the appearance of psychoanalyzing or treating persons as objects rather than as unique persons created in the image of God. This sensitivity needs to be felt for those whom MEs supervise—both volunteers and other staff members. Studies suggest the best style of leadership is determined by the maturity of the worker and the tasks that need to be done.[3] Persons are treated as unique rather than made to fit the same mold. Many potential staff relation problems could be avoided if each staff member had a sensitivity to the needs of others.

• **Ability to get along with others.** Life has many interactions with others. The smoothness with which people can work and relate to others is a significant component in success. Effective educational ministers are diplomats. They know when to push people to go forward and when to permit them to move or work at their own pace or in their own way. It is important to know when and how to confront so that it is redemptive, not punitive. On occasion, other persons are given time to see if their way is better. Conflicts or problems may arise among workers in the educational programs. A choice may have to be made whether tasks or people are more important. Ideally, people are more important than programs unless personality differences drastically affect the work that needs to be done.

• **Create a climate of motivation.** In the sense that motivation is an internal influence rather than external, one person cannot motivate another. MEs help people feel secure and create a climate that allows Christian workers and leaders to function at their highest potential.[4] Another way to create a positive climate of motivation is to see that workers have adequate materials and supplies with which to work.

• **Good communication skills.** Good human relations skills include the ability to communicate well in written and oral form. The message sent is clear and easily understood by its recipient. Terms are selected that do not have multiple meanings or that could be potentially misunderstood. Technical language or jargon is avoided. Good communication is crucial in training or instruction. Whether trying to train a new worker in an unfamiliar task or helping experienced workers in preparation for educational opportunities, educational ministers must be understood. Their verbal and non-verbal communication proves their respect for church leaders and members as persons of worth.

• **A wise delegator.** No one can do everything. Wisdom in knowing what to delegate, when to delegate, and to whom to delegate is a skill practiced and honed by effective ministers. A good rule to follow is delegating to the lowest *competent* level. This principle suggests that the most logical or best qualified person is the delegatee. Find the person who can do it. Unless this principle is used, delegation goes to people at the top. Other persons are never trained or developed in leadership skills. MEs do not delegate tasks because they do not want to do them. Delegation can be used for tasks where they do not feel as competent or skillful. There are usually persons who can handle the task.[5] A recurring task that takes much of the educational minister's time is ordering and distributing literature. Most MEs feel trapped by this responsibility. I cannot count the hours I have given to this twin task. It has taken many Saturday afternoons since I did not have time to do it during the week. Both the ordering and distribution of literature could be delegated to lay members involved in the educational program.

• **A good listener.** The person who can listen well to others makes them feel important. Most ministers need to work on listening skills. John Drakeford wrote *The Awesome Power of the Listening Ear*,[6] describing the influence we have with others when we listen to what they are saying. He proposes various approaches to improve listening skills. One is "creative listening" in which you repeat what you hear or understand the other person to say. At times we are guilty of thinking what we will say rather than hearing what the other person is saying. Remember: listening is not waiting your turn to talk. Good people skills begin with becoming a good listener.

A Growing Christian

Some time ago there was a book entitled *Growing Ministers Growing Churches*.[7] When I saw the title I thought they had placed it in reverse order. On further consideration, I feel that it is in the proper order. Churches grow because ministers are growing. One expectation of MEs is to help the local church grow quantitatively and qualitatively. Educational ministers are usually responsible for helping the church reach new persons for Bible study and for church membership. If they expect to lead the church to grow numerically, they must practice what they ask others to do. MEs are involved in every aspect of the church's outreach ministry—to the unsaved, unchurched, absentees, prospects, and the pastoral care of members. They are also in charge of the church's discipleship program that seeks to help all believers—not just new ones—to grow in Christian maturity. Educational ministers are growing in their relationship to Jesus Christ and helping others to do likewise. Being a disciple and a discipler must be high on their priority list.

In the religious realm it is almost impossible to teach or lead someone to do something that the teacher or leader is not doing. Growth is not an optional matter for the Christian leader. Being an example of what it means to grow in Christian maturity is a part of ministry through the life and work of the church. Jesus set the pattern as reported in Luke 2:52: "And Jesus grew in wisdom and stature, and in favor with God and man" (NIV). The Christian is always becoming more like Jesus Christ; his life is never static but is always dynamic, changing, and growing toward Christlikeness.

Christian growth is not automatic; it is planned. MEs grow spiritually by spending time in Scripture study and prayer, opening themselves up to the changes and corrections needed in their lives. This then prompts growth in their relationships with and their ability to get along with others. Christian growth, or lack of it, is never more evident than in relationships with fellow staff members. Westing suggests eight potential team problems.[8] Avoiding and overcoming these potential problems enhances the ability of a staff team to function together. Nothing destroys church members' confidence in the ministerial staff more than staff disharmony and conflict. All are to grow in their ability to be and do what Christ would have them be and do.

Love for People

An ME's primary tool for getting work done is people. Harris comments, "DREs see themselves as primarily involved in an effort devoted to helping people in very direct and personal ways."[9] A genuine love for people characterizes this ministry. Love for people is matched by the ability to work well with people. Sincere affection both for workers and for participants or prospective members of the various Christian education organizations is necessary. One thing I observed from conversations in class and in personal time with Professor Ernest Loessner was his great love and respect of people. He never talked about his love for people. It was obvious by his speech and personal relationships. Because of his example, I committed myself to seek to lead people through love. Without a deep love for people, MEs may be guilty of manipulation, using the power of persuasion to accomplish personal and program goals and objectives.

Love means considering the personality, needs, and concerns of each worker, treating each one fairly while keeping special needs in mind, being available to listen, and sincerely seeking to provide what each needs. Love for people is shown by private and public expressions of appreciation for quality work. As an ME was leaving a church for a new position, two ladies expressed their regret. They asked the question, "Who will now tell us, 'I appreciate you'?" The ME had affirmed them as persons while affirming their good work. They in turn paid her a high compliment.

Workers can be driven to needed tasks and assignments for awhile without feeling loved, but they are likely to resign when defeats or difficulties come. A good test of love for people is noting the turnover rate of persons with whom MEs work. When workers feel loved, they work willingly and enthusiastically. They also seek to give their best in carrying out the work of Christ through the church. If people feel loved, they in turn are loving people. They also feel the freedom to be creative and realize their highest level of capability.

Healthy Self-Image

Of all the ministers a church has, the ME needs a healthy self-image. Though this work is primarily in the background, in a supportive role for the entire church program, there are many sources to help educational ministers feel a sense of accomplishment. These include:

• **Sense of call.** This ministry is a permanent call, not a stepping-stone to a "more important role as a pastor." MEs need a clear sense of mission; they are called to a teaching ministry. Knowing with certainty God's call strengthens a sense of self worth.

• **Doing what God wants them to do.** Being in the place and doing what MEs feel God wants them to do enhances their sense of self worth. When persons are confident of being in God's will there is a spirit of excitement and enthusiasm about the daily routine of activities. Without this perspective, MEs are bored and unchallenged by the work. They must do and be their best. Their examples calls forth the best in work and behavior from those with whom they work.

• **Affirmation from pastor and other staff members.** Much of the ME's work is not visible to the church at large. They easily feel unappreciated for it sometimes seems no one else at the church is working as hard. They need public affirmation from the pastor, other staff, and church members. It is true it is not important who gets the credit as long as the job gets done; but good work and the accomplishment of goals are worthy of recognition. Everyone needs appreciation. Other ministers get affirmative strokes. Pastors are affirmed for sermons preached. Music ministers are acclaimed for solos, choir specials, and musical performances. Youth ministers receive praise from the youth and their parents. Educational ministers have no one group that regularly and consistently gives strokes for work well done. Theirs is a ministry behind the scenes, a supportive role for the total work of the church. MEs are worthy of receiving affirmation and appreciation from other staff persons for work done so the total church can function effectively. The work of the church takes a team effort, with each member of the staff making a contribution to the success of the church program.[10]

• **Competency, the ability to do the job well.** Self-image is strengthened by doing a good job. Confidence is needed in every facet of the work, even though gifts or abilities are greater in one area than another. Educational ministers who handle effectively and efficiently their various roles have the satisfaction which comes from doing their jobs well with the gifts and abilities God has given them. Such ministers should see the educational work advancing and persons growing in their relationship to Jesus Christ. MEs should know whether they are doing a good job so that affirmation by the pastor, other staff members, and the church membership, especially the key leaders with whom they closely work, is personally meaningful.

• **Periodic performance reviews and self-evaluation.** Periodic performance reviews with the pastor and the church personnel committee enhance self-image if these are positive experiences. Self-evaluation can affirm self-image; most people know when they are doing a good job. This commitment to evaluation procedures helps MEs be realistic about their gifts and abilities and properly assess both their strengths and weaknesses.

• **Growing as Christians and as MEs.** The desire to grow and develop as educators needs to parallel growth in Christian maturity. It is important to be on the leading edge of the profession, to constantly seek to expand and improve their work as educators. At the same time, their motto should be, as it is for every Christian, 2 Timothy 2:15: "Study to shew thyself approved unto God, a workman that needeth not to be ashamed, rightly dividing the word of truth" (KJV).

• **Collegiality groups.** ME's self-image can be greatly strengthened by participating in a collegiality group. I have been part of both a denominational group of educational ministers and an ecumenical or interdenominational group. Sharing with fellow denominational MEs helps build a support base with those who experience similar problems. An advantage to the interdenominational group is that it enlarges educational horizons and introduces different perspectives from which to view educational work. Professional recognition, whether from a denominational peer group or across denominational lines, is a positive influence in helping build a secure, healthy self-image. The key to an effective experience with collegiality groups is commitment as an active member of a group.

Ability to Teach

MEs should be master teachers. Jesus was a master teacher. He embodied what He taught and effectively used a variety of methods, beginning where His learners were.[11] Educators can become master teachers through studying the life and approaches of master teachers such as Jesus. They not only study other master teachers but also work toward developing the skills that result in realizing such a goal. Educational ministers as teachers of teachers should be the best teachers in the church. People learn better by seeing than by hearing. Bingham and Loessner emphasize, "When trying to impart teaching skills to others, showing is superior to telling. The other teachers need to see good teaching in practice. They need to see you teaching them—a teacher of teachers."[12]

Educators are masters of the teaching art; they model excellent teaching both in content and teaching methodology. This comes by understanding and practicing the ingredients of good pedagogy. MEs model good teaching and have the skills and the abilities to help others become master teachers; they are trainers of the volunteer teaching staff, leading workers in studying the purposes of Sunday School, a variety of teaching methods, developmental issues for each age group, and administration of the church's educational program.

Being apt to teach means being ready to teach. It is best for MEs not to teach a particular class on a weekly basis since they relate to the entire church, not just one class or group. However, they must be willing and able to substitute in any age group.

Bingham and Loessner apply the analogy of a coach to educational ministry. They list four key elements:

1. *Intensify* the serious, systematic study done by teachers and students. Magnify the value of first-rate preparation for any class.

2. *Encourage* teachers and students alike to avail themselves of learning aids. People fool themselves who assume their natural instincts are enough.

3. *Participate* in periodic reviews ("game films") with leaders. Talk with them about strategy for the next week's teaching ("game plan"). Do some advance "scouting" for them in the "field" of their next teaching challenge.

4. *Convince* the other "coaches" that winning the game is important. In teaching the realities of Jesus Christ to a lost world, how you play the game is not of ultimate importance as much as whether you win or lose. Many teachers are ineffective because they are not convinced of the importance of the outcome of their efforts.[13]

Bingham and Loessner put the teaching role of the ME in proper perspective when they write:

> A valid criticism of our vocation is not that we are disinterested in teaching, *not* that we do not seek to lead the teaching ministry of the church, *not* that we conceive our labors as promotional. It would be that some of us remain too far from the actual playing field. A coach cannot do his best work from the press box, and a minister of education is not as effective in his office as he is in a teaching situation.[14]

Intellect

MEs not only expect to use technical educational skills and knowledge, but they also must be creative thinkers, using to the fullest the minds God has given them. Their intellectual skills are challenged by the need for analysis. They diagnose needs and then develop plans to meet those needs, whether they are people, program, or methodology needs. MEs must be students—students of the Word of God, the Bible; students of people and what motivates them; students seeking to improve teaching techniques and approaches; students of human development as it affects the teaching/learning process; students of good administration; and students through their devotional lives and personal relationships with God through His Son, Jesus Christ.

They do not perceive themselves as walking encyclopedias but as resource persons for the educational ministry of the church. People expect educational ministers to know the church's curriculum well; in addition, they come for resource suggestions about areas needing study, developmental needs of persons, and methods to improve teaching. Success in this area depends heavily on the ability to know the key, relevant resources available and where they can be secured.

When teaching or speaking, good preparation in understanding what the Bible teaches is important. Only then is it possible to communicate convincingly the truths of God so hearers appropriate them to their lives. Educators use their minds creatively to present these truths in attractive, acceptable forms. They use their intellect.

MEs must be the best they can be for God and for the work God has given them; they must be well-read and well-versed in a variety of subjects. They specialize in learning about the teaching/learning process and its dynamics. Learning is never for learning's sake but for becoming the best ministers.

Enthusiasm

The word *enthusiasm* means "God breathed." MEs' excitement and enthusiasm come from the indwelling of God's Spirit within them. The work they do is God's work and is approached reverently and with a sense that they are sharing the good news of Jesus Christ. Whatever their personalities, they should exude excitement in all they do. They participate in God's work, work with the power to transform and radically change lives for good and for God. Even an introverted person can exemplify this excitement and enthusiasm that come from the confidence that this work can and will change lives for Christ.

A sense of excitement has the potential to motivate and captivate the spirits of those who share the educational ministry. If MEs are enthusiastic, workers feel what is being done is significant and worthy of their best efforts. This role is not that of a cheerleader but a drum major, the leader of the band. They encourage and enable others to give their best in service to Christ, others, and the church.

Christian Model

People in the church watch MEs to see what kind of lives they live. Bingham and Loessner describe this aspect of one's life:

> He is also one who should show what it means to be a Christian. Possibly his finest leadership opportunity in Christian education comes through his daily living among the people who make up the local church. Whether he is conscious of it or not, they are observing his life, his attitudes, his habits, his style of leadership, his language and to a large extent are patterning their lives after what they see in him, rather than by what they hear him say or see him do.[15]

Steadfastness of Purpose

A great hindrance to church growth is ministers who do not have a clear game plan. They often embrace every fad promising to provide magical church growth. Any work worth doing requires hard work. There is no easy road to success. While I was serving as an ME, the Sunday School director and I set a goal to maintain the current Sunday School attendance rather than continue the pattern of decline. Six months later, the Sunday School records showed the worse decline in the church's history. We questioned whether we were doing the right things. After careful analysis, we determined we had the right game plan and would not detour from its pursuit. In another six months, growth was beginning to take place.

Steadfastness of purpose comes when MEs know who they are and where they are going. This ministry and its ministers must have a focus, a sense of direction. They may become discouraged and find the way difficult, but they are willing to risk their professional futures in the pursuit of the educational goals. The apostle Paul expressed it well when he said, "I press on toward the goal to win the prize for which God has called me heavenward in Christ Jesus" (Phil. 3:14, NIV).

I am a goal oriented person. Writing this book is the fulfillment of a goal. It started as a dream, then an outline, and ultimately the writing of each chapter. There have been many interruptions and demands that slowed the progress. I struggled, even labored, to keep at the task. So it is in the church. MEs have dreams of what God wants His church to be. Plans and strategies are devised to help those dreams become realities. Distractions and problems arise that deter quick accomplishment of the dreams. A stubborn resolve to work at the task brings victory in the end.

Ministers who look honestly at the vastness of the job feel overwhelmed. Often when they feel this, it immobilizes them; they do nothing, or work on tasks that require less or can be done in a shorter period. One time management idea is the Swiss cheese approach: take one bite at a time! Instead of trying to do the job all at once, begin nibbling away at it. Do the part that can be done in the time available now. Keep working to complete the task one step at a time. Have a vision of what must be done and the resolve to work at the task until it is completed. When the task is successfully completed, then hope to hear the words of Jesus: "Well done, good and faithful servant" (Matt. 25:21, NIV).

Other Personal Characteristics

There are other personal characteristics that help MEs function more effectively. These are qualities all leaders ought to have as they work with people.

Educational ministers need true humility. They understand who they are and have a high regard for others. While humble in spirit and disposition, they also have enough strength or assertiveness to prompt others to want to engage in God's work through the church.

They have high moral character. Part of moral character is sincerity or honest dealing with others both in behavior and in speech.

MEs are attractive in personality and appearance. Their personality and disposition are such that others are attracted to them.

A good sense of humor is a great asset to MEs. They can laugh at themselves and laugh with others. Humor is used appropriately and in good taste. Humor is a great asset in building strong relationships with others. It can release tension when emotions are high. Humor is never used at the expense of others, to ridicule or put them down.

Patience both with people and with programs is needed. People need to feel led rather than pushed. It is about as easy to push people as it is to push a chain. Both can be pulled but neither can be successfully pushed.

Nothing can substitute for good, old-fashioned common sense. MEs need to consider how decisions and views will be interpreted by others. Sound judgment is part of exercising common sense. People ought to feel that educational ministers can be trusted and that proposals and decisions have been well thought out and are reasonable.

Notes

1. Louis McComb, *DCE: A Challenging Career in Christian Education* (Richmond: John Knox Press, 1963), 70.

2. Maria Harris, *The DRE Book: Questions and Strategies for Parish Personnel* (New York: Paulist Press, 1976), 71.

3. Paul Hersey, *The Situational Leader* (Escondido, CA: The Center of Leadership Studies, 1984). This work emphasizes this point.

4. See chapter 14 in this book for a further discussion of the role of MEs as motivators.

5. For further discussion and guidelines on delegation, see Leonard W. Wedel, *Church Staff Administration* (Nashville: Broadman Press, 1978), 145-47.

6. John Drakeford, *The Awesome Power of the Listening Ear* (Nashville: Broadman Press, 1981).

7. Reginald McDonough, comp., *Growing Ministers Growing Churches* (Nashville: Convention Press, 1980).

8. Harold J. Westing, *Multiple Church Staff Handbook* (Grand Rapids: Kregal Publications, 1985), 44-57.

9. Harris, *The DRE Book,* 30.

10. See Westing, *Multiple Church Staff Handbook,* 15-23. This chapter describes the reasons for and the advantages of teamwork.

11. See J. M. Price, *Jesus the Teacher* (Nashville: Convention Press, 1981) for a good discussion concerning Jesus as a master teacher.

12. Robert E. Bingham and Ernest Loessner, *Serving with the Saints* (Nashville: Broadman Press, 1970), 115.

13. Ibid., 116.

14. Ibid.

15. Ibid., 125.

4

Professional Aspects

This chapter explores the educational training and preparation for MEs. Attention is focused on their attitude toward the church. The need for a commitment to an educational ministry is examined. The necessity of being disciplined and competent in Christian education is described. Also considered is the need for effective team work and the leadership needs of MEs.

This chapter could be used by a pastor or church personnel committee to select the kind of persons needed as MEs. It provides information about the professional training and skills needed to function effectively in the local church setting. This chapter is particularly relevant for persons considering entering the field of Christian education as a profession.

What Is a Professional?

The dictionary defines a professional as "having great skill or experience in a particular field or activity" or "one who has an assured competence in a particular field or occupation."[1] By definition then MEs qualify as professionals. They have great skill and experience in Christian education and are competent in this area of ministry.

Another important question is: What constitutes a profession? Montgomery offers this definition: "A profession is simply a calling or occupation that requires special skills, techniques, training, or continued study to fulfill its functions."[2] Although this definition applies to all professions, MEs fit most of the criteria. The one area not often found among educational ministers is continuing education or study. This is also true of the ministerial profession as a whole. Those who see "ministry as profession do so with the idea of encouraging sound training, adequate education, and responsibility for quality in service."[3]

Glasse lists five characteristics of the professional.[4] First, the professional is educated. MEs have studied both theology and Christian education. They should receive this education from an accredited educational institution. Second, they become competent both in theology and Christian education through the experiences of ministry. As Glasse says, "These skills...can be learned and sharpened by practice under supervision."[5] MEs have a specialty— not an all-encompassing expertise—in theology and Christian education. Third, the professional is an institutional person. MEs primarily work in local churches but also may function in denominational administration and publishing. Fourth, they are responsible and seek to act competently. They function as professionals according to high standards of competence and ethics. Fifth, professionals are dedicated both to the institutions served and to the profession.

Montgomery identifies six general characteristics illustrating ways ministry is a profession. Adapted to educational ministry specifically, they are:

1. *MEs associate with other educational ministers.* They cooperate with other local Christian educators and join state, regional, or national Christian education associations which are denominational and/or interdenominational organizations. Their participation is based on their need to discuss contemporary issues, to share problems and solutions, and to seek the counsel of others. In the midst of these activities, they gain inspiration, share in learning experiences, plan cooperative ventures with other churches or groups, and pray together for God's guidance and assistance.

2. *MEs subscribe to periodicals related to the ministry of Christian education published by their denomination and other groups.* Most professional organizations publish journals designed to keep their members advised of developments in the field, research papers, and other items of interest.

3. *All or part of MEs' livelihood comes from those whom they serve in the church.* Just as pastors are worthy of their hire, so are MEs.

4. *MEs are perceived in their community as professionals by nature of the services they render.* They are well trained in the ministry and show that their lives are dedicated to educational ministry.

5. *Because of their response to a divine call, MEs are dedicated and*

committed to ministry. They reflect this professional concern by ways in which they go about ministry. It is more than a job or a career; it is a calling received from God.

6. *MEs live by Christian values and ethics confirmed through their ministries.* Every profession has an ethical code to govern personal conduct and the way its practitioners carry out their duties. MEs measure their conduct by the life of Jesus Christ and by the clear teachings of the Bible. Ethical behavior is chosen and valued because of God's love and righteousness. Their personal and professional lives are above reproach.[6]

Preparation

Many theological and divinity schools offer courses to prepare persons to become MEs. To work on a degree from one of these institutions, a baccalaureate degree is necessary. There is divided opinion among Christian educators about whether persons preparing for seminary or divinity school should major in religion or Christian education. In college some feel it is better for prospective ministers to have a strong liberal arts background rather than narrowing their collegiate studies to Bible and religion alone. Persons broaden their perspective by majoring in liberal arts even if attending a denominational or Bible college. Not everyone who goes to seminary has a college degree. Some seminaries permit work on a diploma after the age of thirty.[7]

Students in Christian education have many degree plans to pursue. The basic degree is the Master of Religious or Christian Education or a Master of Arts in Christian Education, typically a two year program.[8] The Master of Divinity in Christian Education usually requires three years. Both degree plans are popular. The Master of Divinity degree provides students with the same theological courses taken by persons preparing for pastoral ministry, but adds a heavy concentration in Christian education. The earliest organization for MEs, the Association of Church Directors of Religious Education founded in 1913, required four years of college, three years of seminary with courses in religious education, or two years of approved study in a school of religious pedagogy for active membership.[9] In 1930, Munro wrote, "The academic training of the director should equal that of the minister (pastor), both in scope and content, and in addition should include somewhat more emphasis in religious education."[10] The degree plan may decide whether persons may be ordained by the denomination. The subject of ordination will be discussed later.

Church-Centered

The work of educational ministers centers in the church whether they serve a local church, a cluster of churches, or a denominational position. It is fortunate if they have participated in the educational ministry of a local church. This provides a background of knowledge, attitudes, and appreciation for what the church seeks to do through Christian education. Being able to identify with the workers in leadership positions of the church's educational programs is also an advantage. In working with students, I have observed they find it is difficult, if not almost impossible, to comprehend a Sunday School program, a discipleship training activity, or what missions education can do for a church without having experienced them. Good personal educational experiences in the local church before entering educational ministry is invaluable to MEs. They need a background of understanding and appreciating the goals and programs of the educational organizations of the local church. Persons without this background could get experience participating in a church while attending a college or seminary that has a strong, well-balanced Christian education program. The result of these personal experiences and seminary studies should be a sound biblical doctrine of the church and a deep, abiding love for the church and its mission. This includes knowledge about church polity—how their church does its work and organizes itself to do its tasks—and the ability to lead the church to reach its goals through educational programs.

ME's interpretation of the church's purposes has a direct influence on ministry in the church. They provide leadership to the church's educational organizations that interpret what it means to be Christian. They help the church consistently fulfill its mission and ministry both to other Christians and to persons outside the influence of the church. Church educational organizations are often the entrance into the church for persons who are unsaved or unchurched. Unchurched persons may not belong to a local church but have had a relationship with Christ and His church previously. Educational activities also strive to introduce persons to Christ as salvation is explained and offered. Persons are trained, invited, and encouraged to be a part of the mission of the church. This is true both where the church is and to the entire world.

Committed to Evangelism

MEs are committed to personal evangelism. Not only should they train others to engage in personal soul-winning, they also must be practitioners.

Major time is devoted to work with the Sunday School program. Some denominations have made Sunday School their primary tool for outreach and evangelism. They do not believe that the Sunday School saves a person. They believe if you can get a person into a Sunday School class, the Holy Spirit will use Bible study and the witness of workers and members to lead that person to salvation.

Ordination

Ordination is hotly discussed in many denominations today. The type of polity practiced by various denominations has little to do with the ordination debate. It is not my intent to describe the various issues and concerns related to ordination practices, but to raise the issue as it relates to MEs.

Part of the issue is whether women ought to be ordained. Some denominations and churches have ordained women to ministry. In congregational polity, ordination is in the hands of the local church. If the educational minister has a valid ministry in the church, then he or she should be ordained as other ministers in the church and denomination are.

Some MEs do not seek ordination, primarily because they see themselves as laypersons. Ordination separates them from the laity. Some do not seek ordination because their pastors do not want them to be ordained. Some pastors do not feel comfortable having other ordained ministers on the church staff. Some educational ministers are not that involved in pastoral ministries where ordination would be beneficial. Ordination implies an authority and responsibility which some educational ministers do not want; ordination might force them to function in roles for which they do not feel competent or called. Whether MEs are ordained or not is a decision made by denominations, by the local church served, and by educational ministers.

Montgomery lists four practical benefits ordination accords the church and the persons called:

1. *Ordination is a confirmation of the person's call.* It is God who calls and equips persons to ministry. God uses the church to affirm that call in the individual.

2. *Ordination sets the person aside for service.* A Baptist practice after a person acknowledges God's call to ministry is for their local church to "license" them. This act encourages them to begin doing the ministry they feel called to do. Ordination has followed after a period of time in which the church has an opportunity to observe that person's ministry gifts and abilities. Ordination bestows the church's encouragement, prayers, support, and blessing as the person begins ministry.

3. *Ordination notifies other churches of the person's call and response to a special function in ministry.* Ordination remains in effect throughout a minister's lifetime. As he moves from church to church, his ordination goes with him, rather than being reordained by each subsequent church served. After ordination, other churches are free to use the person as a minister.

4. *Ordination grants legal status to the person as a minister.* In some states, ministers must be ordained to perform weddings or other services expected of a minister. The federal government has also used ordination to define occupational status for tax purposes.[11]

A study of current ordination practices suggests the decision regarding ordination is made more at the denominational level than by the local church. Often the ordination decision focuses on educational qualifications rather than the ministry position to be filled. The key criterion for ordination seems to be whether the candidate has completed a theology or divinity degree. In discussing courses an ME should take in seminary to earn the M.A.C.E. degree, one theology professor stated he would never agree to ordain an ME who did not study systematic theology. This attitude places a premium on certain theological courses rather than on ministerial functions.

In some denominations there seems to be a trend toward ordaining MEs regardless of the seminary degree earned. They do not set out theological qualifications for ordination. Being a professional educator, I, of course, believe strongly in education. Yet the question of ordination should be answered by evaluating both the work of MEs and their academic and theological preparation. If MEs minister in pastoral care, proclamation, conducting weddings and funerals—as pastoral ministers do—the same privileges of ordination should be given. Munro states the issue well:

> The case for ordination of a professional leadership for the Church seems about as strong as for that of pastoral leadership. Religious education is one method and preaching and pastoral work is another method of carrying out the same program. It is

> difficult to see how one method is more sacred or fraught with holier responsibility than the other. There ought to be no difference in spiritual qualifications for the two functions. If it is a question of "the fitness of things" there seems no reason the director should not be ordained.
>
> In giving the educational method and function its proper recognition and in placing upon its leaders their grave responsibility, ordination seems to have definite value. Lack of it causes unfortunate and untrue implications of inferiority.[12]

Part of this problem is perpetuated by theological and divinity schools. In some of these schools Christian education is given either a secondary or inferior role behind the more important theological, divinity curriculum. One reason for this is that the field of Christian education is a young discipline. Several years ago I joined a theological faculty as a special instructor in religious education. A long time faculty member welcomed me by saying he was glad that I was there to teach in a "no content area." In that school there was a radical distinction made between the theoretical and the practical. He felt the theoretical was more important or significant than the practical. Unfortunately this view has carried forward into the present in how seminary curriculum is arranged, and also in the way many seminaries are structured into separate schools.

To use the degree earned as the only criteria for ordination totally ignores the work that MEs do. Interestingly the process of ordination and the determination of who is to be ordained is primarily in the hands of pastors or denominational leaders with pastoral backgrounds. Thus, an appropriate response is for educational ministers to establish some professional standards and criteria. Such standards could include academic training, internships that benefit the ME, and an established criteria for continuing education needed to maintain professional standing. This is in keeping with such professions as medicine, law, nursing, and social work. Such responses have not been forthcoming due to the relative newness of the profession or perhaps a reluctance by MEs to set forth such standards.

Ordination practices vary from denomination to denomination and from church to church. It is not my intent to try to dictate to a church or denomination about ordination. My concern is that fairness be applied in deciding who will be ordained.

Discipline

Self-discipline is essential for successful MEs. They need regular office hours even though their work in the areas of educational ministry, evangelism, and lay leadership enlistment and development often requires working away from the church building and after typical business hours. For example, when they function as counselors, meetings may occur away from the church building or at times outside regular office hours. They spend many nights making home visits and meeting with committees and program organizations. MEs need to balance work and leisure time. When there are night meetings they may leave early in the afternoon or come in later the next morning. In every case, they need to work the expected number of hours, being careful not to abuse the privilege of flexible work hours.

Although MEs are accountable to and report to pastors, in essence they are their own bosses. They set hours and decide what to do on any given day, choosing among tasks such as:

• the administration of the church's educational program;
• planning what to do with the program councils (such as the Sunday School Council);
• planning the agenda with program leaders for organizational meetings;
• preparing adequately when they are responsible for speaking and leading group activities; and
• devoting major blocks of time to studying educational trends, educational innovations, and developmental psychology as they influence Christian education.

They discipline themselves so they have time for family, if married, or for themselves, if single. Family and personal time are scheduled just like the heavy demands on their time from leaders and members of the church. While striving to keep spiritually fit they also need to remain physically fit. They will be unable to be good managers of others if they cannot manage themselves well. They learn to establish priorities or they find themselves pulled in every direction—by family, friends, recreation, leaders, pastor, and denomination.

An additional problem in the wise use of time is that often they are not in control of structuring their schedules. The pastor, church volunteer leaders, and others have agendas MEs are expected to address. As staff members they confront several sets of goals or priorities: the pastor has expectations; MEs have their own goals and priorities; the church's goals; goals of the educational leaders; the goal and expectations of other staff members; and the goals of their denomination. Good communication aids in the resolution of potential conflict between these many sets of goals. The pastor and educational leaders need to know what MEs are striving to do so they can sustain and appreciate the benefits to the church through the educational programs. Educational ministers' priorities and goals are never theirs alone but are adopted through working with the pastor, other staff members, and educational leaders. Thus there is joint ownership of tasks and the encouragement and support of others as they work.

Competency

Being professionals means they are competent and skilled in the total field of Christian education and that they function effectively as both ministers and educators. Although each competency skill needed by educational ministers is discussed in Part II, a brief thumbnail sketch is described below:

• **Administrators.** MEs are responsible for providing administrative leadership and support to the church's educational ministry. They function as administrators in helping each program organization achieve its specific tasks and objectives. This includes working with program leaders in developing budgets, providing necessary equipment and materials used by the educational programs, and securing essential curricula materials. Much of their administrative time is spent working with the Christian education committee or educational councils, helping these program leaders give administrative direction to their programs.

• **Planners.** MEs work with program organizations in making not only long-range plans, but also weekly, monthly, quarterly, and annual plans. They coordinate all of the programs so that the cumulative needs of the church, its members, and the community are adequately met. Coordination skills see that each programs' leaders work within task statements that coincide with the objectives of the church. Stated simply, they lead in planning the church program. They help educational organizations in making plans for the present and the future. Planning is seen as a means to an end, not the end of the administrative process.

• **Equippers/enablers.** This is the heart of MEs' work. Their primary task is to equip and enable the people of God to do the work of ministry. This task requires more than discovering, enlisting, and training potential workers for the Christian education organizations and the church, and can be handled in several ways. They assist the church in the nomination, selection, and election of potential workers. They also are encouragers of persons who currently work and serve. In offering potential leader training programs, persons surface who could provide leadership in the total life of the church. They also discover potential leaders through talent and skills surveys. MEs consult regularly with leaders of adults to identify potential leaders whom they strive to enlist and involve in leadership positions. They work with appropriate program leaders to train properly all workers so they can effectively do their assigned tasks.

• **Delegators.** The ministry of education is training and equipping others to do the work of ministry. All members have a ministry to render. This part of the ME's job is never ending. Enabling others to do the work of ministry can only be done as MEs learn to delegate appropriate responsibility to program leaders and other qualified persons. With delegation goes supervision. Delegation without supervision usually means frustration for all parties involved. Supervisors seek to catch people doing something right and to give positive affirmation. When corrections need to be made they first affirm the person, then correct the problem. In large churches, MEs also have the responsibility to supervise age group staff workers who function as evaluators, supervisors, and trainers of others.

• **Evaluators.** MEs develop evaluation tools and skills for assessing the Christian education program. Evaluation begins when the statement of purpose, or the overarching objectives of the total Christian education program, is examined next to the results actually achieved in the total program. Then each educational organization is similarly assessed according to the task statements assigned to it. The purpose of evaluation is to help the church move forward. Educational ministers need to be experts. The Christian education program needs, such as curriculum, program organizational patterns, and space and equipment needs, are evaluated quantitatively and qualitatively. This evaluation occurs at least annually, but more often as the needs demand.

• **Growth agents.** All Christians need to continue to grow in their relationship to Christ and in their ability to serve Christ effectively. MEs help persons grow in the faith. They also help churches grow numerically. Probably more time and energy are devoted to such church growth than to helping believers grow and mature in the Christian faith. Church growth will occur through evangelism and outreach, but it cannot be sustained unless there is a good training program for new Christians and maturing disciples. Most churches need a more adequate discipleship program; a church cannot continue to grow numerically unless all members are growing in their relationship to Christ. MEs help the church develop a growth strategy so it can reach more persons with the gospel through its programs of outreach evangelism and discipleship training.

• **Communicators and promoters.** First, MEs are communicators, disclosing what they believe about the gospel, the church, and people. They have a responsibility to converse well in oral and written form through speaking opportunities, in letters, and in the church paper. Second, educational ministers promote the total Christian educational program; often they have the responsibility of promoting the total church program. Usually they are responsible for the church's public relations program, working with the church's publications, and helping the church be understood internally and externally.

• **Educators.** By calling, training, and job assignment, MEs are first educators. Because they are heavily involved in the total life of the church, there is the temptation to do more church administrative work. They must guard their time as educators and protect priority time for helping the church function and grow educationally. As educators, they devote most of their time to equipping and enabling people to be more effective in Christian service and ministry. As educators they are curriculum specialists, knowledgeable about new educational trends, educational psychology, teaching methodology, human development, and the theory and philosophy of education. They are constantly designing and completing training programs. Some training helps new persons assume places of leadership. Other training develops the skills and competencies of persons already serving.

• **Motivators.** Establishing a climate for motivation is a needed competency skill. MEs are enablers of persons so they can do the work of ministry. They are encouragers, helping persons to do their tasks well. They establish a climate where every worker and member feels freedom to use their spiritual gifts. Educational ministers are motivators through their excitement and enthusiasm about their work. They also serve as motivators by examples they set and the quality of work done. People decide they can do their jobs because MEs model effective Christian education. MEs' personal motivation is high as they see what is happening in the lives of the people with whom they work.

• **Theologians.** As MEs interpret the Christian faith they function as theologians. They must have an adequate theology to explain and proclaim it to others. If their goal as educators is to encourage the development of Christian believers, they are theologians. Christian education is a practical theological discipline helping form the character of Christian people. Interpreting what it means to be a Christian and how one becomes a Christian are skills used by educational ministers. They know and communicate the great doctrines of the Christian faith both to their workers and to the church membership. They must study theology constantly to interpret it to others.

A Good Team Member

Westing describes the reasons for and the advantages of good teamwork.[13] Becoming a functioning team requires hard work and constant effort by each team member. Each team member is an equal of other team members and has a unique ministry to do. This does not negate the pastor's role as lead servant.[14]

Within two weeks after moving to a new church, a member told me I was the most important minister the church had. This was very flattering to my ego, but it simply was not true. I told her what I did was important but the senior minister was the most important minister in the church. Unless various members of the church staff including the ME see themselves as team members, the church will not be as effective as it could be if they worked together.

In an orchestra there are those who occupy the first chair. They will be ineffective unless those who occupy the second chair make their special, unique contribution. So it is in the church. It takes each staff member doing their job to the best of their ability for the church to move forward in worship, ministry, evangelism, and Christian nurture. For the church to be what it ought to be, educational ministers and other staff members should model for the entire church what good team work is.

Developing a good team depends upon recognition of the part each member of the team plays. The pastor is leader, the administrator of the church, and supervisor of the church staff. Each staff person knows what he/she is to do and has the responsibility and the authority to carry out the task. Various members of the team have different strengths and different spiritual gifts which complement those of other church staff members. Various testing instruments could be used to see how a church's staff members mesh and how they can better work together.

Through effective team work, the staff may lead church members to do the total work of the church and to minister to the variety of needs found in the congregation and the community.

Leadership

Every minister must exercise leadership. People in the church and in the community look to ministers to provide leadership in spiritual, moral, and ethical matters. MEs are able and need to be willing to lead in such areas, too.

Within the church, they provide leadership for the total educational program. Some MEs want also to be the program leaders particularly for the Sunday School program and discipleship activities. My preference is always to work with lay leaders, training and enabling them to carry on the ministry. When I was an ME, my Sunday School director often reminded me I was doing the work he was supposed to do. This danger exists because MEs are full-time and often do the work as the need arises. Remember, too, the unfortunate, rapid turnover rate among MEs that leaves the primary educational programs leaderless if they have done most of the work. Ideally, the ME's leadership roles bring continuity and balance to the church's total educational ministry.

MEs lead in other areas of the life of the church. As they work with various church committees and councils they provide leadership. By virtue of their position on the church staff they are perceived as leaders by program leaders and workers, by church committee members, and by the councils within the church with which they work. If they fail to exercise their leadership responsibilities, others in the church may move in to fill the leadership vacuum. If this occurs, MEs are unable to influence and direct the educational programs or the movement of the church in desired directions.

Notes

1. *The American Heritage Dictionary of the English Language*, s.v. "professional."

2. Felix E. Montgomery, *Pursuing God's Call: Choosing a Vocation in Ministry* (Nashville: Convention Press, 1981), 72.

3. G. Willis Bennett, "Ministry as Profession and Calling," *Review and Expositor* (Winter 1973): 10.

4. James D. Glasse, *Profession: Minister* (Nashville: Abingdon Press, 1968), 38.

5. Ibid.

6. Montgomery, *Pursuing God's Call*, 73-74.

7. This is the policy at the six Southern Baptist seminaries. The reasoning behind this policy is that a person can and should be able to complete college and then enter seminary by age thirty.

8. Some schools use the term "religious" while others use the term "Christian." I will use the term "Christian."

9. Johnie Clifford Tharp, Jr., *"The Parish Minister of Education ... An Examina-*

tion of His Role(s)" (Ed.D. Dissertation, Southern Baptist Theological Seminary, 1970), 52.

10. Harry C. Munro, *The Director of Religious Education* (Philadelphia: Westminster Press, 1930), 171-72. The term "pastor" inserted in the parenthesis is my clarification rather than Munro's word.

11. Montgomery, *Pursuing God's Call,* 90-91.

12. Munro, *The Director of Religious Education,* 36-37.

13. See Harold J. Westing, *Multiple Church Staff Handbook* (Grand Rapids: Kregal Publications, 1985), 14-23; this section describes the team concept.

14. Ibid., 44-46.

5

The Joy of Being an ME

Are there special joys or blessings MEs experience that are not enjoyed by pastors or other church staff members? I believe there are. Working in a support role, educational ministers see the accomplishments of events in the life of the church. Also they observe growth in the lives of workers and members not observed by other staff members.

Data for this chapter came from about fifty MEs who were randomly selected for a non-scientific study. Some had several years of experience; others were new to the work. Both men and women were included and all serve churches or work within denominational structures. I recorded their joys, observations, and insights, with illustrations and examples, as they shared them.

Their statements appear in their words. This experiential approach permits educational ministers to speak for themselves. The issues which they addressed and which comprise the remainder of this chapter are not listed in any order of priority or by the frequency with which the sample of ministers mentioned them.

Opportunities for Evangelism

Every minister and Christian should actively engage in personal evangelism and feel the joy of seeing a person come to know Jesus Christ as personal Lord and Savior. Evangelism involves seeing people make their professions of faith in Christ, join the church, or make rededications to Christ and the church. Joy comes in knowing these decisions are made because of our personal ministry. These are some testimonies:

> The greatest joy is sharing the gospel with a lost person. As I sat with a college student a few weeks ago and shared my testimony

and passages of Scripture, I rejoiced as he asked Jesus to come into his heart. In my twenty-five years on a church staff as a Minister of Education, nothing equals that kind of experience.

Joy is in training people in evangelistic witnessing, seeing them witnessing, and then training others. I can count over fifty men and women I trained in the church I served for 16 years.

Joy is leading someone to Christ, watching them get involved in discipleship, helping them discover their spiritual gifts, and then providing nurture and opportunities to use their gifts.

Another combined hospital ministry with evangelism. He wrote:

One young lady whom I visited in the hospital was very hostile. I said, "I'm only here as your friend, not a minister." I later witnessed to her, and saw her come to Christ. She has just finished seminary and entered the hospital chaplaincy.

Another educational minister wrote:

Pleasure comes from watching the outreach ministry of our church in full circle. It is reaching the lost through outreach and developing them into responsible positions of service through their church. Such was the occasion with one couple discovered by church members going door to door in a People Search. They enrolled in Sunday School, were led to the Lord, and were baptized. Later they went through the Leadership Training Program. Both accepted positions of leadership in the Sunday School program. He was later ordained as a deacon. This began seven years ago with the discovery of a fine unchurched couple with two small children who responded to the invitation to enroll in our Sunday School program.

Personal and Spiritual Growth

MEs are challenged to personal growth. As they minister to and with others, they also need to grow spiritually. As they mature and grow in spiritual maturity, they also enable others to grow in their personal and spiritual lives. They continue to learn more about their leadership styles and skills as they lead others.

One minister surveyed identified joy as the opportunity to set a high personal standard of spiritual sensitivity in a vocation that can become mechanical, rote, and routine. He did this through Scripture memory, study of the original Greek from a devotional and an academic perspective, daily quiet time and spiritual journaling, including a spiritual emphasis as one element of each educational staff meeting, and reading appropriate books and materials. He also set short-term and long-range goals for continuing personal academic growth and reached those goals by taking courses for credit at a local college and a seminary extension center. This continuing commitment to personal spiritual growth brought joy as he observed the positive effects this effort had on the staff and church members.

Growth of Christian Leaders

MEs receive joy as church leaders develop and begin to reach their potential as leaders. They have the joy of discovering new leaders and then seeing them function in a responsible, efficient manner. Joy comes in helping leaders improve their leadership skills. Their experiences include:

> An exciting thing in my ministry is watching people grow in their commitment to the Lord and to His church. I am thrilled as I see a teacher or department director organize a class or department and begin to effectively minister to members and prospects. I remember a class of adult women who recently began working with a blind lady. She responded to their efforts as she began to attend church regularly.

> My greatest joy is discovering the potential people have to serve the Lord. It is a wonderful experience to see a young or old Christian find ways they can be used. Recently I had the joy of seeing a quiet couple discover their gifts. It began with a telephone call followed by a visit. We went over the job description for preschool teachers. I emphasized training and the weekly workers meeting. Both accepted this place of responsibility and exceeded all my expectations. They are now directors of two of our preschool departments. They have excelled in Sunday School work. They are also involved in training activities and have volunteered to help in ministry opportunities. They have publicly given testimonies to what God is doing in their lives. What a joy it is for me to have been a small part of their discovery process.

> One of my greatest joys and pleasures is observing those persons who graduate from our Leadership Training Program. They now fill strategic Sunday School leadership positions. They are department directors, teachers, and outreach leaders in every age group. The Potential Leadership Class does not ask for a commitment to a position upon completion of the course. It calls for a commitment to be available as the leader might lead. My experience is about eighty-five percent of the graduates accept positions of leadership within three to six months. My responsibility as ME is to provide training and equipping opportunities to serve effectively and happily.

> One of the greatest joys of 40 + years of educational ministry was

seeing people I had enlisted to serve in some area maturing in that process, being blessed, and moving into greater areas of service. I even have some "sons and daughters in the ministry." Some have moved into the same or similar fields of vocational callings. Some are in seminary and others are already serving churches. Being in churches for extended periods makes this even more apparent, for such growth takes time.

Another found joy in seeing people grow and become disciples of Jesus Christ. He saw this as people developed from being a "sitting member" to becoming a Sunday School class officer and then a teacher. Happiness is seeing children, youth, and adults grow, develop, and mature from the point of being led to becoming leaders themselves. There is delight in equipping young Christians and then observing their maturation in Christ.

Another wrote:

There is great joy in equipping the saints to be "salt and light" in the marketplace. When lay people risk their faith to minister in the marketplace that is affirming to me as an ME. The *transformation* that I perceive keeps me going.

Assist Believers Toward Spiritual Maturity

MEs must be growing Christians if they are to lead others to grow in spiritual maturity. They should be growing in their faith and relationship to God. They cannot legitimately ask others to do and to be what they themselves are not doing or becoming. Their faith must be so contagious that others want to be like them.

Two MEs commented:

Being the "enabler"—helping persons find their gifts, develop them, and press them into service—brings joy. No one else in the church shares this unique position.

Helping people discover their gifts and providing a community in which they can develop and exercise those gifts makes being an enabler a rewarding vocation.

Others found joy in seeing God come into the lives of people and effect change, or in discipling Christians who valued a more significant relationship with Christ.

Help the Church Grow

There is joy in seeing numerical increase in church programs for which MEs have responsibility. This may be Sunday School enrollment and attendance, discipleship training, Christian stewardship, or many other programs.

One respondent noted joy in averaging a net gain of two per Sunday in Sunday School enrollment over twenty-one years in educational ministry. Another found joy in building a Sunday School organization where none previously existed and seeing it grow and reach out into the community.

Another described her joy:

> It is pure fun to organize, equip, support, and work with people who want to do the work of the church, and even with those who don't when I win them over. Their success is mine. Their joy and satisfaction is mine. Their growth through effort and struggle, success and failure is mine.

Being in God's Will

Every Christian and minister should desire to know the will of God for their lives. There is a powerful, personal affirmation experienced from doing what God wants them to do with their life and ministry. They ought to have a consciousness of being in God's plan for their lives. This is how some expressed this joy:

> I've really found a deep sense of quiet joy in knowing I'm where God wants me to be.

> The joy is being involved in such an important venture and knowing God has called you to this ministry.

> Joy results from obedience to God's leading. He called me to the educational ministry, and it was always a joy to be where God wanted me. I was very sure of this call. Joy also is a result of the Holy Spirit's presence in a believer's life. This is the primary source of joy in my ministry. Joy is an inner condition rather than the result of outward circumstances.

> Often the work was hard, or discouraging, or confusing, but always there was a return to the realization of joy because of God's Spirit of encouragement.

Helping Workers Grow in Skill Development

Much of an ME's time and energy is spent helping persons develop skills to be better ministers of Christ. No greater joy comes than observing a worker have an "Aha!" experience. It seems as if one can see the light of insight flash into the person's mind. This joy was described:

It is a great joy to watch a teacher see the value of using teaching methods that involve class members. I observed a teacher of older women at a weekly workers' meeting. In previewing the lesson, a method was used that she perceived as fit only for school age children. When the activity was completed, she discovered how useful the method was for accomplishing the intended purpose of the lesson. It was like a light being turned on. She realized how valuable involvement of the learner was for deeper learning.

Joy came as I watched the saints in the churches grow in service and as I helped them know how to lead or teach. "Equipping the saints" was what I felt called to do, and this work with people in the church was joyous.

I find joy in creating maps for the laity to use. I see my role as a "map maker." It gives me great joy when lay persons value my maps enough to pick them up and use them in ministry. There is great joy in creating maps!

Starting New Teaching Units

MEs face the challenge of convincing Sunday School leaders of the importance of starting new teaching units. It is even more joyous to help a person become committed to growth by starting a new class. Here are two such experiences:

A doctor had a class of people in their 60s. He loved the class and its warm fellowship. He finally was persuaded to try to create a new unit. It surprised him when he found how easy it was to get new members to join that were never interested in the old class.

I serve in an old historic downtown church. I have experienced joy at starting new Sunday School classes and watching them grow and thrive. Two classes have particularly pleased me. One was a young single adult class that started with six and now has over forty-five. Another class was one of young adult couples that started with three or four couples and in a short time had ten to twelve couples attending regularly.

Enlisting Workers

As equippers and enablers, MEs seek to enlist more workers. While this is both a great challenge and a continuing task, nothing can bring more joy. One said, "I greatly enjoyed the challenge of finding someone with leadership or ministry potential. I would then train them and enlist them in their desired area of service." Another wrote, "I've been particularly blessed in this area. I could sense where various people could serve. I have evidently been persuasive in a Christian way to encourage them to take that place of service." Another expressed joy as:

> Being a facilitator of convergence! It is a great joy for me in putting the pieces of the puzzle together, stepping back, and seeing ministry happen. When organization and relationships converge, that is exciting for me to watch. Convergence results in real growth in the church.

Influencing Others

Everyone wants to influence those with whom they work. One described her joy as:

> Watching people grow at all ages. When a young preschooler in a public place smilingly greets me as "my friend from church," it's joy. It's joy when I listen to a teenager I taught last year teaching another person the same lesson. When a lady who was my inexperienced partner for visitation decides she likes it, it's joy. Spending time with a young couple, struggling through courtship and marriage, "your," "mine," and "our" children, celebrating promotions, adoptions, baptisms, watching them come out on the other side of difficult circumstances is joy. Knowing a sick person has felt God's presence through my presence is joy. Asking a senior adult to do a job and watching the smile of appreciation that results is joy. And it's just plain fun when a teacher who said, "Visual aids? Never!" is covering the wall with them after observing my use of them for a while.

Tenure

The ability to stay in one place for several years brought joy to several MEs.

> I felt this gave me the opportunity to know, minister with, earn trust and respect of the lay people and the vocational staff. Staying in one place allows the opportunity to mature and grow as a person. I also can see long term goals for ministry and programming come to reality.

> My greatest joy is the satisfaction of staying long enough in one place to see my "footprints in the sand." In over twenty-one years many new programs were started and are now stable and successful. The growth of facilities and the Sunday School over the years was a tremendous source of joy.

One described joy at "seeing the church grow from 300 to 1,150 in attendance, offerings grow from $300,000 to $1,600,000, and gifts to foreign missions grow from $5,000 to $94,000 in nine years."

Another quoted the advice of Gaines Dobbins, who said, "The ME should go to a church and stay there, growing his own leadership." His own assessment concluded, "This is a joy many ministers never experience."

Fruition of Plans and Dreams

Tenure brings other blessings and joys. One is seeing the fruition of plans and dreams. One described it as "an idea that began as just a spark is fleshed-out, reworked, prayed over, and refined. The ME's joy comes when the plan becomes a reality and the people think it was their idea!"

Others recounted these dreams:

> It has long been my dream to begin a counseling center at the church. Besides my educational ministry, I was seeing six to eight clients in counseling per week. We've called a full-time counselor, set up our center, and the counselor is already at a full-time load. It is affirming and humbling when God blesses us!

> It's been a joy seeing a problem solved, working with church leaders to plan change, and to cause the change with everyone being happy. In one church because of a lack of space, we went to two Sunday Schools and one worship service. We did some research on this with other churches. We were counseled not to do it. We worked out all the problems with our people and this was very successful.

> Joy is helping church members turn their dreams into realities. It is joy to lead a fund-raising program for a congregation who wants to build. It is a joy to reorganize and begin new units for a Sunday School or Discipleship Training group that wants to reach more people. It's a pleasure to find space for a crisis pantry for people who want to help others.

Planning and Coordination

The task of planning and coordinating the educational and church program is an unseen job. Yet even this is a source of joy. One wrote, "The joy is coordinating the *number one,* life changing organization in the church—the Sunday School—seeing it staffed and working just as it was designed to do." Another noted the use of the staff in planning: "I find pleasure in getting them to work on new ideas. I get their personal support and then get them to use their ministry group for personal growth."

Another wrote:

> I find joy in working with the Church Council as it sets objectives and goals, followed by action plans. I see people really get motivated as they see how the entire Council is leading the church. They then move in a specific way based on needs, visions, etc.

Another's delight came from helping individuals and the congregation develop a philosophy of and gain an appreciation for the essential nature of Christian education. He also noted:

> It is pleasurable to have your finger on the very heart-beat of the congregation. This is in terms of relating to the broadest spectrum possible of persons (even more so than the pastor) and the varieties of ministries they are involved in.

Others said this:

> Ours is a shared ministry in which mutual respect and responsibility form the basis for all that is done. Working with people to chart and implement the direction of the church, not in a competitive but in a cooperative venture, is rewarding.

> It has been a joy to guide churches in planning, and then see the actions that brought the plans to fulfillment. In Houston we got to move to a new location, totally design a new building, watch it go up and then fill it up.

> Another of my greatest joys is to lead our church members to accept their responsibilities of doing the work of the church. This means they love and follow the leadership of their staff. They do not expect the staff to do all the work of the church. One of my goals is to enlist people continuously to serve in various ways. It would often be easier to do it myself, but why should I take the joy away from them? Our church uses hundreds of volunteers.

Ministering to People

MEs have many opportunities to minister to people. This may be to the sick, either at home or in hospitals, or to those in trouble. Part of their ministry is helping people find their way. One ME identified joy as bringing comfort during times of sadness, grief, and loss. Another experienced joy by celebrating with others during times that are happy. Another was always glad for opportunities to make a contact for the church and to minister to a need. This was a way of expressing care for people.

The opportunity to influence others who accept the call of God to educational ministry brings joy. One described it:

Perhaps the most personally rewarding aspect of educational ministry and the most frightening is recognizing one's role as a model for ministry. It is most fulfilling to look at those now in educational ministry because of their observation of your ministry. This responsibility, though frightening at times, is also an excellent opportunity to extend the ministry to which God called you.

Another found great joy as the recipient of persons' ministries to whom he ministered. He wrote, "When I experienced my extended illness two years ago, some of the most comforting support my wife and I received was from people we had led through Master Life."
Another said:

It has been a joy receiving appreciation from those that I worked with. When I left one church, they took up a love offering and it totaled more than three month's salary. The men in the church bought a set of tires for me. When we went by the previous church and I spoke that morning, they gave me a month's salary as we were moving. The joy came from the appreciation more than the actual money.

Developing Relationships

Several MEs pointed out the joy of developing relationships with people you otherwise would not know. A long tenured ME stated:

Another great joy has been the relationships developed with people I have served in the church. Over these years ties have grown very strong. Babies born since I came are now college students. A genuine love has developed.

Another joy was developing a network of friends and colleagues across the nation through professional associations and conferences.

Good Staff Relationships

Working with staff members is a source of great pleasure. One ME expressed it as "the joy of serving with fellow staff members and developing a true 'family' relationship of love, care, and concern."
Another wrote:

It has been a real joy to work with staff members, even though many have come and gone. They are like proteges that I feel have been developed here. Our relationships continue to this day with a genuine feeling of love and respect.

Another joy is working with other staff members and the pastor to create a team approach to ministry. "Some of my closest friends are those I worked with on a church staff in years gone by," according to one. Another joy is mutually supporting each other and being supported. Some wrote:

> The most important relationship in the church for the ME is the one formed with the pastor. Developing a workable approach to ministry and mutually accepting one another's style of leadership is for me the single greatest opportunity for either growth or conflict. Beyond that relationship, learning to supervise the staff members ranging from fellow ministers to custodial staff requires an intentional, professional approach. I learned to listen before speaking, think before acting, and pray before confronting. I do enjoy other staff members because they become my family while serving on a particular staff.

> It has been a joy being a real friend with my pastor. This does not always happen. I believe it is so important that a person ought to consider the pastor more than the church. When one pastor inherited me, this was the finest relationship I ever had.

Receiving Affirmation

MEs do not work for the praise or applause of people. Yet, it is good to receive positive affirmation. They like to feel they made a difference or are appreciated. One described her joy:

> The personal feedback makes me feel like I have been Christlike at least some time. Hearing feedback like the following is joy: "You have shown me that a woman can be her own person and be strong also." "Did you think up this game? It seems like something that would come out of your mind!" "Next time I need someone to rouse the troops, I'll call you!" "You taught me how to teach!" "The kids know you treat everybody the same." "Your marriage is an inspiration to us."

Administrative Joy

Only one ME described joy in helping the church in administrative matters. She wrote:

> Another joy I have is in the area of finances. It's a wonderful feeling to be responsible for overseeing the tithes and offerings people bring to our church. The budget directs me; but I take the responsibility to have a greater dimension—that is, I work with the budget account managers to make the best use of their monies. Because we take this aspect seriously, the use of volunteers, creativity, and bargains are an important part of our work. Every dollar we save, we can use in another area of ministry. Being frugal with the Lord's money is a joy when you

discover you can do quality ministries and sometimes work with less than what was budgeted.

Summary

Two MEs expressed it well. One wrote, "Joy takes time; time deepens joy." One wrote shortly after retiring, "How do you name your greatest joy? All forty years were filled with the joy of my calling, even the mundane, routine, and thankless tasks necessary to being an ME!"

Part II

What Does an ME Do?

Part II seeks to answer the questions: "What does an ME do? What are the competency skills needed for an educational ministry to function effectively?" The skills chosen are germane to the work of Christian education. Many skills selected are broader in scope than presented here. There are other skills that could be considered.

Chapter 6, "Administrator," details the administrative skills needed by the person who administers the church's educational program.

The ME's planning functions are analyzed in chapter 7. Educators plan with the educational organizations by working with each organization's council. This involves various types of planning—weekly, monthly, quarterly, and annually. An important part of planning is coordinating the total church program. Planning is also integrally related to budgeting.

Chapter 8 describes the ME's skills in equipping and enabling others. This task majors on recruiting and training leaders personally and by working closely with the church nominating committee or Christian education committee.

"Delegator" is the topic of chapter 9. This role is crucial to the task of equipping and enabling the people of God to do the work of ministry. Delegation and supervision are closely woven together.

Evaluating the educational program is explained in chapter 10. Evaluation is a key skill needed by the Christian educator. The total educational ministry and its structures are the subjects of evaluation. This skill is essential in making necessary adjustments to the educational program.

The ME as "Growth Agent" is reviewed in chapter 11. Educators expect to help the church grow numerically. This is only part of the growth agent's function. Individual believers need to grow in spiritual maturity. Training in discipleship is needed not only for new believers but as a continuing program for all ages.

Chapter 12 describes the ME as "Communicator." Some see this as the primary task of Christian education. There are three basic functions associated with this role: communicator, promoter, and public relations expert.

"The ME as Educator" is interpreted in chapter 13. They have many educational tasks to accomplish for the church. Some subjects considered are: curriculum selection, recruitment and training of workers, educational specialist, age-group specialists, teaching and learning dynamics, and developing educational skills. To be educators is the calling of the church and the best definition of who MEs are and what they do.

Chapter 14 considers the ME as "Motivator." This chapter examines the issues of internal and external motivational factors. Maslow's hierarchy of needs is related to the Christian educator's work in the church. Their task is to help create a climate where positive motivation can take place.

"Theologian" is the focus of chapter 15. MEs functioned in this role for a long time. The plea made is for Christian educators to be conscientious theologians who lead others in interpreting their faith. This is not a new competency skill for MEs, but many need a new acceptance of this role in the lives of members and of the church.

6

Administrator

Robert serves his first church as full-time ME. It is a new church, about ten years old. The church experienced rapid growth primarily through the evangelistic efforts of the pastor. Many people reached do not know much about the denomination or its educational programs. Most of the people do not have a strong church background. The church is weak administratively although it has a strong Sunday School program. Little has been done concerning discipleship training and missions education and most of it has been done through Sunday School sponsorship. The various organizations do what they want to do. There is much overlap and duplication of efforts.

Robert has some uneasiness going into this situation. He has concern about his lack of experience. Where should he begin? Are there some guidelines or principles he should know and follow? How can he help each organization do its assigned task? What pitfalls should he watch for?

Many educational ministers carry the responsibility for the administration of the church. I acknowledge this role because many MEs spend more of their time doing church administration than educational administration. Harris comments:

> Any parish has within its congregation many persons who could take on the financial business of the parish, or, better, enough persons to form finance committees representative of all parish interests, which could develop new and ingenious approaches to fund raising and spending.[1]

Her analogy applies to other areas of the church's life. Many church committees could handle some of the administrative details assigned to MEs.

This chapter focuses on administration related to the educational ministry and programs. Harris observes, "Administration includes many duties: planning, implementing, scheduling, securing faculty for, and supervising programs for . . . the various age groups. Administration involves the necessary office routine to such work."[2]

Much of the ME's time is given to administering the Christian education program. Part of this responsibility is seeing that all the educational programs function in an efficient, competent manner. A Christian education program cannot run itself. It requires responsible persons to provide administrative leadership. Robert Bower states:

> Administrators must work with hundreds of details when directing a broad educational program. Plans must be made and policies formulated; they must be carefully carried out; data must be gathered showing the extent to which the plans are successful or unsuccessful, so that future policy-making and planning will point toward realistic goals. In essence, a sound program calls for effective administration.[3]

Each program has specific tasks to do which aid the church in achieving its objectives and goals. For instance, Bible study is one assigned task of the Sunday School program. All Christian education programs have a strong biblical base. As administrator, the educational minister sees that each organization is doing its assigned work. This chapter highlights administrative principles that have special application to the Christian education program and the administrative structure needed for a productive educational ministry. It suggests basic administrative guidelines intended to improve administrative functioning. Techniques are proposed to help ministers work constructively with the educational councils and the Christian education committee or board. Organizational, administrative structure is described.

Computers and Educational Administration

Many churches use computers to assist in record keeping and for data bases. MEs must have awareness of how the computer can help in handling educational administrative matters. Computers help in keeping class rosters, attendance, service records, training received, plus a myriad of other tasks beneficial to educational ministers. One does not have to be a computer wizard to make the computer work for the educational program. There are a number of church software packages available to fit the needs of most any church. Once the data is entered, its recall and reports greatly help the ME in his/her work. A number of potential uses of the computer are described as they are appropriate to the ME.

Guidelines for the Administrator[4]

Powers suggests ten guidelines for MEs as administrators:

1. *Determine the purpose and organizational structure for each educational program.* Each program has specific, unique tasks for which it is primarily responsible. The value in establishing the purpose and tasks for organizations is to eliminate overlapping responsibilities and the duplication of efforts. It also helps the church have a broader range of ministries and services. Sample task statements for the various educational programs are presented later.

2. *Use, or establish, a church council or committee of key leaders to plan, coordinate, and evaluate the church's total educational ministry.* Each educational unit has a core of key leaders who are accountable to the church. The church needs representatives from each program area plus some at large members who give general oversight to the Christian education program. This is done best through a Christian education committee or board. This group is for planning, coordinating, and evaluating the Christian education program. Some churches do these tasks through the church council; the problem with using the church council is that so many of its members are in noneducational aspects of the church's life. Much of the church council's work focuses on planning the church's calendar of activities and rarely highlights particular ministries.

3. *Prepare job descriptions...for all positions giving duties, decision-making authority, and person to whom responsible.* Often this task is shared with the Christian education committee which brings appropriate recommendations to the proper church body for final approval. The church's educational ministry depends upon volunteer leaders. These persons are willing and capable, if properly trained, to do quality work. With training they know what particular or special skills are needed to carry out their assignments. They know what authority they have in completing the task. They also know to whom they are accountable. Position descriptions provide this information.

4. *Use approved job descriptions when enlisting and orienting new leaders, planning for enlargement, determining organizational problems, and other similar administrative duties.* Enlistment in-

volves more than convincing persons to accept a position in the church. They must have an awareness of the total purpose for which the organization exists if they are to help it move toward fulfilling its objectives and goals. They also must know the specific tasks assigned to that program, and perceive how the program is structured administratively. In addition, they must know how well the program is currently achieving its objectives and goals, and how it fits into the total work of the church. Written job descriptions help potential workers better understand the tasks to be accomplished, the authority they have in the organization, and the person to whom they are responsible.

5. *Make annual plans for each organization.* In fact, it is better to have a fifteen month calendar; when organizational leadership changes each year, new leaders know immediately the plans for which they are responsible. Annual plans result from annual evaluation and assessment of each program. For instance, the Sunday School can evaluate its work using the following instruments: an analysis of the task statements, denominational standards or goals, or a growth plan.[5] These and other instruments help leaders see what has been done. Areas needing improvement or additional work are noted so appropriate plans can be made. Additionally, annual planning could begin by program leaders examining denominational plan books. These give additional ideas, annual themes, and new resources that spur interest in planning for the next year.[6]

6. *Budget for regular expenses such as curriculum materials and for all special items in the annual plan.* A strong, healthy Christian education program requires an ongoing financial commitment. Most educational activities depend upon curriculum materials for pupils and for teachers or leaders and other resources. A part of the Christian education budget ensures adequate library resources are available for leaders and learners. Budget funds include the cost of training materials, and occasionally, persons needed to conduct the appropriate training. Key leaders are assisted to attend local, regional, and national training opportunities through budgeted monies. The church needs funds for adequate supplies especially for preschoolers' and children's classes. If new classes and departments are started in the new year, equipment or furniture needed is included in the budget. The ME must work closely with various educational units in planning and monitoring budgets during the year. Part of the budgeting process includes noting when funds will be needed; for example, many educational activities happen during special events like Vacation Bible School, camps, retreats, or mis-

sion trips. Thorough planning highlights for the church when adequate cash flow must be available.

7. *Maintain a master calendar listing all plans, person(s) responsible, and budget provisions if any.* The master calendar should include all church activities, meeting places needed, special equipment needs, persons responsible, and budget requirements. Without someone monitoring the master calendar, the church risks two or more groups wanting the same space or needing special equipment someone else has reserved. Churches often receive many requests for meeting space from groups outside the church. The ME usually has a better grasp of building and space needs for the total church program than other staff members. The logical person to be administrator of the church's master calendar is the educational minister.

8. *Maintain a complete record system for each organization listing persons involved, contact information, officers, and attendance records.* Good records are crucial to an active Christian education program. Records, with the exception of attendance records, have been deemphasized in many churches in the past several years. Records have positive benefits for the church: (1) they are essential to a growing church because they provide information about persons to be reached for Christ and church membership; (2) they are essential to building a program of education, training, and Christian nurture available to church members of all ages; (3) they are important if any kind of evaluation is done after projects are completed which will determine if goals were achieved; and (4) they disclose to church leaders and ministers items that need more attention.

I grew up when personal records were important. Both Sunday School and discipleship training records prompted me to do practical things that aided my growth as a Christian. A church sins against its members when they do not help believers grow as Christians. Records help this growth occur by encouraging members to read their Bibles daily, pray daily, study God's Word, be good stewards, and participate in the church's activities. Records are never seen as an end, but as a means to aid individual believers to grow toward Christian maturity. Accurate, up-to-date records also help the church keep track of its members and what is happening spiritually in their lives. Attendance records are kept current so that appropriate contact can be made with absentees. Absence suggests a problem; it may be physical or spiritual, but it is a problem that needs someone's attention. The keeping of service records may prove very valuable to educational ministers as new classes or activities are begun. Instead of having to discover, enlist, and train the needed workers, they may find qualified workers are already in the church who can be relisted. Detailed and current training records keep MEs knowledgeable about the training needs of members in the congregation.

The September, 1969 issue of *Church Administration* magazine carried an article entitled "Parable of a True Church...or Who Needs Records." The article described a dynamic, thriving, growing church. They decided records were not spiritual and thus ceased keeping them. The result was a loss of members, lost ministry opportunities, the inability to pay bills and salaries, and total disarray in the church. Although it is a parable, it does point out what the absence of records does to a church.[7]

9. *Evaluate periodically and annually.* Evaluation is a continuous process in the education program. The only proper way to evaluate is to measure what has been done against stated tasks, objectives, and goals. Educational activities are assessed while they are in process and when they are completed. Failure to evaluate an ongoing program may lead to the program's missing the purpose for which it was intended. Corrections and adjustments can be made while the activity is running. The total program is examined annually to see how effective it has been in reaching stated purposes, objectives, and goals. The evaluation process leads back into the planning process as it reveals areas needing additional work or a new emphasis to begin. Evaluation greatly aids educational ministers in their administrative tasks.

10. *Follow the basic principles of working with, for, and through people in administering church educational organizations.* The three "I's" are a good guide:

> ● *Inform*–Communicate specifically what is happening and why; seek a clear understanding of all plans and procedures; provide opportunities for open discussion of pertinent issues; keep in touch with key leaders in the educational organizations.

> ● *Inspire*–Minister to and motivate the persons with whom you work. Whatever you are as a leader will be the most powerful influence on those through whom you must work. Administration is not doing the work yourself, but eliciting, combining, and guiding the resources of the congregation. What you cause to happen will be multiplied through others.

> ● *Involve*–Share leadership duties widely among responsible persons. This requires giving major attention to: (1) equipping leaders to perform their tasks, delegating to them responsibility, and supporting/encouraging them as they do their jobs; and (2) involving persons in making decisions which will affect their organization.[8]

Improving Administrative Functioning

Bower describes six basic assumptions to improve administrative functioning.[9] They are:

1. *People are more important than programs or organizations.* Jesus placed more importance on the individual than on the organized religion of His day. When Jesus was questioned about His disciples picking grain on the Sabbath, He stated, "The Sabbath was made for man, not man for the Sabbath" (Mark 2:27, NIV). Mark also told how Jesus healed the man with the withered hand on the Sabbath. Jesus asked the religious leaders, "Which is lawful on the Sabbath: to do good or to do evil, to save life or to kill?" (Mark 3:4, NIV). Sometimes educational programs place organization above the individual. Often people are invited to join a religious activity, like the Sunday School, without communicating to them what Sunday School can do for them or what personal needs it can meet. The individual should never be sacrificed for the sake of organizational efficiency.

2. *Every Christian has a ministry to fulfill in the body of Christ.* When Paul described spiritual gifts in 1 Corinthians 12, he emphasized that persons in the body of Christ and their gifts are interdependent and important to the proper functioning of the body. Christian educational administrators have a responsibility to identify and assist each Christian in finding their place of service or ministry so that the church fulfills its mission and ministry.

3. *Church leaders are servant leaders.* Robert Greenleaf shares why he wrote *Servant Leadership: A Journey into the Nature of Legitimate Power and Greatness:*

> The idea of the Servant as leader came out of reading Hermann Hesse's *Journey to the East.* In this story we see a band of men on a mythical journey, probably also Hesse's own journey. The central figure of the story is Leo, who accompanies the party as the *servant* who does their menial chores, but who also sustains them with his spirit and his song. He is a person of extraordinary presence. All goes well until Leo disappears. Then the groups falls into disarray and the journey is abandoned. They cannot make it without Leo. The narrator, one of the party, after some years of wandering finds Leo and is taken into the Order that had sponsored the journey. There he discovers that Leo, whom he had known first as *servant*, was in fact the titular head of the Order, its guiding spirit, a great and noble *leader.*[10]

Jesus Himself functioned much as Leo did in Hesse's story. Yet when He was no longer present, the movement did not die because

He had spent time training and equipping His followers to continue the work He began. In John 13:1-17, Jesus exemplified servanthood when He washed His disciples' feet, a task usually assigned to the lowest servant. Throughout Jesus' life and ministry He practiced servant leadership. The apostle Paul identified himself as a servant of Jesus Christ (Rom. 1:1). He also was a servant of the Corinthian church (2 Cor. 4:5). Christian leaders should perceive themselves as servants, not ones to be served.

4. *Leaders accept the responsibility for guiding and directing the educational program.* Bower wrote:

> Although it may appear paradoxical, the leader must take the attitude of one who serves and yet of one who is willing to assume responsibility for directing and supervising the activities of personnel assigned, even as Christ, who served, also instructed and sent His disciples out with directives to evangelize the world. Administration and supervision become matters of guiding, directing, and helping others in their ministry for Christ. It is direction of a program, however, through planning and through educational supervisory means rather than through authoritarian and dictatorial methods.[11]

5. *Clearly defined structure for each congregational organization is essential.* The New Testament describes church leaders who were selected to carry out general tasks within the church. Church leaders identified in the New Testament were apostles, prophets, evangelists, pastor-teachers, bishops, and deacons. The organization, described in broad, general terms, had this overall purpose: to provide for all the needed ministries. The New Testament does not list the various leaders necessary in the modern church. Some type of organization is necessary so the work of the church may be done as productively as possible.

6. *Every task and position in the church is important.* Some positions carry more responsibility than others, but each is significant for doing the work of the church. In the eyes of God each ministry and position is important. Bower emphasizes:

> It is the faithfulness to one's appointed duties which is of ultimate value, not what position is held, nor how important from man's standpoint one's work seems to be to the organization.[12]

For the church to fulfill its mission and ministry, each member must faithfully execute chosen and assigned tasks.

Working with the Educational Councils

Administratively the ME works in close harmony with the various educational councils. Each educational organization has its own council that is responsible for planning its work. A council is not an additional organization but rather a gathering of key leaders in the structure for consultation or advice. Tidwell notes each organization "needs leaders who will work together to lead the organization in developing and carrying out a comprehensive, coordinated, effective ministries plan."[13] Council members include the director, other general officers, and the key leaders of the major units of the organization. Powers states, "The organizational council does not need to report formally to any other group, but should monitor its planning activities for consistency with the church's total objective(s)."[14] Each council provides leadership in planning, coordinating, implementing, and evaluating the organization's ministries. Tidwell identifies other tasks of organizational councils:

> The organizational councils plan for the resources they will need to carry out the activities and projects their organization will direct. Among the resources they anticipate and try to provide are organization, leaders, training, materials, equipment, space, and publicity.[15]

Normally, each council meets monthly to review plans for the next month's activities. Annual planning is done during a retreat or over an extended period. The ME serves as a resource person to each educational council.

The Sunday School Council

The Sunday School Council members are all Sunday School general officers and department directors. The general officers include the pastor, the ME, the Sunday School director, associate director, outreach director, general secretary, and other general officers. The Sunday School Council plans a year's work. These plans help fulfill assigned tasks, objectives, and goals.[16] The six tasks of the Sunday School are:

- Reach people for Bible study;
- Teach the Bible;
- Witness to persons about Christ and lead them into church membership;
- Minister to Sunday School members and non-members;
- Lead members to worship; and
- Interpret and undergird the work of the church and the denomination.[17]

Discipleship Training Council

All evangelical churches need an active discipleship training program for all age groups. Discipleship training is more than offering basic training to new believers. The Scriptures teach that a Christian is to grow in grace and maturity to be more Christlike. The church provides training opportunities so believers are challenged to experience growth. Members of the Discipleship Training Council include the pastor, educational minister, Discipleship Training director, enlistment director, secretary, age group training leaders, and other general officers. They are responsible to assist the discipleship training organization in doing its tasks. The discipleship training program tasks include:

- Reach persons for discipleship training;
- Orient new church members for responsible church membership;
- Equip church members for discipleship and personal ministry;
- Teach Christian theology and denominational doctrines, Christian ethics, Christian history, and church polity and organization;
- Train church leaders for ministry; and
- Interpret and undergird the work of the church and the denomination.[18]

Discipleship training orients new members, equips members, and trains leaders. The church is greatly strengthened and better equipped for mission and ministry by a quality discipleship training program.[19]

Missions Education Councils

Missions education, like Sunday School and discipleship training, needs to provide for all age groups within the church. In some churches, there is only one missions education council that provides leadership and direction for all missions education in the church. In some churches there is an organization for women and girls and one for men and boys. In both organizations the council is composed of the director, secretary, age level leaders, the pastor, the ME, and other age-group staff members. The tasks assigned to the mission education organizations include:

- Teach missions;
- Engage in mission action and personal witnessing;
- Pray for and give to missions;
- Develop personal ministry; and
- Interpret and undergird the work of the church and the denomination.[20]

The Christian Education Committee or Board

My first experience with a Christian education committee was at First Baptist Church, Greenville, South Carolina. The church had such a committee with which I worked and learned about Christian education for five years. Some denominations call it a committee; others, a board. This group works with the pastor, the ME, and other educational leaders to aid the church in carrying out its educational objectives. A good description of the work of this group is the following:

> The Board of Christian Education is the agent of the congregation set up to deal with the educational needs and problems of the congregation. It concerns itself with education for all age levels and suggests the policies for all educational agencies and groups of the congregation. It considers and acts on the recommendations of the school staff, the Sunday School staff, and leaders of other educational agencies. It concerns itself with the calling or appointment of personnel. In short, the board seeks to advance the total educational program of the congregation for all age levels.[21]

The committee coordinates and gives guidance to the various Christian education activities conducted by the church. They keep the congregation informed about the various needs and developments in Christian education.

The Christian education committee is the center of educational programming in the church; its members provide guidance for the total Christian education program. They lead in planning for the present and the future. They structure a leadership training program for potential leaders and provide in-service leadership training. They are responsible for the enlistment and training of workers for the various educational organizations in the church.

The committee's members represent the various educational organizations by virtue of office held or special interest with additional members from the leaders of each age group. In addition, it is good to have some members from the congregation at large. Size of the total committee is nine to fifteen.

Gangel identifies three basic tasks of the Christian education committee: planning, supervising, and evaluating. The committee evaluates the present program, then projects the needs of the church into the future. This work comprises a continuous program of planning and developing goals toward an adequate Christian education program. When the church has such a committee, they often do the work of the nominating committee, filling the educational programs' leadership slots. Gangel points out:

> In its planning work the board is also a policy-making group. It decides matters of curriculum, organizational procedures, establishment of record systems and the determination of standards in all phases of the educational program.[22]

This group defines and recommends general purposes, objectives, and goals for the Christian education program. They prepare job descriptions for all Christian education positions.

The committee functions in a supervisory role for the Christian education program. Supervision coupled with the planning function brings a sense of unity and the desired correlated program. Gangel makes the point that "supervision includes the provision of all curriculum materials and teaching aids necessary, guidance for all workers in the total church program, and the constant representation of those workers to the congregation as a whole."[23] The committee makes decisions about whether different curriculum material (other than one's denominational curriculum or the curriculum line adopted by the church) could be used by a particular class or age group.

The third function of the committee is evaluation. It is inseparably related to planning. Gangel rightly observes:

> Evaluation thus turns into planning, planning is followed by supervision, supervision by evaluation, and the cycle constantly repeats itself as the board carries out its duties in connection with the program of Christian education in the local church.[24]

Gangel cites four significant results from the efficient work of a board of Christian education:

1. An organized total church program—keeping things running.

2. An efficient total church program—keeping things running smoothly.

3. A coordinated total church program—keeping things running together.

4. An advancing total church program—keeping things running ahead.[25]

Organizational/Administrative Structure

Each church determines its own organizational structure for each educational program. These structures vary from denomination to denomination and from church to church. Powers suggests three major considerations essential in determining how to organize an educational program.[26]

1. *Clarifying the specific, unique purpose of the organization.* Each educational program is assigned specific tasks or functions to do for the church. The statement of purpose tells why the organization exists, what its unique contribution to the church is, and what ministries would be left undone if this program did not exist.

Both Sunday School and discipleship training have tasks of reaching persons for their particular programs. Part of the organizational, administrative structure includes leaders who have responsibility for reaching and enlisting persons to participate in their activities. One reason many churches are not successfully reaching new persons for Sunday School and to hear the gospel is they are not organized or structured to do so. Discipleship training also is weak because its organization is not structured to continue to bring new persons into a systematic program of discipleship training.

2. *Selecting the best way to do the organization's stated purpose.* Powers suggests considering the following questions:

   • "What resources (leaders, facilities, denominational assistance, financial support, and such) are available?"
   • "What are the priorities within and among the educational organizations?"
   • "What structures will provide efficient and effective team work among leaders as well as facilitate the achievement of educational objectives?"[27]

3. *Identifying distinct areas of responsibility and decision making so the educational ministry and each component achieve maximum productiveness.* These questions are beneficial:

   • "What is the distinct responsibility for each position?"
   • "What decisions should the person in each position be able to make without consultation?"
   • "What are the positions that link each level (or unit) with the larger body for purposes of communication, planning, evaluation, and such?"
   • "Do all leaders have someone to whom they are responsible?"[28]

Each educational organization needs a director and a core of general officers to meet its stated purpose and do its assigned tasks. Lines of accountability and responsibility are drawn. Part of administration is seeing the structure is in place and its plan is communicated to the appropriate leaders and to the congregation as a whole.

Notes

1. Maria Harris, *The DRE Book: Questions and Strategies for Parish Personnel* (New York: Paulist Press, 1976).

2. Ibid., 4-5. Here she lists the various age groups and special interest groups found in the church.

3. Robert K. Bower, *Administering Christian Education* (Grand Rapids: Wm. B. Eerdmans Publishing Company, 1964), 12.

4. Bruce P. Powers, *Christian Education Handbook* (Nashville: Broadman Press, 1981), 128-32.

5. Southern Baptists have a Sunday School Standard which examines the program from eight different perspectives. An example of a growth plan is the Sunday School Super Growth Spiral, also produced by Southern Baptists.

6. The Sunday School Board of the Southern Baptist Convention produces plan books for Bible teaching, discipleship training, and family ministries. Woman's Missionary Union, the missions education organization for women and girls, has a *Year Book,* and the Brotherhood Commission, the missions education organization for men and boys, has a plan book.

7. Ida M. Clark, "Parable of a True Church . . . or Who Need Records," *Church Administration* (September 1969): 36.

8. Powers, *Christian Education Handbook,* 132.

9. Bower, *Administering Christian Education,* 18-20.

10. Robert K. Greenleaf, *Servant Leadership: A Journey into the Nature of Legitimate Power and Greatness* (New York: Paulist Press, 1977), 7.

11. Ibid., 19.

12. Ibid., 20.

13. Charles E. Tidwell, *Educational Ministry of a Church* (Nashville: Broadman Press, 1982), 223.

14. Powers, *Christian Education Handbook,* 56.

15. Tidwell, *Educational Ministry of a Church,* 227.

16. Members of the Sunday School Council will get many helpful ideas and suggestions in the *Bible Teaching Plan Book* from Convention Press. A new one is published each year and usually is available by June 1.

17. For Southern Baptists' best administrative guide for the Sunday School, see Robert A. Orr, *Being God's People: A Southern Baptist Church on Bold Missions* (Nashville: Convention Press, 1987), 68-79. See also Harry Piland and Ernest Adam, *Breakthrough Sunday School Work* (Nashville: Convention Press, 1990), 10-18. I strongly recommend that the reader who is not Southern Baptist find the various appropriate administrative manuals from his or her own denomination. If a denomination does not produce such manuals, these concepts in the above resources can be adapted to fit any church.

18. *Discipleship Training Plan Book* (Nashville: Convention Press). Produced annually.

19. Orr, *Being God's People,* 84-91. See also Roy T. Edgemon, *Discipleship Training: A Church Training Manual* (Nashville: Convention Press, 1986), 8-9.

20. Orr, *Being God's People,* 106-15. See also Mickey Martin, *WMU Manual* (Birmingham: Woman's Missionary Union, 1988), 6; and *Baptist Brotherhood* (Memphis: Brotherhood Commission, SBC, 1986), 7-10.

21. The Lutheran Church—Missouri Synod, *Handbook for Local Boards of Christian Education;* quoted by Kenneth O. Gangel, *Leadership for Church Education* (Chicago: Moody Press, 1970), 104-5.

22. Ibid., 110-11.

23. Ibid., 111.

24. Ibid., 112.

25. Roy B. Zuck; quoted by Gangel, *Leadership for Church Education,* 113.

26. Powers, 118-21.

27. Ibid., 118.

28. Ibid., 118-21.

7

Planner

Alice, an experienced educational minister, moved to a new church. Educational programs there have yearly planning calendars on which major events are listed, mostly from the denominational calendar. These activities are poorly attended, but once an activity is held, it becomes an "annual event." The church does not show creativity as they plan.

On the surface it appears the church is doing good planning, but many activities are poorly publicized—often announced from the pulpit the week before they occur. The church talks about their goals but does little planning to help them reach the goals. Their calendar of activities shows few differences from year to year.

Being new to the church, how does Alice help them be better planners? Where should she begin? How does she help the leaders develop planning skills? How does she help them discover church and community needs? What must be done to help them set realistic goals and then plan to meet their goals?

David Hunter identifies four steps in planning for Christian education. First, the planner identifies the situations giving rise to a need. Second, the planner identifies the dynamics operating in these situations. Third, she establishes a set of strategies to deal with these dynamic forces. Fourth, she plans the tactics or steps and resources to carry out this strategy.[1] A definition of planning is: "Planning consists of identifying the overall purpose of a project, the activities to be performed, their sequence, and the resources required to accomplish them."[2]

MEs spend vast amounts of time planning. They are involved in the planning process for the educational ministry and its programs.

They engage in weekly, monthly, quarterly, annual, and long-range planning. They give leadership and direction for the entire church's annual and long-range plans.

Bower states, "Planning is the process of examining the past and the present in order to construct the best program for achieving the church's objectives in both present and future."[3] This views planning as a means to an end, not the end of the administrative process. Looking into the future is essential for significant planning to take place. Bower then concludes, "Planning, therefore, studies the past and the present, gathers data, interprets these, and then makes plans for the future with the ultimate end in mind of achieving the organization's goals."[4]

The Function of Planning

Why plan? Planning takes time and energy, but is essential for any organization. It establishes goals and suggests the means for achieving these goals.

Planning outlines the program to be carried out in the future. The function of planning is characterized by the predictive element. A key to competent planning lies in anticipating future circumstances and then designing the program that aids the church's educational organizations to accomplish the objectives.[5] The planning process moves through a series of basic, logical, sequential steps. These steps are:

• **Statement of purpose or overarching objective.** The planning process begins by identifying the overarching purpose. Rush notes, "A strong sense of purpose helps develop the conviction and commitment needed for the work of planning."[6] The educational ministry's statement of purpose grows out of the church's statement of purpose and is complementary to the church's purpose. It helps the church reach its goals. The statement of purpose or overarching objective is made in broad terms, yet it needs to be specific enough that it becomes a clear guide for charting the course and direction of the educational ministry. Each educational organization has specific objectives to guide the development and program of that organization. It requires time to propose, refine, and revise the statement to accurately reflect the purpose of the church's educational ministry.

I once helped a church work out a statement of purpose for its Christian education program. We worked for several months in arriving at a statement we found satisfactory before presenting it to the church for adoption. We met for three or four Saturdays for about six hours each time before we had a statement upon which we agreed. The statement contained only about thirty words, but each word was carefully chosen so the entire statement communicated what we intended.

• **Objectives.** Once a purpose statement is established, then specific objectives are prepared. Objectives are distinguished from the purpose in that they are more specific. Objectives are measurable both quantitatively and qualitatively. Rush states, "A measurable objective tells exactly what will be accomplished, how much is to be accomplished, and when it will be completed.... An objective must be measurable to be manageable."[7] An educational program should increase numerically. It is equally important that the organization serve its members individually and collectively to grow in Christian maturity. This means believers are growing more like Jesus Christ in attitude and behavior. It is easier to see whether the organization is growing numerically.

Evaluating or measuring qualitative growth becomes more difficult because such growth is not as easily observable. Objective statements are consistent with the overarching objective of the church and of the church's educational ministry. Educational objectives are written by the church's Christian education committee or by representative leaders from the various educational organizations. These objectives are limited in number so that the church can adequately work toward their attainment. The church can learn from major corporations who, with professional planners to guide them, work on three to five objectives at a time.[8] Selecting multiple objectives makes it difficult to track progress, and the energy needed to work on achieving them is too widely dispersed.

• **Setting goals.** The first two steps are completed before realistic goals are formulated. Goals are concrete, observable, and measurable. Goals are challenging and capable of attainment. Good goal setting aids people to move forward in their Christian life. Goals are written so they describe individual progress in the Christian life. For example, instead of having an attendance goal of two hundred in Sunday school, state, "Our goal is to have two hundred persons studying the Bible." Some goals are numerical increases. Other goals include growth or progress in the Christian life, or improved skill development. A church could have a goal of increasing the number of baptisms dependent on other goals that include training and engaging in evangelistic witnessing.

• **Action plans.** The statement of purpose, plannings, and goals is translated into action plans for achievement. Action plans are activities on the church calendar. Good action plans are measurable. They move the educational organization toward adopted objectives and goals. George and Logan note, "You need to decide *what* you are going to do; *when* you are going to do it; *who* is going to do it; *how* you are going to do it; and *what resources* you need to do it."[9]

In essence, the action plans are a form of program evaluation review technique, or PERT. Using the PERT process, the planner decides where the organization is to be on a specific date. This may be an increase in Sunday School attendance. It may include the training of more members for evangelistic visitation. Or it may be encouraging members to increase the percentage of money given to the church and mission causes.

Suppose the church decides they want to increase Sunday School attendance by 10 percent over the next 12 months. What needs to be done if they are to reach this goal? Unless they are already growing at this rate, some definite actions are required. This may require comparing the church roll with the present Sunday School roll. This action does not require scheduling on the church calendar. It is accomplished using the church staff or volunteers. A date is set for it to be finished.

Another action may be a community survey to discover persons who are not already enrolled. This activity is on the church calendar. The next action may be deciding if the present Sunday School organization is adequate to handle more people. Suppose the church determines it needs to start some new teaching units? A start-up date for launching new teaching units is set. Then new teachers and workers must be recruited and trained before this time. Dates are determined for the completion of these actions. Another action plan is visitation of potential members on a regular, consistent basis. The people who do the visitation may need training in how to conduct such visits. Again, these action plans are on the church calendar. Setting the goal to increase Sunday School attendance sets in motion several actions to be completed before the goal is attained. Only action plans that lead to meeting goals are placed on the church calendar.

• **Evaluation.** Every event or activity is evaluated. The fair way to evaluate an activity is to measure it against its stated purpose, objectives, and goals. Therefore, every event needs a defined purpose, objective, and goals. Some activities that run over several weeks or months are analyzed while in process so any needed corrections or adjustment can be made. Some questions that prove beneficial in the evaluation process include:

1. Were the purpose, objective, and goals of the activity accomplished? If so, how? If not, in what ways?

2. For whom was it planned? Who attended? Who should have attended?

3. How did this project aid the educational organization in the achievement of its purpose, objectives, and goals?

4. How did this project help the church in the achievement of its purpose, objectives, and goals?

5. What part of the event served the participants best? Why? How?

6. What aided the participants least? Why?

7. Should this event be held again? If so, what needs would it meet?

8. Were the results sufficient for the expenditure of money? What did it cost per person?

I planned a family enrichment conference for a large metropolitan association. National leaders served as faculty members. Meetings were in two different locations so meeting places were close to the participants. The event was well publicized. The problem was the people stayed away in droves. It was disastrous in almost every way. Our evaluation suggested the program was viable and could meet needs. What was wrong was the format of trying to have all the groups meet at the same time. The initial meeting was more than fifteen years ago. Today, the target groups continue to meet by having various groups meet at different times.

Some Planning Principles

Tidwell suggests ten relevant principles in planning the church's educational ministry.[10] They are:

1. *Begin with God.* All Christian planning begins with seeking God's guidance in what He wants the church to do. Otherwise, planning becomes mechanical. The planning process may be well executed, but the spiritual dimension or the reason for the activity may be overlooked. Christian education leaders need to ask: "What does God want the church to do in its Christian education program?" All planning begins with sincere prayer seeking God's divine leadership.

2. *Include implementors in planning.* Persons who will be involved or instrumental in carrying out the plans should be a part of the planning process. Rush points out:

> People develop a feeling of ownership in the planning process
> when they participate in developing the purpose, objectives, and
> activities. When they are involved, people will work hard to
> succeed because the plan belongs to them.[11]

Failure to include the implementors in the process usually
leads to the attitude, "You planned it. You set the goals. Now it is
your responsibility to carry it out." When there is a lack of ownership, it often means the project will fail or only partially succeed.
Program leaders are involved in all plans that affect that organization. For instance, any plans involving the Sunday School need the
input and the support of its leadership. Attendance goals are often
set by ministers without consulting the appropriate leaders who are
crucial to the achievement of goals. Another reason to include the
implementors is they have ideas and insights that strengthen the
plans.

3. *Plan from ends to means.* MEs who know where they are going
more often choose the proper means of arriving at desired goals.
Many people never reach their intended destination because they do
not know where they are going. It is important to decide *why* something is to be done before planning a major activity. Consider: How
does this event help the organization toward the achievement of its
goals? Knowing the purpose and the objectives aids in deciding
what, when, where, who, and how.[12] Avoiding the end-means inver-
sion keeps the planning process on track and reduces unnecessary
detours. Planning from ends to means avoids having needless activities that do not lead to the completion of the goal.

4. *Emphasize the church.* Often the purpose, objectives, and goals
of the church are forgotten by various organizations. Each component feels their emphasis is more important than the church, the
parent organization. The educational minister strives to see that the
purposes, objectives, and goals of the total Christian education program and its many parts are consistent with, and supportive of, those
of the church. The church consists of all the components of the
church—Sunday School, discipleship training, missions education,
recreation, socials, media library, deacons, church council—yet it is
more than the sum of its parts. As plans are made for the Christian
education program, the question ought to be: "How can this Christian education organization help the church in achieving its goals
and objectives?" The bottom line is that church goals *always* have
priority over those of any organization if there is a conflict of goals.

5. *Plan to meet priority needs.* A church and a Christian education
organization have limited resources. They cannot be all things to all

people. There are some things they should not do. There are some
things they would like to do but for which they do not have sufficient
resources. Priority needs are only established from data and information carefully gathered about the church and community. They
cannot be finalized only from generalized information or desires
within the congregation. The church does its planning based on
identifiable priority needs. Just as the church has a list of priority
needs it seeks to meet, each educational organization attempts to
plan from a sense of priorities. It aids Christian education program
leaders to plan from strengths rather than weaknesses. Problems
are seen as opportunities. Christian education leaders are possibility thinkers rather than those who refuse to tackle difficult but
priority needs.

   6. *Aim for the range of challenge.* Plans need to be challenging but
achievable. As Christian education leaders and workers are enlisted
to work in the church, the opportunities for spiritual growth for
themselves and for those whom they will lead should inspire them to
accept challenges. Goals should have every possibility for success
when implemented through everyone's efforts and hard work. Goals
that are unrealistic or unobtainable demoralize people rather than
acting as positive motivators. When this happens repeatedly, people
tend not to take goals seriously and refuse to work toward their
attainment. For example, some church leaders seek to have a high
attendance day in Sunday School every week. It seems they are
never satisfied. People respond to a challenge if it is realistic. They
give their best when the task summons them to maximum effort.
MEs set the pattern or model by responding to personal challenges
in their Christian walk and in leading the church to respond to its
challenges and opportunities.

   Challenging goals have both numerical and qualitative growth
plans in them. Much Christian education work involves aiding persons first to become followers of Jesus Christ and then growing
them in Christian maturity. Goals for effective, challenging educational work reflect this two-pronged approach of evangelism and
Christian nurture.

   7. *Allow for flexibility.* The purpose of planning is to encourage
or cause change. Planning involves creating a climate or atmosphere for change and carrying out a program designed to cause that
change. Plans are an approach to hasten change. They ought never
be seen as *the* plan. Planners have a clear vision of where they are
going and what they are seeking to do. They are sensitive to people
and the circumstances with whom they work. Changing circum-

stances or events require plans be altered or adjusted to meet changing needs. The educational minister is observant in analyzing data, resources, and people. Therefore, as she plans, she maintains a certain flexibility so plans realistically move toward successful completion. One word of caution: Plans should not be scrapped or altered just because problems or opposition arise. The plan may be valid. Success is not always instantaneous. Good plans are subject to review and revision as need require.

8. *Provide resources for planning.* Christian planning is first based on the direct leadership of the Holy Spirit. Planning includes what God's people believe He wants His church to be and to do. Then, as MEs lead Christian education organizations to plan, they see that necessary resources—lists of tasks, statements of purpose, objectives, plan books, church purposes, objectives, and goals—are available to and understood by those who do the planning.

Each of these resources should represent the church's wishes, not just what has been prepared by the denomination. Planners see denominational goals and plans as resources to serve the local church in implementing its specific plans. Sometimes planners feel frustrated not doing all the denomination suggests, but such plans are intended to assist churches in planning, are not necessarily meant to serve as finished plans. Denominational plans are not carried on conveyor belts directly to the churches; they are more like cafeteria lines where churches pick and choose.

Planning becomes realistic and exciting when planners understand their available resources—people, buildings, equipment, and budgetary funds.

9. *Keep plans simple.* Although some planning processes are sophisticated and complicated, the steps suggested earlier for the planning process for educational ministry produce plans that are simple and easily understood. Plans are prepared so a person who has not been involved in the process can read the plans and understand them. Both the format and the plans are as simple as possible.

10. *Put plans in writing.* All plans are complete when written. This helps in plans being understood and communicated to the rest of the organization and the church. Written plans detail why something is to be done, who is to do it, how it is to be done, when it is to be done, and what resources are allocated for it to be successful. Written plans aid the ME in tracking each activity and seeing where it fits into the organization's and the church's established priorities.

The Benefits of Planning

There is an old saying: "To fail to plan is to plan to fail." Barna suggests five vital benefits to planning:[13]

1. *Planning helps identify and clarify* problems that keep the church from growing and opportunities that might enable the church to grow.

2. *Planning provides a guidebook* on transforming dreams into reality.

3. Considering its problems and opportunities compels the church to *prioritize its ministry objectives.*

4. *Planning aids in maximizing resources* by identifying the church's total needs and deploying them where they can do the maximum good.

5. *Planning pinpoints responsibility and accountability*

The Planning Functions

The educational minister supports the educational organization in making and executing plans. She plans with each Christian education organization and with various church organizations regularly.

Weekly Planning

An effective Sunday School requires a weekly workers meeting. If this weekly meeting is productive and beneficial to the workers, specific plans are made about emphases and activities scheduled in the coming weeks. Usually the educational minister meets with the Sunday School Council to map out strategy for these meetings. The Sunday School is the only organization with a weekly planning meeting. The weekly workers meeting determines whether the Sunday School is productive in providing quality Bible study and reaching and ministering to members and prospects.

Monthly Planning

Each educational organization—Sunday School, discipleship training, and missions education—has a monthly, hour-long planning meeting where specific, definite plans are made. The ME spends time with the program leaders before these meetings making suggestions and offering input. Then, the educational minister's role with the educational councils during their monthly planning meetings is that of an advisor or consultant, not that of running the meeting. A part of such meetings is an evaluation of what has been accomplished during the previous month. Special projects or activities conducted are analyzed and assessed so that future planning is more competent.

Quarterly Planning

Besides the monthly planning meeting, some MEs like to have a quarterly planning time with each program organization. This planning is done in broad strokes and is less specific than the monthly planning meeting. Quarterly planning can be an extended part of every third monthly planning meeting. The purpose of quarterly planning is to give a sense of direction for the organization's next three months. It allows time to prepare for upcoming events. It assures that resources and supplies are on hand when needed.

Annual Planning

The educational minister helps each Christian education organization make annual plans. She is responsible for seeing that each leader has the necessary resources. Annual planning takes place at least one month before the beginning of a new church year. Yearly planning involves examining the stated objectives of the organization and making necessary revisions or corrections. Then goals the organization seeks to accomplish during the next year are set. Usually drawing up a yearly plan takes several hours of concentrated planning either in a retreat setting or an uninterrupted block of time. Annual plans identify action plans (who is responsible for the action, what resources are needed, financial resources required, and any special equipment that will be used); they are specific, but remain flexible since changes occur as the year goes on.

Long-Range Planning

Long-range planning examines the past, evaluates the present, and anticipates the future. Long-range planning projects where an organization wants to be in three to five years. The ME has a definite responsibility to help the educational programs and the church engage in long-range planning. In long-range planning, future building needs are anticipated, additional staff needs are foreseen based on projected program growth, and potential future directions for the church are dreamed and decided.

Coordination and Planning

Coordinating the scheduling of various activities of the church usually is the duty of the ME. Although the graded choir program is also educational, its organization is typically supervised by the music minister. Coordinating a schedule of activities requires consultation and cooperation with all the members of the church staff and the church council.

It takes accommodation to get all the activities scheduled so there is a minimum of conflict and overlap. Usually activities are arranged so that more than one group can meet at a time and members will not have to make multiple trips to the church. Churches with educational ministers usually have a heavy schedule of activities on Sundays and Wednesdays. The biggest difficulty is deciding which meeting or activity is given priority. Coordinating the schedule of activities for a church requires finesse and diplomacy so that all people involved have their needs addressed and are satisfied.

Part of coordinating the church program occurs as the ME works with the church council in its regular meetings. His input is invaluable based on his knowledge of the schedule and the needs for various facilities and resources.

Planning and the Budgetary Process

Often the budgeting process and planning are reversed so that the budget determines the plans made. Providing financial resources is an integral part of the planning process. Therefore an organization plans first, then requests necessary funds. Planning should precede budgeting.

Since churches have limited financial resources, planning ensures top priorities are identified and funded rather than targeting everything people would like to see done. As plans are made, the cost of each activity is estimated and some justification is made for the money requested. Listing what the activity seeks to do, stating what objectives it will accomplish, and enumerating the persons served helps the church in the allocation of funds.

Budgeting is important for the on-going activities of the educational programs, and for the successful completion of special projects or programs.

Notes

1. David Hunter, *Christian Education as Engagement* (New York: Seabury Press, 1963), 32. Also cited in Maria Harris, *The D. R. E. Book: Questions and Strategies for Parish Planning* (New York: Paulist Press, 1976), 13.

2. Myron Rush, *Management: A Biblical Approach* (Wheaton: Victor Books, 1983), 81.

3. Robert K. Bower, *Administering Christian Education* (Grand Rapids: Wm. B. Eerdmans Publishing Company, 1964), 49.

4. Ibid.

5. Ibid., 51.

6. Rush, *Management: A Biblical Approach*, 84.

7. Ibid., 85.

8. Thomas J. Peters and Robert H. Waterman, Jr., *In Search of Excellence: Lessons from America's Best Run Companies* (New York: Warner Books, 1982).

9. Carl F. George and Robert E. Logan, *Leading & Managing Your Church* (Old Tappan, N.J.: Fleming H. Revell, 1987), 60.

10. Charles A. Tidwell, *Educational Ministry of a Church* (Nashville: Broadman Press, 1982), 237-40.

11. Rush, *Management: A Biblical Approach,* 89.

12. Ibid., 238.

13. George Barna, *Marketing the Church: What They Never Told You About Church Growth* (Colorado Springs: Navpress, 1988), 94-96. His ideas are related to preparing a marketing plan for the church but are applicable to the educational ministry.

8

Equipper and Enabler

Mason serves his first church as an educational minister. He feels frustrated because he cannot get all the necessary work done. He works ten to twelve hours a day, seven days a week. He does not feel comfortable in letting other people help with the educational ministry. He feels the church called *him* to do the educational work in the church; therefore, *he* must do most of the work. The church has few persons properly trained to do educational tasks.

Mason's pastor suggests his primary job is to be a trainer, an equipper of people. The pastor developed a strong core of people engaged in personal evangelism by training them one-on-one. The pastor proposes this as a good model. Mason recognizes the pastor's successful ministry through following this approach.

Mason works with the educational organizations to find out their training needs. With the pastor and educational leaders they draw up a list of training needs in the church. He works out a schedule of training events to meet these needs. How can he begin to see himself as an equipper and enabler of the people? Where should he start? How much training should he do? How will this affect his personal ministry? Will this alter his ministry style? In what ways?

Equipper and enabler—this is the ME's heart. His primary task is to equip and enable the people of God to do the work of ministry. He can best do this if he has the right attitude toward people. Means notes, "An enabling philosophy of church leadership always stresses profound respect for people. In the best forms of leadership, people are not treated as subjects or herded like cattle."[1] Peters and Waterman emphasize the same idea to the top companies of

America. IBM's most important belief is respect for people. This idea occupies most of management's time. They write, "Treat people as adults. Treat them as partners; treat them with dignity; treat them with respect."[2]

The ME aids church members to be more competent in carrying out their ministry. This task requires more than discovering, enlisting, and training potential workers for the Christian education organizations and for the church. Means' comment about a spiritual leader is applicable to the ME:

> The task of the true spiritual leader is to promote growth in competence, responsibility, character, and leadership in individuals, to produce a healthy, functioning, ministering body, and to promote the achievement of the church's goals and plans in the community.[3]

An educator has a monumental task—encouraging church members and seeking to support them in the tasks God has given them to do.

He resists the temptation to do the work himself rather than equip and enable others. An educator's great delight is seeing persons whom he has trained begin to function competently. His work is to multiply workers. Through the adoption of an educator's mindset, he is constantly equipping others to engage in the work of ministry.

This chapter explores how MEs are equippers and enablers of persons through the processes of discovering, enlisting, and training them. Suggested topics to include in a training program are described with training models.

Discovering Potential Workers and Leaders

Potential workers and leaders are discovered through keeping good service records either manually or on computer. The ME carries administrative responsibility for seeing that records are preserved and usable. Often persons who have had experience in a particular area are already members. Looking back through service records reveals persons who previously functioned in leadership capacities. Most available church software have files set up to record and track this information. If the service is in the recent past, these persons can begin to function with little or no pre-service training.

Another excellent source of potential workers and leaders is consulting with persons who work with adults in the church. Not everyone should be a teacher in the Sunday School; they may be well qualified to lead in another Christian education organization or serve on a church committee. Getting names from adult church leaders does not mean these persons will be automatically asked to serve, but each person is seriously considered for some position of leadership.

A church commissions the Church Nominating Committee, the Christian Education Committee, a Committee on Committees, or other designated groups to discover potential workers or leaders. The ME works closely with such committees in the selection of workers for the various Christian education organizations. The pastor and other staff members meet with this committee but the educational minister carries major responsibility for this area of ministry. The discovery of potential workers and leaders is a constant struggle for the church if it is to spread the leadership load. Often, the church's leadership is in the hands of too few people. It should be a goal that every member of the church be in a position of leadership. This will not just happen. It must be a goal which is systematically pursued.

Enlisting Potential Workers and Leaders

Enlistment is a significant task the church must do. While this function is most important to the productive functioning of the church, it often is approached haphazardly. The ME takes time to train persons who will engage in enlisting potential workers and leaders. Enlistment is a responsibility the church engages in more than once a year. It is a year long activity as vacancies occur or the roster of needed workers and leaders needs completion.

The enlistment process avoids several traps or weaknesses. They are:

• *Trap #1: Enlistment is done in a haphazard or chance meeting.* Rather, appointments are made when the task can be discussed in private and both parties can give their undivided attention to it.

• *Trap #2: Every task requires identical skills and people to do them.* A false assumption is that teaching and a committee assignment have the same requirements and necessary people skills. A person may have good organizational, administrative skills but lack the ability to relate to people. This person may make a good committee member but probably should not be a teacher or a committee chairperson. Personality differences and skills are matched to the tasks to be attempted.

• *Trap #3: Enlistment is by the person who functions as supervisor.* Ideally this is true; yet the person who makes the enlistment contact should be the person most likely to get a positive response. This person may be accompanied by the supervisor, but not necessarily so. Every attempt is made to match the personality of the enlistee with the enlister. Some people may be turned off by the manner in which they are approached rather than by the task.

• *Trap #4: Enlistment is more a persuasive task than an honest one.* Countless people who have accepted a job in the church discover they did not know what the task involved—the time expectations, the added responsibilities, or the extra meetings they must attend. Sometimes the person doing enlistment is so anxious for *anyone* to assume the task, he does not deal ethically with the enlistee. The enlistee is informed of total expectations. He knows of the opportunities to influence others for good. He also should know he has the possibility for personal growth and development in doing this task.

• *Trap #5: Fill all vacancies quickly.* This sounds good. The problem is finding people who agree to a position may create greater problems for the organization. The enlistment process's purpose is not to complete the organizational roster as quickly as possible. The purpose is to discover and enlist those persons who are best equipped or can be trained. The Holy Spirit's presence and leadership should be felt by the enlisted person and the enlister. Turnover is diminished through the careful matching of persons, jobs, and spiritual gifts.

• *Trap #6: Verbally describe the task.* A church and an organization have a responsibility to prepare written job or position descriptions for every task and for every committee and leadership position. Failure to have church adopted descriptions leads to incompetent work or frustration by persons selected. A written description helps the enlistee have a better awareness of what the job entails. It also can be used as the enlistee prayerfully and thoughtfully considers the position. Figure 1 shows a sample job description for an adult teacher in Sunday School.[4] This job description could be easily adapted for any position in the church by retitling it, and by using the seven categories of information to accurately describe the job given in the title.

Sample Job Description
Adult Sunday School Teacher

Tasks to be done:
1. Understand and use the principles of effective teaching and learning.
2. Prepare to lead each week's Bible study session with your class.
3. Accept personal responsibility in enlistment and witnessing actions.
4. Share in and encourage your class to participate in ministry actions.
5. Be knowledgeable about the role of the class in the work of the church.
6. Lead the total work of the class.
7. Assist group leaders to minister to members and prospects.
8. Plan regularly with class outreach leader and group leaders.

Essential skills:
1. Ability to communicate effectively.
2. Skill in planning and execution of plans.
3. Leadership abilities that challenge others to follow your example.
4. Understanding how to study and interpret the Bible.
5. Willingness to be a learner from the Bible, the Holy Spirit, and class members.
6. Ability to be a personal visitor.

Available Resources:
1. Your denomination's resources will be supplied.

Time commitments:
1. Be in your classroom fifteen minutes before Sunday School begins.
2. Attend the weekly workers' meetings.
3. Participate in the church's outreach program.
4. Attend Sunday School training sessions.

Length of service:
1. Twelve consecutive months (unless elected for longer terms).

Organization objectives:
1. Reach persons for Bible study.
2. Teach the Bible.
3. Witness to persons about Christ and lead persons into church membership.
4. Minister to Sunday School members and nonmembers.
5. Lead members to worship.
6. Interpret and undergird the work of the church and the denomination.

Organizational goals (Each church must set its own. These are possibilities.):
1. Increase enrollment by 10 percent.
2. Increase attendance by 10 percent.
3. Achieve the goal of 50 percent of the class members bringing Bible and studying the lesson.
4. Win *one* person to Christ.
5. Determine a strategy for ministering to members and nonmembers members as needs occur.

Figure 1

• *Trap #7: Seek an answer immediately.* Pressing for an instant response may cause the enlistee to decline the service opportunity. Such an approach implies the job is not very important and does not require much. All the Lord's work is significant for it demands one's best mentally and spiritually. At the interview time, pray with the enlistee that God will guide the decision making process. Covenant to pray with this person about this significant decision. Allow sufficient time for the person to seriously consider whether he or she has the time, the abilities, and the spirituality to be competent in doing the proposed task.

• *Trap #8: When the enlistee says, "Yes," the enlistment process is complete.* Enlistment is *not* complete until the enlistee is functioning competently in the new task. This suggests the enlister must follow up to answer additional questions or provide additional aid. Failure to follow up may be a major cause of a high turnover ratio of new workers.

• *Trap #9: The term of service should be only one year.* Most church committees and deacons are elected for a term of more than one year. Yet Christian education organizations elect their leadership annually. This may be wise when a new person begins serving, but when the stewardship of time is considered, an inordinate amount of time is spent in the enlistment and reenlistment of persons already working in Christian education. Three year terms might be considered with an annual evaluation process conducted to examine the competence of the worker and find out whether continuance is in the best interest of the worker and the organization. The other extreme of this problem is when a person agrees to work in Christian education and assumes he or she will continue for an indefinite period. One Sunday School teacher described it as "a life sentence." A worker should not feel trapped but should know that his commitment is for a specific, limited period. After a person agrees to serve, he is presented to the church for election. In some churches this is by a committee or board.

The entire enlistment process is a crucial activity in the life of the church. How well this is handled greatly shapes the quality of work done by volunteer leaders. Good enlistment helps volunteers see the magnitude and the significance of the task. I describe the enlistment process in detail in *Christian Education Handbook*.[5]

Training

Any task worth doing is worthy of training. Often church people are asked to assume responsibilities for which they do not have adequate skills or adequate knowledge. A church sins against its people when it fails to provide sufficient training so that persons enlisted are assured the best possible chances for success in the job.

A church needs trained, qualified, and capable leaders. This is especially true for the church's educational organizations. No one would consider sending a child to a school that had no qualifications for their teachers. Public school teachers are certified to teach specific subjects and at certain levels. The church should expect that those who work and lead in its life would be "certified." This standard is met in an adequate training program. It will not be a reality unless the church sets qualifications for all leadership positions. Once the church establishes criteria, it follows up by training its leadership.

Training leaders is a task assigned to the educational minister. A good subtitle for the ME is trainer. Much of his work is either leading training events, planning special training opportunities, or encouraging the equipping of others to lead in the training program. Through training he fulfills the role of equipper and enabler. Training includes skill development, special knowledge, spiritual growth, and personal enrichment. Training involves more than preparing people to serve in special areas of ministry. Some training focuses on potential leadership training. Other training opportunities prepare persons to more competently work in a particular ministry of the church. Too often training highlights only the task: a needed balance in training is developing better people skills. In fact, the ME who helps people develop their gifts and abilities encourages them to do their particular job in their own distinctive way. In the past as I led conferences to equip adult Sunday School leaders, I now realize I was putting too much emphasis on the mechanics of adult Bible teaching—almost as if I was attempting to clone them after one acceptable model or duplicate them like photocopies.

Training occurs either pre-service or in-service. Pre-service training occurs before beginning the new task, and it is crucial if the new worker is to feel confident and competent for what is to come. In-service training provides additional skills and helps the worker to improve proficiency. An improperly trained worker usually feels inept, discouraged, or lacks confidence in his ability.

Pre-service Training

Pre-service training occurs in several ways. Some pre-service training attempts to prepare persons for a task they have agreed to do. This could be preparation for teaching in the Sunday School or leading a discipleship training group. This training is task oriented; it develops special, needed skills including lesson development and preparation, understanding psychological and developmental characteristics of an age group, organizational and administrative competence, and strong outreach approaches. The person in training also needs an introduction to the Bible, methods of interpreting the Scriptures, and skills in using Bible atlases, concordances, and dictionaries. This requires more than a brief session before assuming the teaching responsibility. The more time a person has to assimiliate and absorb these various studies, the better equipped he is. Completion may not be possible before he begins to serve. Enlistment begins several months before the expected service date. Such pre-service training requires a minimum of three months with one hour training sessions offered each week plus concentrated study sessions monthly.

A second type of pre-service training is for potential leaders. This training introduces people to specific programs—Sunday School, discipleship training, missions education, church music, or general church leadership. This training combines cognitive and experiential learning. Practical or usefulness are key ideas to consider. Potential leader training helps people see if they have the gifts and abilities necessary to serve in these types of ministries. In addition, a person's temperament and personality are important aspects as they consider working with a particular age group. I can work with preschoolers, children, youth, or adults, but I work best with adults. I welcome short term assignments to work with other age groups, but my temperament and personality are best suited for adults. Pre-service training allows the worker to make this decision through experience with and information about the various age groups. The trainer does not attempt to push or slant a person into one group. In one potential teacher training class, I had a junior high physical education teacher. I knew he would make an excellent youth teacher. In observing various age groups, he felt drawn toward teaching two year olds. He proved to be one of the best preschool teachers in that church.

An area often overlooked in pre-service training is equipping church committee personnel. Churches complain that committees do not accomplish as much as desired. One reason is committee members receive little or inadequate training. They do not know what the task of the committee is or what is expected of them. I developed a three session training module for church committee members. The first session was a visionary one. I believed each committee needed to see how its assignment fit into the total work of the church so that all committee work ultimately moved toward the church achieving its purpose, objectives, and goals. The second session prepared committee chairpersons to lead productive committee meetings. Time was spent on how to prepare an agenda, how to conduct a committee meeting, and how to set goals. The third session was an actual committee meeting. The committee reviewed its job or position description, decided when it would meet and how often, and set some goals for the coming year.

In-service Training

In-service training answers questions workers have after beginning their tasks. At that point, people know what they need to know! In-service training is on-the-job training. Every time an organization meets or plans, in-service training takes place. Planning meetings include opportunities for skill development and personal growth. For example, weekly workers' meetings for the Sunday School offer a setting for training: teachers improve their skills in lesson preparation, lesson development, and teaching methodologies, and gain a better understanding of the age group they teach.

Usually major training activities are calendared at the beginning of the church year. This provides help for new workers and experienced ones. Novices profit from experienced workers; seasoned workers benefit from the enthusiasm of novices. This training creates a spirit of enthusiasm at the beginning of the new year.

Several months into the year workers need a boost in spirit. This is a good time to center on meeting particular needs workers have identified since beginning their ministries or jobs. Some denominations have leadership diplomas workers earn while enhancing their skills. One that I know requires studying and completing assignments in six books. For the Sunday School leadership diploma the books include an introduction to the Bible, an administrative book, a book on teaching, one on outreach, understanding an age group, and denominational doctrine. When study of these six books is completed the worker receives a leadership diploma. They may then work on an advanced diploma. There are also similar courses of study for various church programs and for church leadership positions, such as deacons.

Training is planned with the leadership of the various educational organizations. Planning training events is difficult when the educational minister does not know what courses of study are needed by the workers. Keeping accurate, up-to-date training records greatly expedites this effort. One denomination encourages churches to request credit from its national office. When this is done, the church receives a computer printout twice a year. It shows the course credits earned for that six months by church members plus their progress toward completion of various diplomas, including the courses needed to complete the diplomas. This is useful to the ME and other church leaders in planning training events to meet the needs of the members. A book study usually requires four and one half hours. Books can be studied in a class setting or by individual study. When a class has not been possible, I have combined individual reading and periodic discussion sessions.

Constructive training sessions call for creativity. Be innovative and different to meet your workers' needs. Some good training sessions are in less than ideal circumstances. It helps to get people in a relaxed setting that allows for freedom of discussion and participation.

Continuous training is essential for a church to grow. One Sunday School growth plan insists that one of the ingredients for growth is to have at least fifty percent of the Sunday School workers involved in a training course every three months. Training alone does not produce growth, but combined with other growth ingredients it is a significant part.

The Benefits of Training

There are several advantages to training. One, leaders are challenged by new and fresh ideas. It aids in sharpening skills by presenting new concepts. Second, workers learn from outside persons and each other. The ideas may not be new, but they are presented in current, applicable terms.

A third benefit is new workers are constantly trained. Every church has turnover in leadership. The starting of new Sunday School classes and departments generates the need for new or additional workers. These people bring fresh enthusiasm to the program. They are not afraid to try new ideas. When they prove these work, experienced workers sense permission and encouragement to try new strategies.

A fourth benefit is workers are challenged to grow as persons. Even experienced workers who have several years of seniority doing a specific task need growth in their personal and spiritual lives. All church leaders should be growing persons. They grow in knowledge and in relationship to God and other persons.

Notes

1. James E. Means, *Leadership in Christian Ministry* (Grand Rapids: Baker Book House, 1989), 59.
2. Thomas J. Peters, and Robert H. Waterman, Jr., *In Search of Excellence* (New York: Warner Books, 1982), 14-15, 238.
3. Means, *Leadership in Christian Ministry,* 67.
4. Bruce P. Powers, comp., *Christian Education Handbook* (Nashville: Broadman Press, 1981), 101.
5. Ibid., 105-8.

9

Delegator

Anne wanted to be an ME. In her first church she was surprised it was not what she dreamed it would be. Everyone depends on her for everything. When she tries to observe the Sunday School program on Sunday mornings, she is often stopped by someone wanting to get into a supply cabinet or asking her advice. Weekdays are not much better. Her phone rings constantly as department directors want her to help them get substitute teachers or order supplies for them. Then church secretaries want her to tell them what to do and when to do it. She goes home each day very tired. She feels she has the weight of the world on her shoulders. When she meets with the Christian Education Committee, they want to reelect the same teachers year after year, teachers whose classes had declined in enrollment and attendance, who did what they wanted to do, who were often absent from the weekly workers' meetings, and who seldom participated in the church's visitation and outreach program.

Anne has been an ME for two years. She is thinking about leaving the educational field or finding another church in hopes it would be better. Are there some things she could do to make her work feel successful? Could she get some people to help her with the day-to-day activities of the educational program? How could she encourage her workers to be more faithful and do what they had agreed to do?

In calling an ME, the church practices delegation. They recognize one minister cannot do all the ministerial work. In securing an educational minister, they delegate part of the ministerial leadership and work load.[1] Rush states, "Delegation transfers authority, responsibility, and accountability from one person or group to another."[2] A definition of some key words is in order. "Delegation" is giving others the authority to act on your behalf; delegation is accompanied by specific responsibility for a task or a job. "Responsibility" is the job you and your church are given to do plus the necessary authority to accomplish the desired results. "Authority" is the right to make decisions, take action, and give orders. "Accountability" is your liability to your supervisor and your obligation to accept responsibilities and use authority.

With delegation goes supervision. Delegation without adequate supervision spells frustration for both parties. It is unfair to delegate responsibility without providing supervision or guidance.

Delegation has never been easy for me. Much of my sense of self-worth comes from what I do. I feel I must be busy doing things. I grew up with this insistent work ethic. While I find delegation difficult, I have experienced great fulfillment when I have done it successfully. I delight in finding people very competent and capable. Thus my work greatly expands, and their sense of joy and excitement shows me the value of delegation.

When I became an ME, I had about two hundred volunteer Sunday School workers under my supervision. My job description stated I was responsible for the total Christian education program. I realized I could not provide leadership and guidance to this many workers. Fortunately, the church had a youth minister who was accountable for leading the youth Sunday School comprised of six departments staffed by about forty people. This left me about one hundred and sixty people who looked to me for leadership and direction. Delegating began as I discovered and recruited workers who became age-group division directors. Then I began to work with the four division directors, a much more efficient system. They then delegated responsibility to department directors and department leaders.

The Nature of Delegation

As a church grows, it becomes impossible for a pastor to do all the necessary jobs. Therefore, the church calls other ministers. As the need for help is felt, the pastor must be willing to share responsibilities and opportunities with others. MEs and pastors must trust and have confidence in each other and demonstrate loyalty to each other. MEs are not called to build a little educational kingdom, but to build up the church's members to fulfill their calling and ministry.

The church has delegated educational ministry tasks to the educational minister. As she delegates responsibilities, she coordinates church and educational activities by developing a network of persons to staff and lead the church's various ministries. This network of leaders then potentially touches and involves every member in "the work of service" (Eph. 4:12, NASB).

The Christian education program needs a core of people who assume responsibility to see the necessary service is provided. Responsibility begins with decisions about delegation made by the ME. She may, for example, assign a task to a department director who in turn delegates to a teacher or other department worker. A good Christian education program is a model of the effectiveness and efficiency achieved by delegating responsibilities to leaders and workers. Delegation embodies trust and confidence MEs claim to have that workers can do their tasks and do them competently. Good delegation builds a team spirit. It helps others to have an "ownership" about the ministry and work of the church.

Through delegation, the ME functions as an equipper. People cannot simply be assigned jobs; they must have the necessary skills and abilities to do them. Instruction and training are required for delegation to be productive.

Leaders delegate work to others to extend themselves. An effective leader in the church's ministry prompts ministry actions through others' involvement and inclusion. However, wise leaders do not delegate all their tasks. If other persons can do all the work, there is no need for the leader. When leaders delegate all their work to others, they are merely expediters rather than leaders or delegators. MEs do not delegate all the tasks they have to do. There are some tasks educational ministers are better equipped and qualified to do, such as securing competent persons who become trainers or equippers in the church's many ministry areas. MEs will continue as trainers and equippers in other aspects of the educational ministry or, from time to time, occasionally assume this role.

As leaders delegate authority, others act for them. The definition of authority emphasizes the person who has the right to make decisions, to take action, and to give instruction or direction. Delegation is shortchanged when the person is given the responsibility but not the authority to complete the task. Earlier in this chapter I described my responsibility for the total Sunday School. Difficulties soon emerged, for while I was responsible for the total program, I did not have the authority to execute the total program. The youth Sunday School was controlled by the youth minister. This created many problems in scheduling training activities and having a coordinated, balanced Sunday School. I needed the authority to complete the responsibility assigned. Responsibility without adequate authority leads to frustration.

With delegation comes accountability. Everyone is accountable to someone. The ME is accountable to the pastor, the personnel committee, the Christian education committee, and the church. In most churches she reports directly to the pastor in the daily functions of her office. She is responsible for the program of Christian education. As she delegates to others she grants them the authority to do the job and holds them accountable. Ernest Loessner expressed it: "Give me enough rope to either hang myself or make myself but don't do it for me."

Modern industrial organization has learned that cooperative effort makes them succeed. Delegation provides more complete services and higher productivity. The church cannot meet the myriad needs of its people with only a few doing the work. A Christian education program is severely handicapped if the ME and a few leaders are trying to do it all. Delegation helps the educational ministry provide services and activities that meet the needs of more persons. It aids in the achievement of the tasks assigned to the various Christian educational programs. Delegation of responsibilities is crucial so that the work of Christian education can do what it was designed and intended to do.[3]

Delegation Requires Great Skill and Judgment

Delegation is not easy. Selecting persons to whom to delegate requires great skillfulness and a wisdom in judging other persons to be competent. It requires the ME to assign part of her responsibility to another person. It is made more difficult when she has to give another a responsibility for something she particularly enjoys, for which she is gifted and does very well.

One motivation to delegate is realizing that, as she delegates, she extends her ministry by moving into new areas of ministry. This cannot happen when the leader does not give others the responsibility or authority to make appropriate decisions. Withholding authority may preserve her sense of power, but it also sets her up to be bombarded with minute decisions other persons should make. Thus, effective delegation avoids the danger of abdication of responsibility, but offers no relief from final responsibility for the decisions made.

Since she received her authority through delegation, she in turn knows how to use it in redelegating part of her job to workers she supervises.[4] A good principle to follow is the Golden Rule: "Do to others as you would have them do to you" (Matt. 7:12, NRSV), paraphrased to read: "Delegate to others as you want to be delegated to." Delegation is not easy; there is risk involved. While the intent is to assign tasks to persons who can do them well, they may not do them well, if they do them at all. Still, it is worth the effort, for delegation implies both permission and blessing to grow individually in Christian skills and service and to expand the church's benefits to more persons through leadership and ministry of the body.

Advantages of Delegating

There are many advantages to delegating responsibility. Seven are described here as they relate to the Christian education program.

1. *Delegation gives the ME more time for personal spiritual development.* Rush observes, "To do God's will, the leader must spend enough time with God to find out what His will is. The Christian leader's first responsibility is to God. Therefore, he must make sure he spends the necessary time with God required to manage God's work. Delegation provides that time."[5]

2. *Delegation relieves the ME of less important routine duties.* In Christian education there are many repetitive tasks. Two such tasks are preparing the quarterly curriculum and distributing curriculum when it arrives. These are tasks that could be delegated to division or department directors.

3. *Delegation affords the educational minister more time to spend on goals and projects demanding immediate attention.* Time management studies show that much time and effort is devoted to minor tasks rather than dealing with priority items. Good delegation permits a focus on projects and goals that have major impact on the Christian education program and the church. Rush states, "Delegation helps free the leader, giving him the time and energy to deal with most important aspects of management and leadership."[6] Delegating offers time for dreaming and examining various options.

4. *Delegation frees time to give attention to the professional aspects of ministry.* Educational ministers should primarily be educators. This is why they are called by a church. They must accept their primary function is serving the church educationally, not doing all the educational work. Time necessary for studying educational

trends and preparing for leadership responsibilities are part of the professional aspects of the ME.

Much time and energy are absorbed by the mechanical, routine aspects of educational ministry. Some of these do demand the educational minister's attention, but I now know this: one reason I found myself distributing curriculum material on Saturday afternoons was I was consistently too busy doing many routine things.

5. *Delegation builds a more effective work team.* Church educational work requires building a strong, effective team. The ME develops a core of workers who help in organizing, planning, and carrying out the educational ministry. Delegation involves more than assigning tasks to others. It includes training and equipping others to do the work. Teamwork comes as strong relationships are built and time together is spent planning, praying, and working.

6. *Delegation supports workers in developing confidence to solve problems, make decisions, and use ministry skills.* Rush writes, "Delegation develops leadership ability. It gives people decision-making and problem-solving experience and helps prepare them for greater responsibility."[7] Giving a person a job to do means sharing appropriate authority with him or her to make necessary decisions. As people make decisions, they learn to trust their decision-making abilities. The ME supports the decisions made by workers. Failure to do this undermines their confidence and weakens their desire to make future decisions. If this happens repeatedly, the ME will discover all the decisions are being thrown back to her. When her counsel is sought, she first gathers feelings and insights from other workers before making a decision. Delegation helps develop leaders, particularly as they have greater responsibility.[8]

7. *Delegation helps build trust and cooperation.*[9] Whenever people have significant jobs, they feel a sense of ownership or partnership in what is attempted or achieved. The educational organization and ministry does not belong to the ME but to the church. Delegation is proof of this fact. Trust develops as tasks are assigned, as progress is checked, as assistance is offered, and as faith is demonstrated that those tasks are being done competently.

What Should the ME Delegate?

The ME should not delegate every aspect of every job. There are decisions and tasks she must do. Some questions or principles that aid in determining what to delegate include:

• **Delegate details that recur.** Ask these questions:

1. What keeps repeating itself in my job?
2. Are these tasks that I am better equipped to handle, or could they be delegated to others?
3. Why should I stay involved in this task?
4. What minor decisions do I make most often?
5. Why do I continue to make these decisions?
6. Who else could make them? Who should logically make them?
7. If I delegate these decisions, what effect will it have on the organization?
8. What job details take the biggest single chunk out of my time? Is this the best stewardship of my time and energy?
9. Is this assignment helping fulfill my role as an educator?
10. Why do I choose to do this?
11. How significant is this task to the educational ministry?
12. Who else could adequately handle this task? To what could I redirect the time spent on these details?
13. How would I feel if I delegated this duty to someone else?
14. Is what I am doing worthy of the time given to it? Why have I not delegated these to someone?
15. Are these details beneficial to the advancement of the Christian education program? If so, who should be handling these details?

• **Delegate for the personal development of others.** For educators, ministry is aiding others in doing the work of ministry. Use delegation to train leaders by picking projects involving problem-solving, decision-making, and planning.[10] Some helpful questions are:

1. What parts of my job am I least qualified to do? To answer this question, one must know personal strengths and weaknesses. No one should expect to excel in everything.
2. Who in the church is best qualified to do these things?
3. What job details do I dislike most? Every job has elements not as enjoyable as others. Are these details someone else would find challenging and pleasurable? Of course, the ME should not avoid doing things she does not like; some things are done because of the nature of the job. Restated, the fundamental questions are: Is it an appropriate detail to delegate to others? What job tasks do I do for which I am over-qualified? Some MEs do many times either because they enjoy doing them or because they do not take time to train others. Prior planning and delegating helps avoid these conditions.

4. Are there tasks and duties others can handle as well or better—jobs that use specialized skills? What are the special, peculiar gifts of the people with whom I work? What tasks can be delegated to use these special gifts?

5. Are there activities that lead to the development of workers and test their abilities?[11] What assignments develop workers' skills? Am I willing to permit people to fail? A person's abilities may not always lead to success. Although people are never placed in a position where failure is certain, they learn their strengths and weaknesses through trying to see what they can do.

6. How can I best use the gifts God has given me to advance His work?

What should the ME not delegate? There are three general principles concerning what not to delegate:

1. *Handle the "hot potatoes."* Emergency situations, or those that have serious consequences, arise that require the ME's skill and knowledge. She is the only one to handle such situations; to delegate is an abdication of her leadership and responsibility. Failure to follow this principle leads to chaos and frustration for workers. It does not prove a lack of trust in others, but proves her determination to do her job. Any changes in policy or general procedures are issues she handles herself.

2. *Conduct performance reviews for her people.* Regular evaluation sessions are essential for paid staff and volunteers. People need to know how they are doing, and they need to hear it from her. Issues related to supervision are discussed later.

3. *Do not delegate disciplinary actions.* She provides encouragement and evaluation for those doing a good job; reprimands of Christian education workers are also her responsibility. Reprimands are handled with the utmost care and delicacy.

How to Delegate

How delegation takes place determines how work proceeds and how workers feel about it. Several principles help in the delegation process. They are:

• **State the objectives of the job being delegated.** Know what needs to be accomplished and what actions achieve those ends. The ME has the clearest understanding of what is being delegated. She must describe the results desired in measurable terms, but avoid imposing specific actions that hinder the individual from using her gifts and strengths in meeting the need delegated to her.

• **Be sure there is mutual understanding about the nature and scope of the task being delegated.** Clear communication between the ME and the worker is crucial and must be as direct as possible. Once a definite, mutual understanding concerning the nature and scope of the task is in place, the worker has freedom to act. Nothing demoralizes a worker more than completing a job, only to realize the delegator had something else in mind.

An ME was once asked to work with the Church Property Committee to acquire a new bus. After two or three months work by the committee, she discovered that the pastor had a different idea than the committee. He never told her what he wanted, but he expected the committee's work to reflect a decision he had already made. She learned that as a delegator, she not only helps workers understand what is being delegated, but also how free they are to decide how the task is done.

• **Describe the job in writing.** Delegate clearly and concisely. A one page statement keeps it sharp and to the point. Writing it down clarifies what the job is, defines problems, limitations, and any boundaries involved, and guides periodic checks on how well the job is progressing. Written statements of the task and the objectives benefit all concerned.

• **Make sure there is agreement on budget, personnel, and materials needed.** Delegating a task may be interpreted as "carte blanche" to the worker unless details are explained or defined. People may not understand that there are any restrictions or limitations.

A lady was asked to plan and direct a children's camp. It was a good camp experience for the children, but it was very costly. She purchased many prepackaged crafts and had an adult for every three children. There was no agreement beforehand about the budget, workers, and supplies. The time to clarify these issues is at the time of delegation. The money problems which resulted were avoidable if only the limits for children's camp had been written down and communicated to her.

• **Explain the limits of authority, if applicable.** Some tasks do not require major decisions to be made. The conscientious ME communicates the decisions people can make and those they cannot make without further consultation. Generally, delegating involves responsibility with the commensurate authority to complete the job.

• **Assign clear responsibility for the task.** There is an old saying, "Everybody's job is nobody's job." Workers should know for what they are responsible.

• **Set a target date for completion.** Determining a reasonable completion date for the project and securing agreement to it from all involved persons is part of delegation. The worker who knows when the task must be completed can also work at her pace. It is unreasonable to expect a job to be completed when a date has not been determined.

• **Let workers do their own thinking.** If an ME has fully delegated the task, she allows workers to do it their way. Too much supervision or guidance destroys the advantages of delegation. Workers need to think for themselves. Delegation begins when the results required are clearly stated; delegation progresses as workers invest themselves in the process of obtaining those results. Failure to let workers do their thinking robs them of creativity and does not use them to their full capability.

• **Set up a system of reporting.** Get reports on problems with and progress of the task, and reports on completion of the task delegated.[12] Receiving periodic and final reports eases the need MEs often have to direct or control the project.

• **Delegate to people who are trusted and trustworthy.** Educational ministers should delegate to persons they believe can do the job; otherwise, they are tempted to take over what they delegated. Since an ME cannot know everyone to whom she delegates, there are some risks involved; but it is important to project a basic spirit of trust. Sometimes, it is appropriate to seek the counsel of others who have worked with the person in other capacities. Delegating tasks to competent people enhances an ME's conviction the job will get done.

• **Match delegation to a worker's special abilities.** Knowledge of the spiritual gifts and abilities of workers is invaluable. Delegation challenges people to do and be their best; however, the task could either be too easy or difficult for the person if it does not match well with his or her abilities.

• **Whenever possible delegate a whole task, not a part of it.** Delegation cannot be done piecemeal. Delegating part of a task does not permit the worker to see clearly the objectives and goals of the task, and may inadvertently communicate a lack of trust or faith in the person to do the task.

• **Delegate to develop persons.** God's work requires the best people have. When people are asked to do a job, they should feel it will benefit others and prompt their growth as persons and as Christians.

• **Delegate to the lowest level at which a job can be done.** Sometimes MEs delegate to people at the top of the organization, thus overworking them, while the majority of the organization's workers never develop skills. Much valuable people power is wasted or poorly utilized unless delegation is to the lowest level. This is not the time to say, "It will not require very much of you." Be guided by Jesus' words to His disciples:

> Whoever wants to be great among you must be your servant, and whoever wants to be first must be your slave—just as the Son of Man did not come to be served, but to serve, and to give His life as a ransom for many (Matt. 21:26-28, NIV).

Delegating at the lowest possible level helps persons develop leadership skills that may lead to more demanding positions and greater service opportunities.

• **Caution workers of any potential pitfalls or problems they can expect to encounter.** Some tasks carry more possible problems than others. Dishonest delegation makes people feel manipulated. It makes it more difficult to enlist them to work at future tasks.

• **Don't delegate the same authority to two people.** This conveys a lack of trust in one or both persons. It also creates conflict. When this occurs, no one knows to whom to turn for leadership. This means the task goes unfinished.

• **Don't delegate and then, by discussing limitations and restrictions of authority, make the worker reluctant to tackle the job.** If the ME imposes restrictions out of fear the person will misuse authority, it is better not to delegate to that person. Placing too many restrictions and limitations on workers is asking them to do the task with handcuffs on or hands tied behind their back; worse, it robs workers from the outset of their enthusiasm for and commitment to the job. They need the freedom to do the task in a way consistent with their distinct calling and personality, and complementary of the teachings and principles of the church and Christ.

• **Don't delegate to the impairment of general staff morale.**[13] Both volunteers and paid staff need to feel they are doing their share of the work. Too much delegation gives the impression ministers are better at delegating than doing the job the church called them to do. Delegating unenjoyable tasks hinders good staff morale. No one wants to do the dirty work or the unpleasant tasks. Wise delegation develops a team spirit that affirms all are important to the work of the church.

To Whom Do You Delegate?

Choosing to whom to delegate is not an easy matter. One purpose of delegation is to extend the leader; another is to develop people.[14] If these are educational ministers' primary aims, then they use caution in selecting persons to whom to delegate. Listed below are several matters to consider:

• **Delegate to persons immediately under you.** Do not bypass lines of accountability and authority in delegating tasks. Rather than going directly to a department director, assign the task to the Sunday School director who delegates to the department director. Delegating to the person immediately under you recognizes the significant job that person holds. It shows respect for both the person and the position held. Others may also delegate until the lowest level is reached.

• **Avoid the obvious—the temptation to delegate to the most capable.** This places an undue burden on the competent person; in some ways, this punishes them by giving them all the work. It also forms the habit of delegating only to certain persons who are quickly overloaded while others do little or nothing. Violating this principle explains why few persons have leadership positions in the church. Part of the problem is these very competent people are willing to serve and feel a great responsibility for the church, but this hinders the development of other leaders. Many persons are willing to accept responsibility but are never asked. Gardner and Davis observe about enlarging the leadership pool: "This has the advantage of bringing new points of view to bear upon situations, developing new skills, and preventing the overloading of the person who is particularly adept at a certain kind of job."[15]

• **Delegate to the person with the most available time.** Seek to delegate to persons who are not busy. The opposite is often the case. MEs often prove their belief in the old saying: If you want something done, ask a busy person! Yet as an equipper and enabler, an ME must consciously delegate to as many different people as appropriate. Sadly, many persons in churches want to be needed by their church or serve through its programs, but lack the specific skills required, or are too shy to volunteer.

• **Delegate to the person who needs the experience.** Since one purpose of delegation is to develop people, adhering to this principle helps persons take on more responsibility and gain needed, valuable leadership experience. Moreover, delegating to provide experience overcomes the oft-stated reason for declining a job: "I've never done it!"

• **Delegate to the person whose ability you wish to test.** People's potential surfaces in many ways: through a check on an interest survey, through a deacon family ministry visit in the home, through a hallway conversation, through recommendation by a friend. It is at least negligent, if not criminal, not to follow-up in such situations as these with a chance to serve. Here the *ministry* of education is most apparent.

Problems of Delegation

By now, the many advantages of delegation in developing leadership and ministering to and through those leaders should be apparent. The work load is spread more evenly. Then, why are leaders reluctant to delegate? Part of the problem lies with the leader and part with persons not accepting delegation. Then why do some leaders persistently avoid delegation?

Some leaders suffer with feelings of personal insecurity. Do you? They do not feel competent without the burden of overwork and the power of final authority to prove it. Small wonder they are reluctant to delegate.

Some leaders conclude they are more competent than their workers. Have you? Whatever the answer, this is not the key question MEs need to ask and answer. The ministry of education is not about the minister's competence; it is much more the empowering of God's people with the competence only God gives. Paul's words to the Corinthians are applicable to ministers personally and should guide their ministry among people in the church:

> Such confidence as this is ours through Christ before God. Not that we are competent in ourselves, but our competence comes from God. He has made us competent as ministers of a new covenant (2 Cor. 3:4-6a, NIV).

Some leaders are afraid of not knowing the answers. Are you? No one wants to look bad by not knowing an answer, particularly in areas of their expertise. This is where delegation has the opportunity to bring persons who have particular skills and abilities into the process. When leaders use this excuse, they are trying to stay in control of the work by avoiding challenges to it or questions about it.

Leaders struggle to define objectives with sufficient clarity.[16] True of you? It is difficult to delegate what cannot be defined. Not being clear about objectives sabotages the delegation process.

There is the possibility delegation fails because workers are reluctant or unwilling to accept responsibility. MEs should be sensitized to the important concerns implied in these statements:

"I don't understand the task." Neglecting to clarify objectives makes workers reluctant to accept delegation because they fear failure as much, if not more so, as ministers do. Mishandling a church responsibility engenders a global-sized guilt for failing friends, the church, a minister who trusted you, even God.

"It's easier to ask you than to figure it out!" Some workers expect the leader to explain everything; this may say more about the leader's style of leadership than it does about the worker. The worker may not have the competency skills necessary to do the job; if so, then she is an incorrect match for this task. More likely when you hear this statement, "You figure it out," you've enlisted someone with a high rate of dependency; they do not want to make decisions, but want every decision to be made for them.

"Everyone won't like my way of doing this." This worker is afraid of making mistakes and being criticized. She does not want to feel ridiculed or made fun of in front of her fellow workers.

"I don't think I can do that." Delegation considers more than the competency of the person. It must also seek out persons whose attitude is, "With God's help, I believe I can do it and do it well."

"I've got enough to do, thank you!" May I reemphasize two principles already stated—delegate to the person with the most available time, and delegate to the person who needs the experience.

"I've never been involved in that." The person lacks identification with the program. People are unwilling to assume responsibility for programs with which they do not personally identify.[17] They may support the total church program, but have no interest in this specific program for themselves. They feel their gifts and talents are in other areas.

Supervision

When functioning as delegators, MEs are also supervisors. To supervise is to oversee and direct workers in the performance of their work. Supervision determines the productivity of an organization and the morale of the workers. Often, leaders either under-supervise or over-supervise; either extreme causes persons not to produce expected results or fail to develop leadership skills.

The amount of supervision required depends upon the maturity and competence of workers. The less mature and skilled workers are, the more supervision is needed. *The One Minute Manager* encourages supervisors to catch their workers doing something right and praise them for it.[18] This gives workers positive feedback while an activity is in progress. Positive affirmation is a great motivator and builds worker morale.

When persons fail in a task, they are affirmed as persons while their actions are corrected. A good supervisor builds up people and improves the quality of their work.

How do MEs provide ongoing supervision to persons to whom they delegate responsibility? Lyle Schaller describes a plan for working with staff members that is applicable and adaptable to volunteer leadership.[19] I have adapted his process to be used with key program leaders. Three sheets of paper are used with a vertical line drawn down the middle of each. On the first sheet the person responds to the question, "What is my job and what support do I expect from the church and the ME?" On the left side of the page, volunteers write their understanding of "My responsibilities to the church." On the right side they explain "What I need from the church and the ME to fulfill my responsibilities."

What is my job and what support do I expect
from the church and the minister of education?

My responsibilities to the church...	What I need to fulfill my responsibilities...
1.	1.
2.	2.
3.	3.

Figure 2

The second sheet deals with achievements and the needs for improvement. On the left side is listed what has been done during the last three months. The ME may add to this list. On the other side they identify the needs for improvement in personal and church deficiencies. The ME also may add to this list.

Where have we been?
Where are we going?

What has been done in the last three months?	How can I improve? How can the church improve?
1.	1.
2.	2.
3.	3.

Figure 3

The third sheet asks: "What does the future hold?" It lists on the left side the goals for which they have responsibility for the next three months. The right side enumerates the action steps necessary to achieve each goal.

What does the future hold?

Goals I am responsible to implement in the next three months . . .	Actions necessary to achieve these goals . . .
1.	1.
2.	2.
3.	3.

Figure 4

Schaller points out that by sitting down with the worker once every three months and using these three sheets of paper, "the burden of supervision can be transformed into a very creative and productive shared experience."[20] I have adapted Schaller's list of benefits in this approach to supervision:

• The ME gains a clearer understanding of each worker's task and achievements.
• The personal and support needs of the worker surface and are met before inattention to them becomes counterproductive.

- Internal communication is enhanced.
- Barriers to goal achievement are identified in advance.
- The worker leaves each supervisory session affirmed.
- Each supervisory session has a defined beginning point.
- Both the ME and the worker know the procedures.
- Regular opportunities are available to redefine the responsibilities of the ME and the worker to each other and to the church.
- Accountability is established between the ME and the worker.
- It creates periodic opportunities for handling deficiencies in performance.
- Each worker receives the attention of the ME at least four times a year.
- The ME becomes better informed about the total ministry and program of Christian education.[21]

MEs supervise the total educational program through the twin roles of being a friend and a sympathetic observer of the activities of the leaders of the educational ministries.[22]

Bingham and Loessner list eight personal characteristics of the supervisor. They are:

> 1. *The effective supervisor is approachable.* He is interested in people and is concerned with their personal problems and growth. He seeks opportunities to be helpful in the solution of their problems and in helping them to grow in usefulness. He values and protects confidences as privileged communication.
> 2. *The effective supervisor is patient.* He tries to be understanding of those struggling to become more effective Christian workers. He seeks to empathize with them and discover the necessary facts to help them solve their problems.
> 3. *The effective supervisor is adept in communication skills.* He tries to speak on the level of his hearers. He seeks to speak intelligently and clearly concerning the area under discussion, and he tries to bring into the discussion the best of knowledge and resources available.
> 4. *The effective supervisor maintains a sense of humor.* He can laugh at himself and with others and appreciates a humorous story.
> 5. *The effective supervisor has confidence in himself and in the people with whom he works.* He seeks to understand the problems that exist and tries to approach them with confidence and honesty.
> 6. *The effective supervisor is an expert in friendship.* Above all, he seeks to be a friend to all he is trying to help and to gain their confidence and understanding. He does not force himself upon others but seeks through conferences and personal interviews to help those growing as leaders and as Christians.

7. *The effective supervisor seeks to work with the persons supervised* in developing a plan for meeting those persons' needs and for the further development of their fullest potential.
   8. *The effective supervisor must be an effective Christian* in his daily life and in his witness to the lost.[23]

Notes

1. Harold J. Westing, *Multiple Church Staff Handbook* (Grand Rapids: Kregal Publications, 1985), 149-50. Westing also provides several guidelines for determining when to add new staff, and discusses some occasions when staff members should be added on pages 145-48.
2. Myron Rush, *Management: A Biblical Approach* (Wheaton: Victor Books, 1983), 132.
3. Neely D. Gardner and John N. Davis, *The Art of Delegating* (Garden City: Doubleday and Company, 1965), 1-2.
4. Leonard E. Wedel, *Church Staff Administration* (Nashville: Broadman Press, 1978), 145.
5. Rush, *Management: A Biblical Approach,* 136.
6. Ibid., 135.
7. Ibid., 135.
8. Ibid., 135.
9. Ibid., 145-46.
10. Ibid., 141.
11. Gardner and Davis, *The Art of Delegating,* 21.
12. Ibid., 40.
13. Wedel, *Church Staff Administration,* 146-47.
14. Carl E. George and Robert E. Logan, *Leading & Managing Your Church* (Old Tappan: Fleming H. Revell, 1987), 117.
15. Gardner and Davis, *The Art of Delegating,* 86.
16. Ibid., 96.
17. Ibid.
18. Kenneth Blanchard and Spencer Johnson, *The One Minute Manager* (New York: Berkley Books, 1981), 50-60.
19. Lyle E. Schaller, *The Multiple Staff and the Larger Church* (Nashville: Abingdon Press, 1980), 119-20.
20. Ibid., 120.
21. Ibid.
22. Robert E. Bingham and Ernest Loessner, *Serving with the Saints* (Nashville: Broadman Press, 1970), 122.
23. Ibid., 123-24.

10

Evaluator

William recently went to a large metropolitan church as ME. Church attendance has declined for the past several years, although on the surface, the church is doing well. They are using the same organization as when attendance was much larger. The pastor wants William to halt the decline in Sunday School. There are no identified reasons to explain the decline.

One of his priorities upon arriving at the church is to delve into the Bible study records. He discovers the decline has been gradual over the past ten years. Looking at the other Christian education organizations, he finds one probable cause. There is a significant decline in the educator's discipleship training program. One discipleship group, primarily composed of older adults, currently meets. The church also has difficulty finding workers to staff the Sunday School.

William also discovers the denomination is coming out with an entirely new curriculum line for all age groups in a few months which changes the grouping/grading plan, so a new organization is now necessary. Where should William start? Are there some places where he could find help? How does he decide what to do first? What criteria can he use to evaluate the present Sunday School organization? How can he evaluate the new curriculum? How does he assess the new grouping/grading plan?

Constant evaluation is essential for the Christian education program to advance and meet changing needs. Evaluation is qualitative and quantitative. It is easier to do the latter. It is easier to see if the Christian educational program grows numerically.

Many educators feel that comparing this year's attendance with last year's record is evaluation. Often they are not deeply concerned since more people are attending.

A part of qualitatively evaluating the educational process is measuring what people learn. Neither education nor evaluation takes place unless someone assumes responsibility for them. Young suggests evaluation should be considered by persons in the Christian education program within the following context:

> (1) Evaluation is a humane process involving an assessment of strengths and weaknesses in the performance of individual human beings. (2) Evaluation is the only way to determine whether objectives and goals of the educational program are being accomplished. The process helps administrators, teachers/ leaders, and learners clarify the objectives and goals. (3) Evaluation is a process that, hopefully, will promote an attitude of self-improvement. It provides opportunities for persons to diagnose difficulties and to establish ways and means to test new approaches to erasing the problems. (4) Evaluation is a process that requires personnel involved in utilizing a variety of assessment techniques to determine levels of accomplishments. Thus it is a tool that serves as a basis for developing alternatives to ongoing ways of doing things. (5) Evaluation is a process that enables teachers/leaders and learners to determine the amount of success that each exhibits in the teaching-learning process. (6) Evaluation provides a means whereby the need for and utilization of facilities, equipment, materials, and supplies are seen in relationship to the total educational program.[1]

Educators are responsible for evaluating church activities. Lindgren proposes eight questions as a guide for evaluation:

1. What are the goals toward which the activity is supposedly moving?

2. Are these goals in harmony with the nature and mission of the church?

3. Will the activity contribute to achieving the goals?

4. Is the activity in conflict with any other equally valid projects of the congregation?

5. Are sufficient personnel and resources available to carry out the activity? Or, will the congregation be overburdened by it?

6. Will all the techniques employed bear examination in the light of the gospel?

7. Is there a danger that this activity, as a means to an end, will become an end in itself, thus obscuring the real goal by its very success?

8. Are there other more basic goals that require prior attention?[2]

A basic question is: "What do we want or need to know about the Christian education program?" Some issues to consider are:

- What are people learning?
- How do we know they are learning it?
- Is the curriculum material constructive?
- How well are the workers using the curriculum material?
- Are we organized to reach our desired goals?
- How conducive is our building to a good teaching/learning experience?
- Are our teachers adequately trained?
- Does the church provide the necessary supplies and equipment for good teaching/learning to take place?
- How accurate are the records?
- What areas of improvement do the records suggest?

This chapter explores the purpose and scope of evaluation, and some principles to guide evaluators in creating a climate for evaluation.

What Is Evaluation?

Wychoff describes the evaluation process. He states:

> Evaluation is a process of comparing what is with what ought to be, to locate areas and directions for improvement. The existing situation is first described and analyzed. Standards are then set up by which to appraise the situation. Compare the two. Note the things that are weak, strong, omitted, and overemphasized. From these notations, implications for improvement develop into a plan or strategy for the future.[3]

Evaluation is not a simple, easy process. It requires an indepth look at problems, needs, and objectives.

The beginning of evaluation of Christian education is the statement of purpose or overarching objective. Wychoff feels that the standards for Christian education are rooted in three elements: the basic understandings of the objective of Christian education, curriculum principles, and principles of administration.[4] A potential statement of objective or purpose is:

> The objective for Christian education is that all persons be aware of God through his self-disclosure, especially his redeeming love as revealed in Jesus Christ, and that they respond in faith and love—to the end that they may know who they are and what their human situation means, grow as sons of God rooted in the Christian community, live in the Spirit of God in every

relationship, fulfill their common discipleship in the world, and abide in Christian hope.[5]

This statement was adopted by sixteen denominations in the United States and Canada as part of the Cooperative Curriculum Project. One denominational statement of the educational objective of a church reads:

> To help persons become aware of God as revealed in Scripture and most fully in Jesus Christ, respond to him in a personal commitment of faith, strive to follow him in the full meaning of discipleship, relate effectively to his church and its mission in the world, live in a conscious recognition of the guidance and power of the Holy Spirit, and grow toward Christian maturity.[6]

These statements enhance and guide curriculum development denominationally. The church also should have its own statement of objective, not that of another church or even its denomination, although these models show what areas need to be addressed and what work needs to be done. It needs to consider the uniqueness of that church and help evaluate its total Christian education program. Each Christian education organization is evaluated by examining its task statements and the standard for that organization.

Coleman describes the evaluation process as involving three steps. The first step sets up a standard by which to measure. Educators attempt to answer the question, "What ought to be?" The second step analyzes information and data about the present condition to answer the question, "What is?" The third step interprets the information or data according to the standard comparing "what is" to "what ought to be." The standard is the key to measuring whatever they want to evaluate. The purpose of these three steps is to cause improvement in the Christian education program.

What Is the Purpose of Evaluation?

After agreeing on what evaluation is, the next question is: What is the purpose of evaluation? There is a need for evaluation. Its value is what it does to help the Christian education program. Some evaluation is always taking place. Leaders profit from an understanding of the purpose of evaluation. Evaluation standards are set before plans are completed. Evaluation helps the planning process. It helps in the assessment of the total Christian education program. Learner progress is also addressed through evaluation. Johnson identifies these other purposes of evaluation:

1. Evaluation should serve to provide a *comprehensive* view of the educational ministry.

2. Evaluation should assess the *consistency of the program* with the educational philosophy of the church.

3. Evaluation should provide a chance for a *cooperative effort* by everyone involved.

4. Evaluation should serve the church continuously as *a part of the planning and implementing process.*

5. Evaluation should *highlight quality and growth.*

6. Evaluation should provide *a serious look* at teachers/ leaders, learners, and the learning process.

7. Evaluation should *identify strengths* and feed this information into the total planning process for inclusion when expanded ministries are considered.

8. Evaluation should *identify problems* and focus upon them with a view toward proper solution.

9. Evaluation should help *clarify good objectives* and point out weaknesses in poor ones.

10. Evaluation should *provide accurate and relevant information.*[7]

The Scope of Evaluation

The Christian education program involves a dynamic interchange among many groups and persons within the church. Young identifies the program:

> The scope of the interchange that constitutes the education program of a church is: the church itself, its members and constituents; the denomination and its distinctive character, purpose, mission, and program; the community in which the particular church resides, its problems, opportunities, and challenges; the curriculum that is in use, its purpose, scope, context, process, and design; the participants in the program with their education, aims, interest, needs, and Christian experience; the parents of the children and youth who are participants in the program, and the homes from which they come; the leadership of the program including teachers/leaders, administrators, staff and other leaders; the buildings and equipment that are available for the program; the personnel and financial support of the program; and the organization and management of the program.[8]

Simply stated, the scope of evaluation is as diverse and far-reaching inside and outside the church as the educational program and the mission of the church which sponsors that program.

Principles of Evaluation

Evaluation helps the educational program and organizations move forward. Some evaluation may hinder rather than aid an organization. The following principles strengthen the evaluation process:

• **Evaluation grows out of objectives or standards.** The objectives come from the church. They grow out of what the church expects Christian education to do. The church defines its educational mission. The same is true for each Christian education organization. Examine the objective statement in the previous section. With such a statement as a guide, evaluation is more than a statistical analysis or an examination of the attendance record, even if it is only a comparison to last year's record. The purpose of Christian education is more than simply getting people to attend. Educators want to help Christians grow in Christian maturity through various Christian activities which benefit them individually and help the church.

• **Evaluation standards are understood by all involved in the process.** It is unfair to evaluate people by standards they do not know or approve. It is best to share evaluation standards with everyone involved; otherwise, they rarely lead to improvement, and they may create poor morale.

Good evaluation standards are prepared by those who are evaluated. When the evaluator alone determines standards, he is tempted to take all the credit for successes, and assign blame for all failures. For example, most teachers plan to involve class members in a discussion only to discover no one studied the Bible lesson for the day. The teacher goes from the class discouraged because class members have not done what was expected. The teacher is evaluating the class members by a standard—each member comes to class prepared for a participative teaching/learning experience. Teachers need to know the standards of evaluation used for them. They should be as thoughtful with their class members.

• **Evaluation covers every aspect of the Christian education program.** Evaluation is comprehensive. It covers every organization and every age level. Individual organizations are assessed by their departments and classes. Individual growth of participants needs evaluating also. Leaders and participants are a part of the evaluation process, and evaluation uses a variety of approaches and techniques. Some evaluations seek to measure knowledge learned through giving Bible knowledge tests; others plot attendance patterns.[9] Coleman suggests:

It also should take into account such things as the attitude of members toward the Bible study experience, the flow of interpersonal communication within classrooms, changes in attitudes that might result from Bible study, and the condition of teaching-learning facilities.[10]

Creating a Climate for Evaluation

People use evaluation in every area of life. Industry, schools, and community organizations employ evaluation tools and techniques. If the Christian education program is going to improve, evaluation must occur. The idea of measuring what is done must be sold to the Christian education organizations and the church. Here are some suggestions for seeing this is done:

• **Conduct an annual Christian education evaluation retreat.** Schedule it before the time for annual planning and involve the general leadership of the Christian education organizations. The purposes of this retreat are to examine what has been done and to set up criteria or standards to measure the quality of work. While attending the retreat, people agree upon the standards by which to evaluate. They identify areas of fulfillment for the past year. They list their dreams for the coming year and decide what has to happen for them to fulfill their dreams. This enables them to set specific goals and agree upon the evaluation procedures. Evaluation is not difficult or threatening when the goal indicators have been agreed upon. This process benefits each Christian education organization— Sunday School, discipleship training, missions education, and other educational programs.

• **Keep the notion of evaluation before regular Christian education committee meetings.** People have a tendency to feel things are going well if attendance is up and there are few problems, but evaluation does not go on feelings alone. What tangible evidence is there that goals are being reached? MEs help Christian education leaders develop ideas for planned evaluation procedures. They lead them to make definite plans to use the evaluation procedures during the church year. Events and activities need assessment as they are happening. Doing it annually means evaluation is general and not very specific. Regular evaluation identifies areas done well and areas not done well.

• **A variety of short tests can popularize the suggestion of evaluation.** The church has been reluctant to use written tests. Some feel this would turn off adults, reminding them too much of school. Some try to evaluate what is happening in Christian education through excessive testing. Testing has its place in the evaluation process. Most tests measure cognitive learning, what facts or information the learner has mastered. Here is the rub: too much emphasis in Christian education is on the cognitive/knowledge level. Religion is not a cognitive process but primarily involves the "affective" area of learning. Testing in the church needs to measure how people feel about issues, whether they are growing in their relationships to God and people. Affective learning focuses on appreciations, attitudes, philosophy of life, acceptance of a way of life, Christian ethics, and morality. Testing measures the total Christian experience, not just what people know. Tests can be an effective part of evaluation if they are designed to measure one's growing Christian life.

• **Discuss evaluation with Christian education leaders in personal conferences.** Personal conferences permit the opportunity to discuss the importance and the criterion of evaluation in a non-threatening setting. Questions and personal concerns are open for discussion. Some questions to consider in the personal conferences are: (1) How do you feel about what is happening in your organization? (2) Are you encountering any particular problems? (3) How could I help you with these problems? (4) What are your hopes and dreams for your organization during the next three months, six months, year? (5) What are your ideas for improvements in the teaching/learning process? (6) What attitudes need improvement among your workers? (7) What are your goals in the learning area (knowledge, behavior, habits, attitudes, life-styles)? (8) How do you plan to measure progress toward the realization of these goals?[11]

Kinds of Evaluation

There are various kinds of evaluation that occur to assess the competency of the Christian education program. Areas examined are the content of learning, the process of learning, worker performance, facilities, the organization and the program, and the level of participation or non-participation.

The Content of Learning

In the learning process, the cognitive and the affective levels of learning are both present. Persons engaged in Christian education learn knowledge, information, theory, and principles. However, it is important for Christian educators to know that religion has more to do with the affective (or feelings) and attitudinal levels of learning. This learning has to do with feelings, attitudes, emotional responses, appreciations, and values. Evaluating learning at the knowledge level is not difficult. A person either knows or does not know. Learners prove understanding of the material by memorization, understanding background information, drawing certain theological truths from the Scripture, or knowing what a certain truth has to say about human history. Evaluation of knowledge learned comes by testing, simulation, personal interviews, or observation.

Evaluating affective learning is not as easy. Most persons who describe affective learning outcomes acknowledge there must be a secondary outcome. One way to measure this level of learning is to ask people what they "feel" or "think" about a particular subject. Questionnaires, interviews, and observation are used. A good method to measure affective learning is to use "projectives," working with puppets, movies, modeling clay, wire sculptures, drawings, or other art materials, or even occasionally, keeping a journal. Manipulating such materials becomes the concrete method for persons to explain abstract feelings or the implications of their actions. How can educators evaluate whether the teaching/learning experience has seeped into everyday life? This comes by asking the learners themselves to report on what is happening in their lives during the process of learning.

The Process of Learning
All teachers and leaders wonder "Are my class members enjoying the class? How do they feel about me as a teacher? Do they feel the subject matter is relevant? Is it helping them in their Christian experience? How do they feel about each other?" These questions relate to the learners' attitudes toward the teaching/learning process. A brief questionnaire, offered periodically, discovers the attitudes of the learners. Another way to evaluate the teaching/learning process is to observe the flow of communication in the educational experience. At times most educators wonder if everyone feels personally engaged in the class. Others wish they could control the people who monopolize the class. One way to objectively evaluate the class is to appoint an observer who records the number of times people speak. The class members' names are written on a sheet of paper. Each time a member speaks, a tally mark is placed by their location on the chart. Near the end of the session the observer

makes a report to the class identifying the number of times a person spoke.

I worked with a teacher who felt his class members were not participating in the class sessions. I attended this class regularly and was amazed at how many class members took part. I suggested he list the class members and draw thirteen lines beside each name. After the session each Sunday he was to place a mark by the names of each person who spoke. After about four weeks he stopped tallying as almost every member of the class had overtly shared in each week's class.

Occasionally, class members may want to rate themselves on how well they participate in the class sessions and discuss the insights they gain with the class or with the teacher.

Worker Performance

The evaluation of the educator—whether professional or volunteer—is a very difficult area. Adams describes the difficulty and the necessity of such evaluation:

> Any organization, including the church, would be presumptuous to suppose it could deal with the relation to God's standards of a member's work or as yet unrevealed effects of that activity known only to the Deity. Instead, the appraisal is addressed to the Christian's performance in activities designed to accomplish purposes and goals established by the church to which the member has made a commitment in accepting a responsibility.[13]

Bowers identifies four reasons to evaluate leadership ability. (1) The interest of the leader starts out at a high level. It decreases with time and marked inefficiency results. (2) A person has served well, but as they have gotten older their mental and physical capacities hinder success. (3) A person begins with a small group that has grown. Some leaders who are skilled in administering or teaching smaller groups do not have the energy or commitment level required for larger ones. (4) A person needs help but will not ask for it. Bowers cautions, "It is *not* the responsibility of the evaluator to judge or recommend dismissal; rather, it is to encourage, to guide, and to help every member of the church in his God-given ministry."[14]

Evaluation must be very tactful and done with the full cooperation of those involved. A wise first step is to have the workers evaluate themselves before being evaluated by someone else. Before evaluating a teacher, first decide what good teaching is. Teachers themselves ought to assist the ME in defining the standards by which they are judged.

I recall an ME who decided he would rate his teachers each Sunday. He did this through installing a two-way communication system in each classroom. During the morning he listened in on class sessions. Before the teachers left each morning he gave them his rating sheet. The teachers were incensed and rightfully so. This went on for several Sundays with the tension mounting each week. It was not long before the church asked for his resignation. One teacher said, "I am for evaluation. I need to be a better teacher. This was not the way to do it."

The ME or church program leader helps teachers in agreeing upon some basic skills a teacher should possess. Remember the attempt is to define teaching skills, not abstract traits or character qualities. Coleman suggests:

> Such skills might include: (1) the ability to formulate specific lesson aims, (2) the ability to listen to learners carefully, (3) the ability to ask good questions, (4) the ability to use a variety of teaching methods appropriately, including audiovisuals, (5) the ability to introduce a lesson in such a way that it motivates learners, (6) the ability to guide group discussion without dominating it on one hand, or letting it get off track on the other hand, (7) the ability to prepare for and direct Bible learning projects, (8) the ability to accept and use the remarks of learners in a constructive fashion.[15]

The list would be very specific in relating to the particular age group with which a teacher works. The key benefit accrues when the teachers develop a list of teaching skills and evaluate themselves on a self-rating scale. The scale might be calibrated to rate each item listed as highly skilled, skilled but could be improved, much room for improvement, not skilled.

Another excellent way to help teachers evaluate themselves is to videotape a class session. Many churches and members have video cameras. We use this in the seminary to train pastors, musicians, and educators. Introduce this at a weekly worker's meeting as your effort to evaluate your effectiveness in conducting meetings. Then, videotape only those teachers who request it or agree to it.

Self-evaluation is important, but we never see ourselves as others see us. Other skilled teachers can help by evaluating teacher performance periodically. A caution given by Coleman:

> For teachers to accept the idea of evaluation by observation, four principles must be incorporated into the process:
>
> First, the person doing the evaluating must have the respect of the teacher as someone who "knows what he is doing." Teachers

very understandably reject the idea of being observed by someone who has not shown his competence as a teacher.

Second, teachers must enter into the process voluntarily, with the attitude that this kind of evaluation will be helpful to them.

Third, the evaluation observation must be planned in advance and carried out unobtrusively.

Fourth, a post-observation conference must be carried out as a mutual evaluation, rather than as an occasion for "telling the teacher what's wrong."[16]

Learners should occasionally participate in evaluating the performance of a teacher since they are the persons most directly involved in the teaching/learning process. This kind of evaluation must be handled tactfully, with full knowledge and consent of the teachers involved. It is best that the teacher not handle the evaluation instrument directly. This works best with an entire age group or large group of learners where the identity of the learners is not known by the teacher. In designing learner evaluation forms, the learners evaluate the teacher and themselves as learners. It is not so easy to rate a teacher poorly when the rating instrument also reveals the learner has exerted little or no positive effort in the teaching/learning environment.

Evaluating the Facilities

The physical setting of the teaching/learning situation contributes to the quality of teaching and learning. Space and facilities need to be reviewed and evaluated annually. This is a task the workers can do themselves. It is wise to have someone other than the teacher who uses a room to evaluate it.

As in other areas already discussed, the beginning point is determining the standard by which facilities are judged. Most age group study books list the required amount of floor space plus recommended equipment. When crowded conditions exist, it has an adverse effect on the quality of teaching that occurs. Equipment designed for the specific age group is essential.

For example, the first step might be to identify the total floor space in the room and to note who uses the room. Second, list the average attendance for the past six months. Then show how many people the room can adequately handle if used by adults, youth, children, or preschoolers.

Observers are knowledgeable about the kind of teaching for the various age groups, plus the equipment and proper setting for good teaching and learning to occur. The program leaders analyze the entire building. After examining the physical plant, the findings are discussed with the appropriate people who use these rooms.

Evaluating the Curriculum

This section examined two primary issues: how to select a curriculum line and how to evaluate the curriculum currently used. Churches have many options about which curriculum to select. The church may choose its own denominational curriculum or some produced by other denominations or independent publishing companies. The choice is based on previously established criteria. A basic consideration is: "What are the characteristics of good curriculum?" Colson and Rigdon list seven characteristics:

1. *Biblical and theological soundness* are important to assure that what is taught in the curriculum is genuine Christianity.

2. *Relevance* has to do with suiting the teaching to the nature and needs of the learners in their current situation.

3. *Comprehensiveness* means that the curriculum will include all that is essential in the scope and all that is essential to the development of well-rounded Christian personality on the part of the learners.

4. *Balance* means that the curriculum will have neither overemphasis nor underemphasis of the various parts that make it up.

5. *Sequence* is the presentation of portions of curriculum content in the best order for learning.

6. *Flexibility* is important if the curriculum is to be adaptable to the individual differences of the learners, adaptable to churches of different types, and adaptable to the varying abilities of leaders and teachers.

7. *Correlation* is the proper relation of part to part in the total curriculum plan.[17]

Comparing various curriculum lines or producers raises other issues. Tidwell suggests a checklist that aids in this process. See Figure 3.

Evaluating Organization and Program

Much of the success of the Christian education program depends upon the skills and efforts of individual workers. These efforts are enhanced or restricted by organizational decisions. The way learners are grouped for teaching/learning influences what happens during their time together. Class and department size also influence the quality of teaching that takes place. Some questions to consider are:

1. Do we have enough units and the right kinds of units to carry out the work?

2. Do we have an adequate corp of workers?

3. Do we have enough of the right kinds of meetings to plan and carry out the program adequately?

4. Are we making the proper use of resources, including budget, curriculum materials, facilities, personnel, and time?[18]

Organizational patterns will either strengthen or hinder the program. A common task assigned to the Sunday School and discipleship training programs is reaching people. Often outreach or enlistment officers are absent from the general officers structure. If the task is to reach people, someone has to have this as a primary responsibility. Organizational evaluation points out weaknesses like this one, or areas that need strengthening, if it does its assigned tasks. Organizational patterns are found in the manuals for various programs. The designated officers and leaders are not ends but means to help the organization realize its intended objectives.

The program of each organization needs evaluating also. The purpose of the program is to enable the organization to realize its intention. Various planning meetings are essential for program leaders to plan jointly and strive to move the organization forward. Coleman has seven questions about planning for the Sunday School. They can be adapted for evaluating other Christian education programs, too.

1. Does every administrative leader (general and department officers) have opportunity to meet with his working associates periodically for face-to-face planning?

2. Does the Sunday School council do annual as well as monthly planning?

3. Is an annual Sunday School calendar developed, approved by the church, and widely distributed? Is it available to all Sunday School workers?

4. Does every department in the Sunday School conduct a weekly workers' meeting? A monthly meeting? Do department directors make careful preparation for these meetings?

5. Do Sunday School teachers preview curriculum units in advance? Do they engage in joint planning for Bible study week by week?

6. Does your Sunday School have annual and long-range goals which are well-publicized and understood by the members of your congregation?

7. Are well-planned Sunday School reports presented to all regular church business meetings?[19]

Curriculum Selection Checklist

Use this checklist to compare lines of curriculum you might consider for use with a given age group. Secure samples of each line you wish to consider. Examine the materials carefully. Check each item on the list below. Indicate by __X__ which line is best on each factor. Compare the basic pieces of each line: the pupil's material; the teacher's material; and any additional teaching aids offered. Choose and use the curriculum that best meets your needs.

Factors to Consider   **Curriculum**

                                                           A   B   C

1. There is ample, appropriate use of the Bible.   ___ ___ ___
2. The teachings are doctrinally sound.   ___ ___ ___
3. Doctrinal emphases are balanced.   ___ ___ ___
4. Coverage of the Bible is comprehensive.   ___ ___ ___
5. The educational philosophy is valid.   ___ ___ ___
6. Concepts presented are suited to the age group.   ___ ___ ___
7. Content addresses life needs appropriately.   ___ ___ ___
8. Teachings encourage appropriate responses.   ___ ___ ___
9. Methodology is properly related to content.   ___ ___ ___
10. Methods are suited to our workers' skills.   ___ ___ ___
11. Training materials are available to develop
    workers' skills.   ___ ___ ___
12. Learning activities are right for the age group.   ___ ___ ___
13. The materials support the church program.   ___ ___ ___
14. Materials advance purposes of this organization.   ___ ___ ___
15. Quality teaching/learning aids are readily available. ___ ___ ___
16. Supplementary commentaries are available.   ___ ___ ___
17. Art use is in good taste.   ___ ___ ___
18. The layout is attractive to the user.   ___ ___ ___
19. The binding is sufficiently durable.   ___ ___ ___
20. The paper quality is adequate.   ___ ___ ___
21. The print size is right.   ___ ___ ___
22. The print is clear and easy to read.   ___ ___ ___
23. Use of color in materials is attractive.   ___ ___ ___
24. Service for ordering, receiving, and paying is good. ___ ___ ___
25. Consultation in use of materials is available.   ___ ___ ___
26. Number of pages in each piece is adequate.   ___ ___ ___
27. The cost in relation to the benefits is suitable.   ___ ___ ___
28. The cost is less per comparable item.   ___ ___ ___
29. _____.
                (Other factor we consider important)
30. _____.
                (Other factor we consider important)

Based upon this comparison, curriculum line ___ seems best for us. It is available at the following address:

_____
_____
_____

Figure 5

Notes

1. William E. Young, "The Minister of Education as an Evaluator" in *The Minister of Education as Educator*, compiled by Will Beal (Nashville: Convention Press, 1979), 80.

2. Alvin J. Lindgren, *Foundations for Purposeful Church Administration* (Nashville: Abingdon Press, 1965), 30-31.

3. D. Campbell Wychoff, *How to Evaluate Your Christian Education Program* (Philadelphia: The Westminster Press, 1962), 9.

4. Ibid., 10.

5. *The Church's Educational Ministry: A Curriculum Plan* (St. Louis: The Bethany Press, 1966), 8.

6. *Church Curriculum Base Design 1984 Update* (Nashville: The Sunday School Board of the Southern Baptist Convention, 1984), 13.

7. Bob I. Johnson, "How to Plan and Evaluate" in *Christian Education Handbook*, comp. Bruce P. Powers (Nashville: Broadman Press, 1981), 60.

8. Young, "The Ministry of Education as an Evaluator," 86-87.

9. Lucien E. Coleman, "How to Evaluate Bible Teaching-Learning" in *How to Improve Bible Teaching and Learning in Sunday School* (Nashville: Convention Press, 1976), 42-43.

10. Ibid., 43.

11. Ibid., 44-51.

12. Ibid., 51-65.

13. Arthur M. Adams, *Effective Leadership for Today's Church* (Philadelphia: The Westminster Press, 1978), 158-59.

14. Robert K. Bowers, *Administering Christian Education* (Grand Rapids: Wm. B. Eerdmans, 1964), 131-32.

15. Coleman, "How to Evaluate Bible Teaching-Learning," 63.

16. Ibid.

17. Howard P. Colson and Raymond M. Rigdon, *Understanding Your Church's Curriculum* (Nashville: Broadman Press, 1981), 50.

18. Coleman, "How to Evaluate Bible Teaching-Learning," 65.

19. Ibid.

11

Growth Agent

Cheryl accepted the call to be ME at a large church. The church, more than a hundred years old, is rich in tradition and strong in educational ministries. However, the church has declined gradually for several years. For various reasons the church cut back on educational programs. Educational ministry focuses on the Sunday School and missions education. Very little is done in discipleship training. Each year it becomes more difficult to staff the Sunday School. The pastor is concerned about the decline and wants Cheryl particularly to grow the declining Sunday School.

What could she do to help this church begin to grow again? What should be her priorities? Can she work only with the Sunday School or can she seek to develop an active discipleship training program? What about leadership development? Is there a need for a potential teacher class?

One task of MEs is to lead the church to grow. Many churches call them with the expectation they will bring additional persons into the church believing they will more than pay for their salary with new people.

In most churches they direct the visitation and evangelism programs. The Sunday School is structured so a class or department is responsible for every prospect. MEs provide leadership to the church's visitation and outreach emphases. Often the Sunday School accounts for more new church members than any other church program. One task of the Sunday School is to reach persons for Bible study. The belief is once a person is in Bible study, the Holy Spirit uses the study experience to convict of sin and prompt decisions to become a Christian. Another task is to witness to persons about

Christ and lead them to church membership. Churches grow using this approach to evangelism and outreach.

Many churches lose more people through "the back door of non-involvement and inactivity" than they reach through evangelism. Evangelism without discipleship training creates this revolving door pattern. People are reached through evangelism but do not remain because of faulty or poor discipleship training. This is poor evangelism. New believers need discipleship training at the beginning of their Christian lives; they also need discipleship training for the remainder of their Christian lives. Discipleship training has three aspects—new member training, member training, and leadership development. When such training is available, the church assimilates or "folds" the new believer into its fellowship. Such training proves a church's commitment to every member's "faith development."

This chapter addresses these three critical issues. First, the ME has responsibility for evangelism. She helps the church grow numerically by reaching more persons for Jesus Christ. The second issue is discipleship training. How can the church help people become grounded in the faith? How can believers live effective Christian lives? The third issue is faith development. How can the church aid its members to mature in their faith? How can they be more like Jesus Christ?

Growth Through Evangelism and Outreach

Most major denominations experienced membership declines from the 1960s through the 1980s. One contributing fact was the emphasis upon Christian nurture in their Christian education programs to the neglect of evangelism. How a Sunday School perceives its purpose is a major difference between growing and not growing. Arn, McGavran, and Arn note, "In most declining Sunday Schools the 'reason for being' is exclusively ministry to existing Christians and nurture to members of existing churches."[1] They then describe the result:

> What happens when the priority of Christian education focuses exclusively on nurture of existing Christians? People are urged to participate in the Sunday School because it will help *them*. The church is thought of as a refuge for intimate fellowship with other believers; a personal and spiritual center where *believers* are nurtured to spiritual maturity. Programs, activities, and curricula focus almost exclusively on the personal concerns of existing Christians.[2]

Evangelism and outreach must be major priorities for the church to continue to grow. One denomination had only minor decline during the past thirty years because they emphasized evangelism through the Sunday School. Churches grow through using their Sunday Schools for evangelistic results. Churches who want to grow must learn to use the Sunday School as their vehicle for evangelism.

One way Sunday School reaches new people is through class activities and bringing new persons into the class. Arn, McGavran, and Arn observe:

> The activities of inward-focused Sunday Schools also reflect an introverted concern toward their own members. Social activities are member-oriented with little or no effort to find and bring in non-Christians. Visitors often have difficulty crossing "barriers" of existing social relationships or exclusive tradition. Growth, if it occurs at all, happens almost entirely because of *transfer* growth of existing Christians.[3]

Growth objectives in the inward-focused Sunday Schools do not mention reaching unchurched persons in the community. They assume it is an automatic by-product of Christian nurture.[4]

The outward-focused Sunday School has a different emphasis. Its purpose is to obey Christ's Great Commission (Matt. 28:18-20) and to equip God's people for ministry (Eph. 4:11-12). There is concern for spiritual growth and nurture of Christians—it is a crucial part of all curricula and activities—but it is a means to an end, not an end. Arn, McGavran, and Arn write:

> Outward-focused Sunday Schools . . . see evangelism and education as two sides of the same coin; two tasks to achieve one goal. Carrying out Christ's commission—to reach and disciple lost people—is the motivation for Christian education in most growing Sunday Schools.[5]

Byrne declares, "Evangelism is the chief work of the Sunday School. In fact, Christian education cannot be *Christian* unless it is evangelistic. To fail here is to fail in our primary reason for existence."[6]

This posture permeates the entire Sunday School. It is the attitude of the general Sunday School organization. It is also the emphasis of classes and departments. Arn, McGavran, and Arn observe:

> In outward-focused Sunday Schools, each class and each department gives high priority to seeking, reaching, teaching, and discipling men and women, boys and girls. The focus of the entire organization, events, classes, curriculum, and activities of growth-centered, outward-focused Sunday Schools is toward one goal: making disciples.[7]

Growing churches have one common denominator: they have an effective, active visitation program. The Sunday School is the evangelizing, reaching arm of the church. If the Sunday School achieves its mission, visitation becomes the established priority. All Sunday School classes and departments are units for outreach and witness. Braden asserts, "The Sunday School should make a commitment to quality Bible study and ministry as well as to reaching unsaved persons, unchurched Christians, and their families."[8]

MEs are responsible for organizing and leading the church visitation program. Although the ME has the responsibility, other church leaders are important to its success. The necessary steps to a successful visitation program are described by Braden in *How to Set Up and Conduct a Weekly Visitation Program.*[9]

Most MEs feel maintaining an effective visitation program is their most challenging assignment. What can be done to keep interest, enthusiasm, and participation at a high level? Braden has several suggestions to accomplish this task.[10]

Discipleship Training

The need for discipleship training was noted in the Thirtieth Anniversary issue of *Christianity Today*. Kantzer points out the danger faced by evangelicals from the penetration of secularism:

> The key to meeting this challenge is doctrinal and moral instruction of its converts. . . . The greatest challenge to the church during the next 30 years, therefore, is the need for both evangelization and discipleship. We are surrounded by a materialistic, self-centered, pleasure-seeking society of individuals. As Christian witnesses, we must enter that environment to reach the lost. To the degree that we are successful in introducing them to the Savior, our task of discipleship becomes all the more urgent. It will be wonderful to fill our churches with new believers. But it is equally important to nurture them in the faith. If we win the battle for evangelism but lose the battle for discipleship, we have lost the church of the next generation.[11]

Many denominations have declined in the total number of baptisms for several years. Coupled with either weak or nonexistent discipleship training, the problem is acute. Discipleship training has a positive effect on evangelism. As persons are discipled, they do the work of evangelism.

Many churches have good discipleship training programs for new converts. This is helpful but it is inadequate to sustain believers throughout their Christian experience. One excellent tool is *Survival Kit for New Christians*.[12] While this is useful, it is only a beginning for the new Christian. Without further discipleship training, it is like throwing a life preserver to a person in the middle of the ocean and hoping they make it to safety. New church member orientation is a step in the right direction if it is more than indoctrination. It is most effective when it assimilates new members into the body of Christ, the local church, gives information about the local church—how it functions, what it believes—and explains how new members are to function as responsible members of the church. Part of this orientation involves introducing persons to the life-long task of growing as a disciple.

Said another way, new member orientation is a plan for introducing new members into the fellowship they have joined. It is a link between the church's evangelistic ministry which seeks to win the lost and its educational program which helps church members become more mature and effective Christians. Orientation is also the church's planned approach to ensure a valid church affiliation for redeemed persons seeking church membership. New members are guided and encouraged toward effective Christian discipleship. Orientation is basic, initial training for new members. The members' new relationship to Christ and the church is interpreted to them. It helps persons become meaningfully involved in the life of the church and its witness to the world.[13]

The church's primary mission is leading persons to Christ and bringing them into the fellowship of the church. Evangelical churches believe the Bible teaches a regenerate church membership. A church seeks to maintain purity while increasing the strength of the church. Through its commitment to evangelism, the church strives to achieve three objectives. Waldrup lists these as:

> 1. To help ensure the church that each new member understands the nature of the covenant relationship he is entering and that he is committed to it wholeheartedly.
> 2. To help each new member gain a basic understanding of, and commitment to, the specific privileges and responsibilities of membership in the church he has joined.
> 3. To help each new member become a growing participant in the life and ministry of the Christian fellowship which he has joined, so that he may bear an increasingly effective Christian witness to the world.[14]

Three activities grow out of these objectives:

1. A church seeks a regenerate church membership. A church makes a conscientious effort to see each new member understands the nature of this new relationship. This requires every person seeking church membership be counseled.

2. A church needs to deepen the new member's understanding of that church. This involves the church's covenant, its programs, and the privileges and responsibilities of membership.

3. A church seeks significant involvement of new church members. New member orientation involves counseling and instruction. It also is a laboratory for good churchmanship. New members are guided by other church members to participate in other phases of church life. This helps in translating into practical experience what is presented in other orientation activities. Participation establishes the climate and context for significant study. Additional help comes in personal counseling, work of new member sponsors, enlistment in activities, and through appropriate recognition.[15]

What to include in a new member orientation program varies from church to church and from denomination to denomination. Some programs are for four weeks, others thirteen weeks. A church designs its new member orientation plan in keeping with its objectives for such a program.

Discipleship training just begins with new member orientation. Church members need to live and serve as effective members of the body of Christ, the church. The church answers the question: What understandings, skills, and relationships are needed by church members enabling them to be effective Christian disciples? The church is believing people. The church deals with the growth and development of individual believers, equipping them to function as Christians in all aspects of life. Thus discipleship training helps church members develop corporate understandings, skills, and relationships that build up the church. Church members need to know how to work in harmonious relationship with one another.

Discipleship training also includes Christian theology and church doctrines, Christian ethics, Christian history, and church polity and organization. By studying Christian theology church members deepen their understanding of biblical teachings. Out of this study they organize their beliefs into a personal theology. The primary objective in studying Christian theology is to help church members know, express, and apply what they believe. By studying church doctrines members communicate what they believe and why they believe it.

Every person is responsible to God for moral choices. Christian ethics is concerned with God's ideals for living. Christian ethics speaks to issues with which the Christian is confronted. These issues influence Christian conduct. Studying Christian ethics helps church members to act according to Christian principles.

Christian history starts with the revelation of God in Christ. The Bible is the primary witness to the origin and earliest development of the church. Christian history examines the problems of church and state, economic motives in Christian behavior, and the influence of society upon the life of the church. Christian history considers the church struggling with its own internal problems of discipline.

The study of polity and organization helps church members know how and why a church does its work. This includes a study of the church's internal and external relationships. It assumes when church members know the why and the how, they are motivated to be good stewards of their time, talents, and money in fulfilling the church's mission.

Discipleship training also includes training church leaders for ministry. Discipleship training in this area includes any type of leadership role held by church members. Training intends to develop increased competence for members to serve effectively and efficiently. Training enables people to understand better the type of leadership role in which they will be most effective. Leader training is one of three types: (1) Potential leader training provides basic knowledge and understanding about leadership. (2) New leader training enables a person to function in a specific leadership role. (3) Experienced leadership training enables a leader to improve or gain additional knowledge, understanding, skills, or attitudes, or to develop as a leader beyond the point of functioning in a specific job.[16]

The assumption made is that a systematic program of discipleship training leads to spiritual maturation. While this is partially true, does it address the knowledge we now have about "faith development"?

Faith Development

Two names are identified with our understanding of faith development. John H. Westerhoff, professor at Duke University Divinity School, was the first to write about faith development.[17] Most people feel the definitive work is James H. Fowler's *Stages of Faith: The Psychology of Human Development and the Quest for Meaning.*[18] Bruce P. Powers, professor at Southeastern Baptist Theological Seminary, also did some research in the area of faith development.[19]

The need for faith development was identified by a study of six major Protestant denominations in America. The study indicated only a small percentage of youth and adults have an integrated, vibrant, and life encompassing faith that congregations seek to develop. For most youth and adults, their faith lacks many key elements identified as needed for mature faith.[20] The study stated, "The primary aim of congregational life is to nurture ... a vibrant, life-changing faith, the kind of faith that shapes one's way of being, thinking, and acting."[21]

Faith development is a significant part of discipleship training. How can MEs design a Christian education program that helps individual believers move forward in their personal faith development? The present curriculum designs will not necessarily accomplish this goal. Too much of current curriculum is designed with cognitive outcomes programmed into them. Although knowledge plays a part in faith development, the whole area of religion involves the affective area of learning more than the cognitive. Religion is more than what a person knows; it is an attitude toward God, Jesus, the church, humanity, the world, involving appreciation of these and a philosophy of life that includes these. All are in the affective domain of learning.

Educational ministers must understand faith development and the process by which people grow in spiritual maturity. Much of this is programmed into an active, effective discipleship training program. By understanding and identifying where people are in their faith development, they can design programs to move them forward in their Christian experience. This means a variety of growth opportunities are made available in which people can participate. Faith development comes through stretching people beyond their past and present religious experience. Faith development will not happen by itself; it must be planned.

Notes

1. Charles Arn, Donald McGavran, and Win Arn, *Growth a New Vision for the Sunday School* (Pasadena: Church Growth Press, 1980), 40.

2. Ibid.

3. Ibid., 41.

4. Ibid.

5. Ibid., 44.

6. H. W. Byrne, *Christian Education for the Local Church* (Grand Rapids: Zondervan, 1963), 56.

7. Arn, McGavran, and Arn, *Growth a New Vision for the Sunday School*, 45.

8. Doyle W. Braden, *How to Set Up and Conduct a Weekly Visitation Program* (Nashville: Convention Press, 1982), 5.

9. Ibid., 7-19.

10. Ibid., 21-39.

11. Kenneth S. Kantzer, "Time to Look Ahead," *Christianity Today* (October 17, 1986): 17.

12. Ralph W. Neighbour, Jr., *Survival Kit for New Christians* (Nashville: Convention Press, 1979).

13. Earl Waldrup, *New Church Member Orientation Manual*, rev. ed. (Nashville: Convention Press, 1970), 4.

14. Ibid., 6

15. Ibid., 6-7.

16. Ibid.

17. John H. Westerhoff, *Will Our Children Have Faith?* (New York: Seabury Press, 1976).

18. James H. Fowler, *Stages of Faith: The Psychology of Human Development and the Quest for Meaning* (San Francisco: Harper & Row, 1981).

19. Bruce P. Powers, *Growing Faith* (Nashville: Broadman Press, 1982). Powers has a good summary of the findings of both Westerhoff and Fowler. He also presents his own ideas about faith development.

20. Peter L. Benson and Carolyn H. Eklin, *Effective Christian Education: A National Study of Protestant Congregations—A Summary Report on Faith, Loyalty, and Congregational Life* (Minneapolis: Search Institute, 1990), 3. There is also a report for each denomination who participated in the study.

21. Ibid., 9.

12

Communicator and Promoter

The second day on the job as ME of a large metropolitan church, Joanne put the four-page church paper together. It seemed like a simple task. Copy was received from various staff members. The problem was, she had never put a paper together. When she began to paste it up, it was almost a half page short of copy. When she wrote additional copy and pasted it up, she was two hours late getting to the printer. She learned this job requires more time than she anticipated. Thereafter every Tuesday morning was set aside for the church paper.

When Joanne accepted the church, she knew it would soon be moving to a new location. The church used as its logo a picture of the present church. The church building had columns, high steps, and a steeple. The new building had a temporary sanctuary. Architecture was modern. Once the move was completed the old logo was no longer appropriate. She had the task of getting new logo designs to convey the church's mission and purpose. A building picture was inappropriate as the permanent sanctuary was not built. She decided to use a Christian symbol as the new logo.

MEs are communicators. They have a personal message to share about what they believe about people, the gospel, and the church. Communication skills are oral and written. Good communication involves good content and good presentation.

They are also promoters. There are a variety of activities and events they promote. Their goal is to make people aware of approaching events that benefit their Christian lives. They also promote the church's educational ministries and church activities. This task relates to the church's public relations program.

MEs also are public relations experts combining their roles as communicators and promoters. The objective of public relations is to present an organization attractively. It helps people accept and understand the church's program and ministry.

Communicator

Communicate means to make known or impart. It also means to express oneself, and to be readily understood. Much time is spent in communicating or being a receiver of communication. Sometimes communication is the process by which a communicator transmits symbols to modify the behavior of others. Every message communicated, however, does not generate a response or action. Interestingly, a person may speak or write—that is, express oneself or transmit symbols—without communicating.[1]

Craig identifies the significance of communication:

> Who was the most effective communicator ever known to man? Who had the most to communicate? Who has continued to communicate? There is no question about the answer. It is Jesus.
>
> His message, his deeds, his methods—they all communicated. When Jesus communicated, he disturbed the religious leaders; but the common people heard him gladly. He did not use a billboard, newspaper, or a church paper to impart his message; but his methods were contemporary. He used language people understood. He used techniques of his day and invented some of his own.
>
> Jesus wrote in the sand, read from the Scriptures, questioned and was questioned, painted word pictures, and selected his audience from every class of people.
>
> His every move communicated his purpose. During his Galilean ministry, the word of his coming spread by word of mouth through more than two hundred villages.
>
> As Jesus went from village to village, he communicated his concern by:
> ...healing a paralyzed man
> ...enlisting a publican
> ...restoring life to a ruler's daughter
> ...curing a diseased woman
> ...opening the eyes of two blind men
> ...restoring the voice of a dumb man...
>
> Nineteen centuries later, Jesus' mandate is still the same—communicate the good news. Twentieth-century Christians are to convey the gospel, using all the proven means at their disposal.[2]

What then is the purpose of communication in the church? A church must correspond with its members. Non-members visiting the church must know all about it if they are considering membership. Communication should tell other organizations, inside and outside the church, who the church is and what it is doing.[3]

MEs communicate with various forms. One is transmission of information—what Barna calls "giving a rational message"—which seeks to offer information by using data and logic to inform or persuade.[4] Transmitting information assumes sharing between the speaker and the listener. MEs communicate using this method when they teach. Various teaching methods also use this kind of communication: debate, discussion, and symposium are processes for sharing information. Educators share information as they work with the Christian Education Committee, the Church Council, and various educational councils. They share information as they move toward decision-making. Lesch observes, "The effectiveness of the communication depends upon the quality of the information possessed by the individual members and their ability to communicate the information efficiently."[5]

There are types of communication other than sharing information. Barna describes the emotional message that seeks to touch people through their emotions. The purpose of the emotional message is to secure a behavioral response growing out of one's emotional energy. A third message is the moral one. It appeals to a person's sense of right or wrong. There also is the reward-based message, trying to convince people they will benefit from specific responses.[6] No matter its form or message, the most effective communication accesses interpersonal relationships.

Some believe impressive communication is a gift with which some people are born. Communication specialists believe everyone can learn the basics of interpersonal communication.

Promoter

Communication is a significant part of promotion. Promotion is the act of furthering the growth or development of something, to help bring it into being. Ezell and Businaro state, "Promotion is a planned strategy for making persons aware of an event, emphasis, program, activity, action, or resource."[7]

The intended result of forceful promotion is to move people from an awareness (a static response) to involvement in the emphasis, program, activity, action, or resource (a dynamic response). Promotion stimulates people and arouses interest. When promotional activities arouse sufficient interest, the person is motivated to act, become involved, and to participate.[8]

Most churches programs and activities have room for more persons to participate. The attempt to involve people who need what the church offers makes promotion all the more important. Because many people are uninformed or reluctant to participate, promotion is essential. Because members and prospects need acquaintance with what the church is doing, promotion is necessary. Because more people need to participate in church activities, promotion is important. Because people need what the church has to offer for Christian growth, promotion is crucial.

All church leaders should understand promotion. Since MEs are heavily involved in planning activities, they are often seen as promoters. Those who plan activities with evangelism and Christian nurture or growth in mind want as many people as possible to participate in these activities. Experience suggests church activities need promotion from the pastor and other staff members to give them both visibility and credibility. MEs acknowledge they are promoters. They are promoters of the Christian faith, promoters of the church, promoters of the pastor, promoters of the church's activities, and promoters of the educational ministry. They believe in what the church is doing. Their promotion is sincere and enthusiastic. Promotion is regular. It is continuous. It is unending.

Promotion does not just happen. Planned promotion is essential for awareness and involvement in the church program. When promotion is planned it generates the results that make the time investment in planning worthwhile. A promotional strategy requires that the emphasis be defined and that a description be given of what the emphasis can do for potential participants.

Promotion uses different methods. Promotion is visual, oral, printed, or a mix of these three. Good promotion evidences a variety of approaches.[9] Promotion is making people aware of what the church and its organizations are doing and planning. Promotion is attractive and in good taste. It describes the positive results that may happen to people if they participate in an activity. Too often promotion focuses on the benefit to the church or the organization rather than the benefits to participants.

Public Relations Expert

Usually MEs are responsible for the church's public relations. What is church public relations? Lesch writes, "Church public relations is understanding and evaluating the church program, and communicating to those inside and outside the church to gain their understanding and acceptance of the program."[10] Stoody observes:

> In the framework of religion good public relations can be thought of as doing whatever contributes toward making a church deserve and receive the confidence and cooperation of increasing numbers of people—in still simplest form: making friends for Christ and his Church.[11]

Craig notes public relations has five elements. First, it begins with the leaders. The chief leader gives it major consideration. The pastor leads the church's public relations program. While this is assigned to a committee or a staff member, the pastor is the key. Second, public relations is evaluative. It answers the difficult questions: What are the objectives and purposes? Who is doing it and for whom? Why is it being done? Asking "what," "who," and "why" is part of the beginning of good public relations. Third, it is public minded. The older the organization, the more difficult it is to hear and understand the world outside its immediate area. Being a "people advocate" is essential for the effective Christian communicator. Fourth, it is persuasive. It plans for action and selects communication tools aimed at the right audience with a specific purpose in mind. It is also within the budget. Fifth, public relations requires improvement. What are the strong and the weak points in the program? What corrections might be made? Evaluation starts the process of public relations over but with an improved program.[12]

MEs are responsible for the church's publications and for the church's promotion of church activities. Communication is inside and outside the church.

Getting Started as a Communicator and Promoter

Public relations is communication at its best. It begins with stating the purpose or objective for which the organization exists and deciding which details about that purpose need to be communicated. The next step is to decide whom you want to reach with this information—this is the target audience. The final step determines how to disclose this message.[13]

Determining the Target Audience

Church public relations has two primary audiences—inside the church and outside the church. These are the church's "publics."

Inside the Church[14]

Different and various media are available to most churches to convey the message of public relations. Inside the church, "a large part of the message is transmitted by impressions, feelings, emotions, and implications."[15]

Talking is a useful public relations strategy and is used widely in smaller congregations. A good "grape-vine" distributes information quickly and easily by word of mouth. People use spoken language to influence the thinking of others. Interestingly, businesses recognize word of mouth as the most productive means of advertising.

The written word is valuable to a church public relations program. Everyone likes to get personal letters. With the use of the computer, personal letters can be generated for almost any occasion.

A letter's look is as important as its content; therefore, designing the church stationery, arranging its text on the page, giving attention to style, grammar, and punctuation—all are important. Its language is today's language, the same language used in speech. Short sentences, short paragraphs, and small words are clearest and best. A letter from the church needs to be friendly and genuine.

Church publications are another form of the written word. Usually a church starts with publishing the order of service for worship. It is not long before announcements and other information are added. Sometimes, the church bulletin or order of service is mailed to absent members. Before long the calendar is included with announcements of coming events, and maybe a note from the pastor and other church leaders. Thus the church paper is born. The church paper meets the following purposes: information, inspiration, encouragement, and promotion. Knight's *How To Publish A Church Newsletter* offers practical suggestions.[16]

Some churches also include the following in their publication program: a yearbook, a pictorial church directory, roster of members, the annual church calendar, information brochures about the church, visitation pieces, or talent survey cards. The more publications a church has, the greater the public relations budget needed.

Visual presentation is very important. While person-to-person communication best transmits information leading to understanding of the church program, visual presentations enhance understanding and prompt retention of information. Consider these examples:

• **Budget information.** Nothing bores most church members more than financial figures. Using visual presentations helps present the annual church budget in an attractive and informative manner. The message becomes clearer when pictures of church activities and of state, home, and foreign missions are used. Charts and graphs help people visualize where the money is going. Color slides or a videotape describing the church's ministries also enhance a budget presentation.

• **Routine business.** Most church business meetings are conducted in a routine, humdrum manner; consequently people do not attend because the meetings are dull and lifeless. Graphs and posters help reports and presentations come alive. Dramatic skits and role-playing may be appropriate. The interest of the members is stimulated through adding visual presentations to the sharing of information.

• **Special events or fellowship occasions** offer a church other opportunities to communicate visually and creatively with its internal public.

Outside the Church[17]

Communication or public relations inside the church is directed to a friendly, yet captive audience. These persons are already involved in the church in some way. Communicating to those outside the church can be very similar. Although word of mouth communication is not always as easy or systematic, what the members know about the church is very important to the external public. Daily, based on what they know and understand of the church program, members decide what to disclose to those outside the fellowship.

Various signs aid the church in communicating to its external public. Attractive directional signs placed at prominent intersections help people locate the church. Identification signs on the church property are helpful to outsiders if they are attractive, freshly painted, and in good repair. As one who visits churches regularly I know how difficult it is to find a church even with directions. A sign in disrepair hinders my search and sends me a powerful, non-verbal message from that church about its interest in me.

Some churches place bulletin boards on their front lawns to provide information about their services and to make special announcements. The information must be kept current and the messages kept brief but catchy.

A church makes other impressions on the external public. The church's architecture tells a story at a glance. The church can use electronic chimes, streamers across the street, billboards, tracts, taxi and bus posters, menu notes, and other media to share its message and ministry beyond church walls.

Getting the Most for Your Money

Market surveys reveal practical ways to convey the church's message. An in-house survey of new members reveals how they found the church and what attracted them to the church. Churches who spend large sums of money on newspaper, radio, and television advertisements depend on the person reading the paper the days the ad runs or listening to radio or watching the television program when the ad runs. Good human interest stories are more convincing than paid advertisements. They clearly convey that a church is not a place, but a group of individual people living redeemed lives. The ME or chairperson of the church public relations committee needs to make friends with religion or feature editors and public service announcers.

A large newspaper ad or a radio or television spot in prime time is very expensive. Some churches use billboards to good advantage. Placed in a strategic location the billboard is seen by several thousand people each day for a month. A "teaser" billboard captures interest. Placing the message in bits and pieces on the board helps people remember the message. A billboard is cheaper than major newspaper, radio, or television advertisement with a much larger potential viewing audience.

Notes

1. Gomer R. Lesch, *Creative Christian Communication* (Nashville: Broadman Press, 1965), 12-15.

2. Floyd A. Craig, *Christian Communicator's Handbook: A Practical Guide for Church Public Relations* (Nashville: Broadman Press, 1969), 6-7.

3. George Barna, *Marketing the Church: What They Never Taught You About Church Growth* (Colorado Springs: NAVPRESS, 1988), 135-36.

4. Ibid.

5. Lesch, *Creative Christian Communication*, 21.

6. Barna, *Marketing the Church*, 137-38.

7. Mancil Ezell and Charles Businaro, *Promotion Handbook for Church Media Libraries* (Nashville: Convention Press, 1983), 9.

8. Ibid.

9. Ibid., 9-10.

10. Gomer R. Lesch, "Organize for Church Public Relations," *Church Administration* III (March 1961), 8.

11. Ralph Stoody, *A Handbook of Church Public Relations* (Nashville: Abingdon Press, 1959), 10.

12. Craig, *Christian Communicator's Handbook*, 13.

13. James A. Vitti, *Publicity Handbook for Churches and Christian Organizations* (Grand Rapids: Zondervan Publishing House, 1987), 20-24. This is a helpful book. The author has chosen to use many illustrations from the business world. Sometimes it is not easy to follow his ideas in making the application to the church.

14. Lesch, *Creative Christian Communication*, 91-109.

15. Ibid., 91.

16. George W. Knight, *How To Publish a Church Newsletter*, rev. ed. (Nashville: Broadman Press, 1989).

17. Lesch, *Creative Christian Communication*, 111-25.

13

Educator

Jean goes to a large church as ME. In working with the pastor and the personnel committee, they talked also about being ME and church administrator. They suggested the church might call a church business administrator. The church business administrator began working one month before she arrived. Her work and job description made her ME only.

As she began her work, she gave her time to getting to know the educational leadership. Her denomination was making major curriculum changes and revising the grouping-grading plan. She gave much time to helping workers work with the new curriculum that advocated some new teaching approaches. Workers were having a hard time dealing with the unusual terms and approaches. She learned as much as the workers. She worked with the Christian Education Committee and the educational councils in drafting plans for the coming year. Everyone was amazed at how quickly she began to make a difference in the church's educational ministry. She was grateful the church called her to be the ME without the additional church administration responsibilities.

By calling, training, and job assignment MEs work primarily as educators. An analogy that helped me understand the role of MEs is they serve in the local church much like public school superintendents do. Both positions offer administrative leadership which involves enlisting and training people, selecting and explaining curriculum, providing training opportunities for new and experienced workers, serving as a consultant and purchasing agent for equipment and supplies, and directing the budgeting and financial aspects of the program. The difference between MEs and school superintendents is they have little or no professional staff while superintendents have professional staff members.

Recent critics of the educational ministry feel there has been a shift from promoting church growth to a preoccupation with administrative detail. When this happens, it leaves little time or energy for growth, evangelism, or enlistment. Graves responds by stating these hopes of the church educator:

> Stated more positively, churches expect the church educators— ministers of education, ministers of youth, children's workers, and denominational educational leaders—to understand and support the basic nature and purpose of the churches and the denominational educational programs. Church members expect them to be able to develop and evaluate educational programs that respond to the needs of each church and community, to be able to work together with other staff members under the leadership of the pastor, to understand and be able to give competent leadership to volunteers in the congregation whom they enlist and train for service and ministry.

> Educational ministers should be productive agents of change, bringing about changes in the lives of the people reached, won, taught, and enlisted in service.[1]

The ME's role as educator is often not understood within the church. Jokes about MEs describe them as "ministers of announcements" or "ministers of etcetera." Churches that do not use their MEs primarily as educators do not get the full value of this useful staff member.

What do MEs do as educators? Beal suggests eight functions: lead in the selection and research of educational curriculum; keep abreast of educational trends; know each age group's teaching/learning processes; supervise the paid and volunteer educational staff; train potential church leaders; develop the educational workers through systematic training programs; secure educational supplies and equipment; and offer library and media services.[2]

Harris describes the work of the DRE as:

> Education includes such tasks as the selection and distribution of curriculum materials, the formation and actual instructions in programs where teachers are trained in pedagogy, the design of suitable educational environments for particular programs, the screening, choice and purchase of library and audio-visual equipment, hardware and software, and the supervision and observation of faculty in actual teaching situations, with the meetings, conferences and evaluative reflection involved in such activities.[3]

Here, education is the total task, seen in every function of the educational minister.

How Are MEs Perceived?

During the 1980s, MEs lost sight of the primary tasks of outreach and church growth, some accuse, due partly to the increasing scope of and development of their educational work. Sadly, some neglected these primary tasks when they succumbed to the pressure to become maintenance oriented. Many MEs are seen by their pastors, the church, and themselves in roles other than that of educator.

Is this problem just a matter of perception? In a recent religious education meeting a national ME consultant asked the participants how they saw themselves. Surprisingly, most did not see themselves as educators. I view MEs first as ministers of Jesus Christ and second as ministers serving through education in and of the church.

Part of this predicament is that a large percent of MEs oversee work other than education. One survey shows 91 percent of MEs surveyed were responsible for areas of work other than education.

The findings were:
54%—Administration
38%—Associate Pastors
30%—Work with youth
20%—Music Ministry
12%—Recreation

What is not known is the percentages of time MEs devote to these other assignments. Often MEs have titles that includes another area, i.e., Minister of Education and Administration. Even churches that keep the educational title often assign responsibility for overseeing the administrative functions of the church. This is not a new challenge faced by educational ministers. Many years ago, W. L. Howse cautioned that "care must be taken in enlarging the supervisory activities of the minister of education so as not to weaken his opportunities for maximum service in his major field."[4] His warning still needs heeding.

Harris notes that the DRE is a master teacher or educational resource person. She states, "The DRE is a catalyst for much of what occurs educationally, both formally and informally, in the parish."[5] Yet much of their time and energy is often required to oversee the office and custodial staffs. This takes away from the primacy of the educational role. It also causes the staff and church members to perceive MEs as administrators, not educators. Instead of acting as personnel managers, they should devote most of their time and energy to the educational ministry of the church.

Part of this problem is created when church personnel committees and pastors bring someone on the staff to relieve pastors of the details of the daily operation and functioning of the church. Thus MEs are not only assigned the task of administrating the church program, but also implicitly are expected to give it primacy over educational opportunities.

The training for educational ministry prepares MEs to function primarily as educators. Whatever churches, pastors, and committees might have done to blur the clear focus on education, MEs also share responsibility for not perceiving themselves that way and functioning primarily as educators.

Why Should MEs Be Educators?

The primary reason MEs are educators is in keeping with their calling from God. To do or be anything else is a denial of that call. Even their title suggests this.

A church calls educational ministers with the expectation the church will grow. The more they function as educators, the greater the potential for church growth. Through the ministry of training, more persons are equipped for practical service, for evangelism and outreach for Christ and the church, and as forceful teachers and leaders. Being educators helps the church and the kingdom of God to grow.

As persons train and are equipped as church leaders, they grow in Christian maturity. Educators model this ministry after Jesus Christ. They follow the example of Jesus who saw people not as they were but as they could become with His help and guidance. When Jesus saw Simon Peter, He saw more than a rough, coarse fisherman. He saw the latent leadership skills and the deep commitment and dedication Peter could give to Him. When He met the woman at the well, Jesus was aware of her sinful nature but saw her capacity to change.

MEs design educational experiences to challenge and develop people to reach their potential under God. Jobs in the church are not only tasks to be done; workers and leaders need to see what they do in the church as a needed function and as a chance for personal growth into Christlikeness.

The educator's ministry helps the church grow quantitatively and qualitatively. By studying statistics and church records, numerical growth is easily tracked. Educators design programs to help churches have the kind of organization that makes numerical growth possible. They develop in members and workers those skills and abilities necessary to experientially grow in the Christian life, and to competently function in the life and work of the local church, the larger Christian community, and in their everyday setting.

While numerical growth is measured easily, qualitative growth is more subtle and harder to assess. Qualitative growth requires a long term plan to lead church members to spiritual maturity. An ME recently showed me a three-year, detailed plan for her church's discipleship training program. She knew where she wanted to lead the church to meet the members' needs. It is a false assumption that all church members possess the same understanding of Christian maturity. The goal of Christian maturity is what was said of Jesus in Luke 2:52: "Meanwhile Jesus grew constantly in wisdom and in body, and in favor with God and man" (Williams).

Educational ministers are responsible for the well-rounded spiritual development of believers in the church. People are led to increase their knowledge of the Bible and how its truths are applied to life events; knowledge or wisdom for its own sake is not the goal. The purpose is to enhance the Christian's ability to live life at the highest possible level and to help those around her do the same. Spiritual maturity includes the ability to make ethical and moral decisions in keeping with the Christian faith.

Educational areas MEs influence are: number of persons trained for leadership; tenure of persons serving in educational activities; evangelism and outreach ministries of the church; and the stewardship commitment of the people. Most of the these are not observable immediately but take time to become evident.

Functioning as Educators

Recall the job functions MEs have which are similar to a district school superintendent cited earlier in this chapter. MEs are specialists in each of these areas, providing leadership to these specific areas and the entire Christian education program. These areas are now examined.

Curriculum Specialist

The curriculum presents many potential problems for MEs. Harris' *Fashion Me A People* is helpful in looking at curriculum issues.[6] One is the number of available curriculum materials. Many denominational and independent religious publishers offer a variety of curriculum lines. Ideas for rating the curriculum are in chapter 10. When all the Bible teaching classes and departments use the same curriculum, an ME's work is easier administratively and in planning for the weekly workers meeting. However, one line may not meet the diverse needs of all Bible teaching classes and departments. Then MEs have to plan with more groups, but the program appeals to a larger audience of people by using different curricula. Choosing curriculum may be the most difficult task facing MEs in the 1990s.

Many workers do not know how to use curriculum effectively. MEs are generalists in knowing the features of the various curricula plus the ways they are used by the age groups. I am a specialist in adult Christian education. By default, one year I had to be the director of the second grade Vacation Bible School department. I had never used the children's curriculum. Studying the material, I found out how well it was written. I also learned the teaching procedures were useable and practical. From that point on, I was of more help to the children's Bible study workers. I concluded educators should volunteer to substitute teach in any age group. This provides first hand information and insightful experience about how the curriculum functions.

MEs lead the Christian education committee and the Sunday School Council in regular reviews and evaluation of the curriculum. Input from teachers and other workers is secured. The users of the materials, the pupils, share their feelings and insights about the curriculum. One curriculum line is selected for a lengthy period. A complaint some people have is the replication of Bible passages in a short period. Generally this happens when frequent changes occur in curriculum choices.

Educators study the attributes of good curriculum. They know how to plan and prepare curriculum material. Part of curriculum planning is understanding the objectives desired. What does the material seek to do in the life of the individual and the church?

Educational Specialist

With the myriad information about education and the educational process, MEs are well read. They keep up with new trends and research in Christian education. They seek awareness about what is happening in teaching methodology, educational psychology, human development, and theory and philosophy of education. Their specialty is education.

They continually study the trends and major research in education through a guided reading program. Professional journals in Christian and secular education keep them informed about new trends, important research conducted, and people who make major contributions to the educational field. Additional knowledge is gained by enrolling in continuing education courses offered by a seminary or college. Even a few days studying in a seminary or university library could prove very useful.

MEs cannot be educational specialists by wishing to be so, it requires discipline, a definite plan, and time devoted to this purpose. One good way to find out what is happening in educational circles is to ask those who are leaders. As a seminary professor, I get several requests a year for syllabi and bibliographies. Over the years, I have befriended some people who read interesting and helpful books in my fields of discipline. When I see or talk to such a friend, I ask what they have been reading, how it was helpful, and thus continue to broaden my educational scope.

Another way to be an educational specialist is to take part in a collegiality group within one's own denominational lines or across denominational lines. I joined such a group that met for two hours twice a month. Sometimes a member led a dialogue about a book they found helpful. Other times an educational guest was invited. Periodically, someone in public education would tell us what was new and innovative in that field.

MEs, even with age-group specialists also on the church staff, provide leadership to the total Christian education program through their knowledge of education. This means being aware of educational history, of the current status of religious and secular education, and of the trends predicted for education.

Age-Group Teaching/Learning Processes
Insights from human development and educational psychology confirm that people learn in different ways. This is certainly true at different age levels. Preschoolers learn through activity; knowing this suggests preschool teachers rely on learning centers or activity areas rather than tables and chairs for effective teaching. Children also learn through activity, particularly younger children. They still do not understand abstract concepts but are very concrete thinkers. Consequently, teachers of children learn quickly each child wants to share his or her experience, even though it is similar to one already shared by another, because they cannot generalize yet.

Youth education moves into more abstract territory. As youth mature, they deal with moral and ethical issues. They can now discriminate between options and seek solutions to complex situations. They can make deeper, more long-term commitments. They can assume more responsibility for what happens in the teaching/ learning experience.

Education at these three levels—preschool, children, and youth—is preparation for life. Adult education is life itself. It focuses on equipping adults to deal with complex and difficult decisions about their lives, their families, and people with whom they work. Religious instruction is life-applicable.

Educators learn how different age-group teaching/learning processes function through guided reading, observation, and by attending conferences especially designed to demonstrate teaching/learning at various age levels.

Supervise the Educational Staff

MEs lead the educational program and the educational staff. This involves working with age-group specialists, if the church has them, and volunteer workers. Guiding the Christian education program requires time and attention. Refer again to chapter 9 on delegation.

Train Potential Leaders

MEs are trainers of leaders. Once new leaders are trained and begin to function in new leadership roles, the task of discovering, enlisting, and training new leaders starts over. This function of the ME is developed in chapter 8.

Developing Educational Skills

Every educational worker involved in an orderly training program should be every ME's goal. Educational workers need new insights into learners, and new, different, and varied teaching approaches to enhance the teaching/learning process. Teachers in public education take part in continuing education courses to maintain their credentials and update their skills. Participants in the church's Christian education program likewise deserve instruction from people who are trained and qualified to work with a specified age group. Only through a systematic training program involving all workers can this possibly be attained.

Securing Educational Supplies and Equipment

Christian education requires adequate equipment and supplies for the teaching/learning process. Some churches feel if they provide a classroom and chairs, this is all that is needed.

For maximum teaching/learning results to become reality, a classroom needs proper, adequate equipment. MEs take the lead in securing this equipment. Having adequate space is essential; inadequate space limits growth. Age-group manuals describe equipment needed for skilled teaching to take place. Tables and chairs of the correct height, chalkboards, tackboards, pencils, varieties of paper, and a myriad supply of art materials will be used in the educational experiences throughout the church.

A strategy for purchasing supplies is essential. Some churches permit each class or department to buy what it needs and then provide reimbursement. However, teachers do not always anticipate what supplies are needed, and buying in quantity is less expensive than buying as needed. It is good to keep a supply of construction paper, pencils, chalk, posterboard, scissors, paste, and paints stored in supply closets or cabinets that all organizations can use. This approach has the advantage over each organization having its own supplies. Someone inevitably will borrow materials from one organization to use in another. Then the organization leaders who planned for and purchased supplies do not have what they need, and hard feelings often result.

This problem once arose in a church kindergarten whose supplies were frequently taken by preschool workers on Sundays. The ME discussed it with the kindergarten director who placed a large order for supplies in August. They decided to double the usual order and split the cost. This solved many problems related to the use of supplies and having adequate quantities on hand.

Coordinate the Church Media Library Services

The church media library does not exist solely for the benefit of educational ministries. Yet it is hard to conceive of a quality Christian education program without a functioning church media library. The media library provides printed, audio, and visual resources valuable to the teaching/learning process used by teachers, workers, and members to enhance the learning environment and experience.

MEs work in close cooperation with the church media library director. This assures new books and other resources are available and known to educational workers. Workers, as they begin new units of study, need awareness of resources the church has that can strengthen their preparation.

Emler has a good discussion of the work of the ME with the church media library. He expands the concept of the media library from a repository of materials only to also include producing of materials.[7]

The church media library is the best place in the church to keep audio-visual equipment. Its staff helps workers set up the equipment and show them how to use it. The church media library catalogs and is the repository for filmstrips, movies, videotapes, and slides so they can be located and made available for distribution and use.

Notes

1. Allen W. Graves, "Education as a Function of the Church," *The Minister of Education as Educator*, compiled by Will Beal (Nashville: Convention Press, 1979), 10.

2. Will Beal, comp., *The Work of the Minister of Education* (Nashville: Convention Press, 1976), 30.

3. Maria Harris, *The DRE Book: Questions and Strategies for Parish Personnel* (New York: Paulist Press, 1976), 5.

4. W. L. Howse, *The Minister of Education* (Nashville: Convention Press, n.d.), 7.

5. Harris, *The DRE Book*, 5.

6. Maria Harris, *Fashion Me A People: Curriculum in the Church* (Louisville: Westminster/John Knox Press, 1989).

7. Donald G. Emler, *Revisioning the DRE* (Birmingham: Religious Education Press, 1989), 149-54.

14

Motivator

Scott is ME in a middle-sized church in a stagnant community. He discovers people accept jobs, but few finish them. Committees start with much enthusiasm, but it is not long before committee members do not show up for scheduled meetings. Sunday School leaders promise to come to the church's regular visitation program but do not. Prospects' names are given and accepted by Sunday School classes. Months later, the people have not been visited. The people lack motivation.

Scott learned that if a job was to be done, he had to do it himself or depend upon a few who were already motivated. It affected his morale when people didn't complete tasks they accepted. He tried to discover why the people were not sufficiently motivated. This led to even greater frustration for him.

He began to ask himself: How can I motivate these people? What appeals can I make so the people will follow through with their commitments? Am I guilty of trying to manipulate the people rather than persuade them?

"Motivate" means to stimulate to action; provide with an incentive or motive; impel; incite. "Motive" is an emotion, desire, psychological need, or similar impulse acting as an incitement to action. As MEs function as equippers and enablers, their ability to motivate others to act is an important element in their success and their major task. Means states, "Spiritual leaders inspire people to recognize their own spiritual needs, values, and objectives, and then facilitate growth in these vital areas."[1]

Knowing why people behave as they do helps in setting a climate for motivation. Motivation, a hard task particularly with volunteer leaders, is an internal force which gives energy for action and defines the course of that action.

What Is Motivation?

Why do people work better or sustain higher levels of loyalty to½ the group? Psychologists list these primary findings:

1. *Motivation is psychological, not logical.* It is primarily an emotional process. Studies have shown people are not more highly motivated because they receive more money or more benefits.

2. *Motivation is fundamentally an unconscious process.* The behavior we see in ourselves or others may appear to be illogical, but somehow, inside the unconsciousness of the individual, what he is doing makes sense to him.

3. *Motivation is an individual matter.* The key to a person's behavior lies within himself.

4. *Not only do motivating needs differ from person to person, but in any individual they vary from time to time.*

5. *Motivation is inevitably a social process.* We often depend on what others think for satisfaction of many of our needs.

6. *In most of our daily actions, we are guarded by habits established by motivational processes that were activated many years earlier.*[2]

External and Internal Motivational Factors

Motivational theory falls into two broad groupings: external and internal. Generally, it assumes volunteers are not motivated by external factors. Although external components differ with each volunteer, they are present.

External Motivational Factors

External or extrinsic explanations of motivation assume a person acts to gain rewards or avoid punishment. Sometimes volunteers drop out when rewards are sensed as artificial or they feel threatened by manipulative penalties. When volunteer workers feel they are driven or pushed, they become dismayed and often drop out.

Volunteers receive "pay" through notice of their efforts and their personal growth. The purpose of volunteers is to help others and to grow themselves. Volunteers enjoy what they do or they would not volunteer. MEs and church leaders ought to avoid or be careful in the use of external motivational approaches.

Internal Motivational Factors

Internal motivational approaches are better suited to the church setting and meet volunteer needs better. They generally follow two models. One is the "deficiency" model. The emphasis is on the strong pull of wants, needs, tensions, and discomforts. Some are motivated by the internal drive to excel, to succeed; others want to exercise power over and influence their followers. On the more positive side, some want warm, positive relationships. They need a sense of belonging and thus they reach out for group participation.[3]

The second model of internal motivation is the "growth" model, popularized by Abraham Maslow's hierarchy of needs. This approach identifies five major groupings of needs. The needs are physical, safety, social, ego, and self-actualization. This theory holds that the most basic unmet need is the motivator. Once the need is satisfied, that need no longer motivates. Then the next higher level becomes the motivator. Motives usually move upward unless a lower level need occurs again. Ideally, persons move up the hierarchy. In actuality some people never get to the highest level of self-actualization.

Needs and motives in the church can shift rapidly because church members will mirror the larger cultural picture; church leaders must be sensitive to the emerging needs of members.[4]

Maslow's hierarchy of needs has great implications for MEs.[5] They need to understand the hierarchy of needs if they intend to motivate others. They must know the real needs of their workers; otherwise, they miss key motivational drives. A problem some leaders face is that their followers are not as highly motivated as they are. However, the opposite is also true: some workers are more motivated than their educational leaders or ministers!

Level one: Physiological needs. These are the most basic human needs. If a person has enough food, then food is no longer a need or want. MEs have few leaders or workers whose physiological needs are unmet.

Level two: Safety needs. Maslow identifies the safety needs as security, stability, dependency, protection, freedom from fear, freedom from anxiety and chaos, need for structure, order, law, limits, and strength in the protector, to name a few.[6] These needs express themselves as persons prefer the familiar to the unfamiliar, or the known to the unknown, when they want to feel secure in the church setting. They do not fear for their physical safety. Their fears are more psychological. Positive motivators which acknowledge these needs are:

• the assurance leaders are supportive of what workers are doing;
• a sense of stability is provided through organizational and administrative pattern;
• good interpersonal relationships are maintained even when discord surfaces;
• decision-making skills and conflict resolution strategies are modeled when problems surface.

Level three: Belonging and love needs. These needs are felt by the person who recently moved to town or to a new church and is hungry for caring relationships. Such persons need to be a part of a family or a group. They strive with great intensity to satisfy this need. They accept places of leadership to feel they belong. They try to avoid feeling the pangs of loneliness, of ostracism, of rejection, of friendlessness, of rootlessness. The church and especially its educational organizations help meet these deep needs. Some people are highly motivated by this hunger for contact, for intimacy, for belonging and are strongly motivated to overcome the feelings of alienation, aloneness, strangeness, and loneliness. For example, people who get over-involved in church activities, who take on more duties than they can keep up with or do well, are satisfying their belonging needs. Sometimes these people know how to give love but are incapable of receiving love. The love need truly met involves giving and receiving of love.

Level four: Esteem needs. Maslow states, "All people...have a need or desire for a stable, firmly based, unusually high evaluation of themselves, for self-respect, or self-esteem, and for the esteem of others."[7] These needs subdivide into two sets. The first set is the desires for strength, achievement, adequacy, mastery and competence, confidence, and independence and freedom. The second set is the desires for reputation or prestige (respect or esteem from other people), status, fame and glory, dominance, recognition, attention, importance, dignity, or appreciation.[8]

When the self-esteem needs are satisfied, feelings of self-confidence, worth, strength, capability, and adequacy emerge. When these needs are thwarted, feelings of inferiority, weakness, and helplessness result.

There is danger in basing our self-esteem on the opinion of others rather than on real capacity, competency, and adequacy for the task. A stable and healthy self-esteem is based on deserved respect, not on external fame, celebrity status, and unwarranted adulation. The church meets this need through its affirmation of people. An annual leadership appreciation banquet meets some esteem needs. Public and private notice of workers and their work meets esteem needs. Through equipping and enabling people, MEs affirm that people are important to God and His work, and to the church and what the church strives to do and be.

Level five: Need for self-actualization. When the previous levels of needs are met, people often feel a new discontentment and restlessness. These develop because they are not doing what they are fitted to do. What people can be, they must be. They must be true to their nature for this is the only way they are "self-actualized." Self-actualized persons have certain qualities. They see reality clearly. They can accept themselves at all levels—love, safety, belongingness, honor, self-respect. They are spontaneous in behavior. Individual differences are greatest at this level.[9] For them, motivation is character growth, character expression, maturation, and development. They feel they have some mission in life, some task to fulfill. This task is one they feel is their duty or obligation. They are concerned with basic issues and eternal questions. Maslow says, "Self-actualizing people have the capacity to appreciate again and again, freshly and naively, the basic goods of life, with awe, pleasure, wonder, and even ecstasy."[10]

Not everyone reaches this level. This does not mean people who do not attain self-actualization do not do quality work. Educators assist people to reach their maximum level by encouraging them to use their God-given spiritual gifts to the best of their ability.

The ME's Own Motivation

Motivating others is hard if MEs are not motivated themselves. Means describes how MEs motivate others:

> Good spiritual leaders infuse others with an animating, quickening, and exalting spirit of enthusiasm for the task of the church and the person of Christ. They do this primarily through their personal optimism, authenticity, enthusiasm, and example.[11]

How does an ME determine if he is highly motivated for his tasks? Some questions that help the educational minister determine personal motivation include:

- Have I set specific goals?
- Do I have written plans for achieving my goals?
- How realistic are my goals? Can I do them? What are my chances of success?
- Do I have a starting point? What have I done to begin?

● What is my peak time of accomplishment each day? Do I do my toughest tasks then?

● Have I established a deadline for each goal? Do I have checkpoints to see how well I am doing?

● Is my goal broken down into small projects or tasks? Do I feel overwhelmed by the bigness of the task?

● What are the general benefits of reaching my goals? Do I reward myself for successfully reaching my goals?

● What do I do when I get stuck on a project?

● Am I optimistic?

● How enthusiastic am I?[12]

Building a Motivational Climate

What can MEs do to build a climate for motivation? Creating the motivational climate is not the unique duty of MEs; this is shared with other church leaders. Yet MEs work with may different church groups at a variety of levels. This work gives them opportunities every week to build this climate throughout the Christian education organizations.

McDonough notes, "A leader's role in motivation is to be sensitive to the needs and gifts of persons, to help persons understand their needs and gifts, and to help them live out their Christian calling in satisfying and fulfilling ways."[13]

A motivator throws away old bags of tricks. There is no one way all persons are motivated. People are different in their needs, hopes, dreams, and fears. MEs are sensitive to the needs of persons. Below are some ideas that build a motivational climate where workers desire to invest their time and energies.

● **Keep the workers' ministry dreams defined and openly communicated.** If groups define their goals and values, they will act to help these dreams become realities. Dale notes, "Leaders who keep the dream keenly focused, advocated, and expressed in words, actions, and symbols create a motivational climate."[14]

● **Workers need recognition and appreciation.**[15] People want to work in an atmosphere of affirmation. Quality work deserves this; otherwise, workers may feel they are overworked and underappreciated. Engstrom and Dayton emphasize, "People are motivated by achievement, by recognition of their efforts, by challenging work, by being made responsible, and by experiencing personal growth."[16] People are either motivated or demotivated. Some demotivators include poor administration, weak or inept supervision, deficient working conditions, poor interpersonal relationships, and a lack of a status and security.[17]

• **Locate energy reservoirs.** Who in the church has the greatest ardor? It is exciting to be around these people. Individuals and groups within the church both can display enthusiasm. These people and groups need identifying. They respond more quickly and creatively to crucial ministries.

• **Align individual needs with the goals of the educational ministry.** The educational ministry strives to complete specific goals. Everyone is not motivated, challenged, equipped, or called to a particular task. Not all people are interested in every task. This lack of interest should not be mistaken for antagonism. The beginning place is a clear vision of what needs to happen and why. In putting people to work, MEs recognize their capabilities. The task is matched to the gifts of the person. Accurate information about people helps motivate them.[18]

• **Help workers recognize and meet their legitimate needs.** People want to be part of an organization from which they get something. Everyone needs structure in life. It helps manage anxiety and change. Identifying genuine needs aids workers in knowing why they want to do specific tasks and thus meet their perceived needs. People volunteer for a variety of reasons and motives. Some volunteer to serve others. This is a way they put their concerns into actions. Helping and serving people are proper ways to live out one's Christian calling. Others volunteer because of their needs for love and approval. These needs are good and bad. It is good everyone needs love and affirmation; it is bad when they become dominating needs and cause people to assume positions for which they are not capable.

Many persons have a deep hunger for recognition and volunteer to gain recognition and status. It is an unhealthy situation when people accept a position to advance their status or power.

Others volunteer to obtain a sense of accomplishment from reaching a goal by putting into practice the talents and skills they possess. They feel a sense of mission about most all they do. Their jobs, vocationally and in the church, are a joy, not a burden. Their highest motivation is to serve God. They know God gives gifts to equip Christians for service; they serve because they feel gratitude for God's work in their lives. McDonough writes, "To serve others is to serve God. To see a position as an opportunity for influence is a service to God. And certainly to fulfill a divine mission is to serve God."[19]

• **Build a ministry team.** Workers want to feel they are making a real contribution to a team effort. MEs have this opportunity with various Christian education groups working together to reach plans and goals they created. A Sunday School class or department is part of a team ministry. They accept assigned duties because those duties match their skills and interests. A key element in a motivational climate is a sense of "we-ness" or "this is ours."

• **Encourage and practice joint decision-making.** A sense of ownership comes from working on projects one created. An old saying states, "A person is always lazy in working another person's goals." When workers give time and energy to plans they make, usually they are highly motivated.

• **Covenant for action.** MEs help people know what is expected of them. At the time of assignment, some agreement is reached about both privileges and duties. This is covenant-making, and it provides handles on the working relationships and clarifies expectations about who is to do what and when it is to be done.

• **Use positive motivators.** Sometimes negative motivators hinder participation of workers in a project or assignment. MEs strive to eliminate those elements that keep people from being highly motivated. Means suggests:

> Real leaders are always encouraging; they are constantly offering a word of appreciation, writing thank-you notes, cheering on one who stumbles, picking up the bruised, and mending the shattered egos of those who have failed. Spiritual leaders do not miss opportunities to inspire, hearten, elevate, and brighten.[20]

Manipulation or Persuasion?

The act of motivation seeks to influence others. The question is: Who is in control? Are persons choosing for themselves goals they find helpful, or is the leader seeking to control others by imposing goals the leader finds beneficial? Stated another way, the question is: Are MEs actualizers or manipulators? Control gets the job done without regard for people; actualization does the opposite. Actualizers appreciate themselves and others as persons of worth, created in the image of God, having unique gifts and abilities. The actualizer's goal is to help persons discover and release their potential. Means writes, "Tremendous motivational power is brought to bear on people who are believed in, entrusted with responsibility, and summoned to participate in shaping the future."[21] Most people are combinations of actualizer and manipulator with a tendency to function primarily in one direction or the other. MEs' goal is to become more actualizer and less manipulator.

Walking the tightrope between actualizer or manipulator is a treacherous journey. MEs can fall into the trap of being manipulators by adopting the "end justifies the means" philosophy. Their need to succeed leads them to use controlling tactics. This temptation is hard to resist when egos and self-esteem are at stake. They fall into this trap because of a strong urge to prompt persons to choose God's way for their lives; they may become vulnerable to the manipulation trap when they believe harmony is a goal worth achieving at any cost.

Why does a person resort to manipulation? The root problem is self-esteem. It expresses itself in several ways. Power helps some people prove their self-worth. The inability to love is another issue. Persons who do not love themselves are trying to prove their worth. Fear of failure is another influence. Some people feel they must be in charge so they resort to manipulation. Fear of being vulnerable is yet another reason. A person protects insecurity through manipulation.[22] McDonough concludes:

> A person who does not have a sense of self-worth will find it very difficult to rise above manipulative patterns of behavior. Because few persons are not plagued with insecurity in some areas, the road to more actualizing behavior must include a continuing examination of who we are and the environment in which we live.[23]

Everyone is motivated. Helping persons be motivated toward a worthy goal is the purpose of the actualizer. Motivation comes from within. Persons, not the leader, are responsible for their actions. The leader's basic task is to create a climate in which persons become motivated.[24] Since motivation comes from within, Christian educators seek to build a climate in which fulfilling needs brings joy and wholeness to persons. McDonough describes this climate:

> Stability, teamwork, and affirmation provide the nurture that persons need to be motivated; but challenge provides the dynamic. Visionary leaders who can verbalize the mission and lead with confidence provide a stimulating climate for motivation.[25]

The power of the Holy Spirit, which grants an extra dimension, operates in the Christian's life. McDonough notes:

> The Holy Spirit does not change the process of motivation. Persons continue to be motivated because of needs. The Holy Spirit works through those needs to add to the quality of a

person's motivation. . . . Persons are need-seeking organisms. . . . The indwelling of the Holy Spirit enables us to transcend this self-centeredness. As a Christian, a person has the capacity for security, love, esteem, and mission that he did not have before accepting Christ.[26]

Notes

1. James E. Means, *Leadership in Christian Ministry* (Grand Rapids: Baker Book House, 1989), 65.

2. Kenneth O. Gangel, *Competent to Lead* (Chicago: Moody Press, 1974), 84-85. Gangel quotes Dr. Mungo Miller, President of Affiliated Psychological Services. This material first appeared in an article by Miller, "Understanding Human Behavior and Employee Motivation," *Advanced Management Journal* (April 1968).

3. Robert D. Dale, *Pastoral Leadership* (Nashville: Abingdon Press, 1986), 149-51.

4. Ibid., 151-53.

5. Abraham H. Maslow, *Motivation and Personality*, 3rd ed. (New York: Harper & Row, 1987), 15-22.

6. Ibid., 18.

7. Ibid., 21.

8. Ibid.

9. Ibid., 22.

10. Ibid., 136.

11. Means, *Leadership in Christian Ministry*, 69.

12. Dale, *Pastoral Leadership*, 156. Dale lists several positive statements. I have changed them into questions.

13. Reginald M. McDonough, *Working with Volunteer Leaders in the Church* (Nashville: Broadman Press, 1976), 58.

14. Dale, *Pastoral Leadership*, 154.

15. Carl E. George and Robert E. Logan, *Leading and Managing Your Church* (Old Tappan, New Jersey: Fleming H. Revell, 1987), 125.

16. Ted W. Engstrom and Edward R. Dayton, *The Christian Leader's 60-Second Management Guide* (Waco: Word Books, 1984), 55.

17. Ibid., 55-56.

18. Ibid., 53-54.

19. McDonough, *Working with Volunteer Leaders*, 12-18.

20. Means, *Leadership in Christian Ministry*, 176.

21. Ibid, 179.

22. McDonough, *Working with Volunteer Leaders*, 40-41.

23. Reginald M. McDonough, *Keys to Effective Motivation* (Nashville: Broadman Press, 1979), 40-41.

24. Ibid., 71-73.

25. Ibid., 82.

26. Ibid.

15

Theologian

Jennifer serves as ME in a fast growing church with many young families. She enjoyed studying theology in seminary and continues to read in this area. She is often asked theological questions. They are in the nature of "What do you believe about...?" or "Where is God in...?" Parents and Sunday School leaders ask her how to tell a child about salvation or what it means to be a Christian. Other issues that confront her are forgiveness, grace, faith, and the problems of pain and suffering.

Her seminary studies did not adequately prepare her for these questions. She knows the major doctrines of the Christian faith and knows the theological issues which Christian education addresses. She learned how theology influenced the methodology of Christian education. She often feels baffled at being unable to interpret adequately the Christian faith to persons in the Christian education program.

Now a new role for the ME is added—theologian. For many years I searched for a theology of Christian education. Several sources deal with theological issues Christian education ought to consider. Others describe how theology affects educational methodology. None provides a theology of Christian education. C. Ellis Nelson portrays the educator as theologian in *Changing Patterns of Religious Education*.[1] Daniel Aleshire further stimulated my thinking in this area in a conference in 1988.

Being theological is characteristic of every Christian, for a theologian seeks to grasp and declare what God is doing. The role of religious leaders and ministers is to help people make their theology and their theological conclusions more conscious.

Adding the role of theologian to the educational minister presents some problems. He or she is typically overworked and carries diverse roles. In some seminaries and divinity schools, education students choose between a two-year and a three-year program; the longer program involves additional study in theology and biblical studies. Both programs equip educators to function as theologians, yet religious educators, feeling the persistent challenge to keep up with various branches of education—curriculum, educational psychology, human development, pedagogy—are also taught they need another discipline, theology, with its variety of doctrines and approaches.

Teaching and nurturing processes raise theological issues. The preacher may choose to avoid these issues by not preaching on them, but the educator does not have this choice. Theological subjects occur regularly in the curriculum. As children grow in the Lord, they make professions of faith in Christ raising issues related to conversion, repentance, and faith—all a part of that special moment. MEs deal with such issues continually because some direction and guidance is needed by children, their parents, and the adults who work with them. Children and youth ask MEs theological questions and expect answers. Deaths of family members, friends, or even pets raise theological questions. Life by nature is theological.[2]

Early training emphases for educational ministers were psychology and pedagogy. Religious education students took Bible, historical studies, and theology as electives. They majored in what some liked to call "practical theology." These courses dealt more in function than in the essence of the Christian faith. Munro saw the need for religious educators to be well prepared in both methods and content. He felt developers of curriculum materials and their teachers should have a complete knowledge of the Bible, history, and theology. He believed:

> The director of religious education who is qualified to be the teaching minister of the church which he serves must be as well trained in the Old and New Testaments—from the standpoints alike of history, literature, and theology, in Church history, in Christian doctrine, and in principles of Christian worship and Christian service—as the preaching minister and pastor.[3]

Being a theologian requires more than knowledge of biblical and historical theology, more than the ability to identify and explain the traditional Christian doctrines. A theologian has the important ability to think theologically about the world and everyday experiences. It is impossible to avoid being a theologian.

As early as the 1940s, some educators began to see that theological thinking was part of the Christian educator's task.[4] In 1940, Harrison Elliott published *Can Religious Education Be Christian?* It was answered the next year by H. Shelton Smith's *Christian Nurture*. Elliott proposed that religious education be more than a conveyor of doctrine. Out of its own existence it should do its own theologizing and make its own contribution to theology. Smith felt modern religious education had become a follower of John Dewey. In so doing, it had lost the essence of the orthodox Christian faith. Smith reasoned that religious education was to teach the basic doctrines. It was not a theology itself but a vehicle for teaching theology. These two books stimulated debate and influenced the evolution of religious education theory.

In the 1960s the religious educator became a "teacher-theologian." Furnish writes:

> The director was challenged to approach the task from a theological point of view or in terms of organization, method, and program. When the director helped the church understand its own nature and the nature of its mission in the world, then the director was seen to have performed a theological task.[5]

She is more idealistic than realistic. Even today, in some denominations, curriculum writers are chosen for different tasks. One prepares the lesson based on the assigned biblical content; another writes the teaching/learning procedures. Even when one is prepared theologically and academically to write both the lesson content and the teaching procedures, this seldom happens.

Some feel Christian education has focused on educational techniques and methods, neglecting the essential message of the Christian faith.

Theology and Christian Education

Theologians and educators debate the place of theology in Christian education. Williams make this point: "Therefore theology does not come to Christian education as a completely independent discipline. Theology must reflect upon those activities which involve Christian nurture."[6] The discussion focuses not on whether theology is a part of Christian education; it is on how and what theology is taught through Christian education.

Little proposes five possible optional relations between theology and education:[7]

• **Theology is content to be taught.** Theology is the rational interpretation of religious faith, practice, and experience. Thus theology offers the basis for a common language and understanding to a religious community. If theology is neglected, the community loses its identity and sense of mission. Indoctrination is not the goal. Theology is appropriated through the exploration of meaning.

• **Theology becomes the norm.** When church officials predetermine either creeds or theological statements as subjects to be learned, then they function as a kind of norm.

> Educators are to take the stance of a theologian, as it were, and engage in the critical work of analysis and evaluation of the practices of the church in its teaching work in the past and the present for the sake of the future. Because theology serves as a point of reference both for what is to be taught and the methodology, it functions in a normative way.[8]

• **Theology is irrelevant.** The first two views drastically oppose this one. This view holds education itself as essentially religious. Its purpose is personal growth and the search for truth. Education is unrelated to theology because it is seen as a means to an end. Reflection on the relationship between means and ends is unimportant. Education becomes autonomous.

• **Doing theology is educational.** This view means one educates as one theologizes, based on the assumption that God is still active in human history. If one wants to be educated, it means "to inquire about the meaning in the events, about God's presence and activity in the past and his purpose for the future."[9]

• **Education is dialogue with theology.** The various disciplines are independent. Each discipline has recognizable functions. Theology exists alongside sociology, psychology, anthropology, and others. Each discipline influences and is responsive to the other disciplines. Little summarizes this approach as:

> Decisions about the educational task emerge from the dialogue. They do not emerge from some "application" of theological or theoretical formulations. Decisions are constantly adapted and indeed remade as the dialogue continues. . . . The significance of a discipline varies according to the situation and the nature of the decision to be made. This calls for a collegial approach to education.[10]

Little has described five classical theological options. The first one holds that theology is a cognitive process. It *is* this, but it is much more. The second option uses theology to judge church creeds. A person learns theological statements. The third option is rejected as it makes education stand alone. Christian education must consider doctrinal and creedal statements. The fourth option asks the meaning and purpose of world events. The fifth view sees education as dialoguing with theology. Options four and five could be blended to help the educator be more of a theologian.

There need not be a wide separation of theology and education. Williams points out:

> All Christian practice must maintain its integral relation to the ultimate source of faith in the word of God made personal in Jesus Christ, and in theology full weight is given to the special insight which comes from the appropriation of the word of God in the activities of Christian nurture.[11]

Theology in Education

Is there a direct relationship between theology and educational methods? What use is theology in Christian education? Education is more than methods. Nelson states, "Education is a process by which more mature people nurture, care for, and lead less experienced people."[12] Some Christian education takes place in planned activities, other learning events take place in informal relationships. Christian nurture is the sharing of faith in the midst of life. Nelson concludes, "All people who make a confession of faith in Jesus Christ are both theologians and educators."[13]

Educator as Theologian

Because ministers and educators interpret faith as they share it, they are theologians. How adequate is their theology? The adequacy of the educator as a theologian is judged by the same standard as the adequacy of a theologian's theology. Nelson writes, "Educators' first concern about theology is that they have an adequate theology so that they may explain their faith in God to other people."[14] How the educator functions as theologian is important. Some feel theology is doctrine to be memorized or learned as "what Christians believe." Thus theology is handed to the individual and accepted. With this approach, educators use parts of the doctrine as they fit what they are doing at the time. If educators recognize themselves as theologians, then they have a personal stake in theology. Theology is not something to accept; it is a thought and a life process in which they engage. Harris points out:

> The relationship between theology and the religious qualities of human life tend to be seen as mutual and complementary.... Their

presence as a religious man or religious woman tends to cata-
lyze others in the community to live out their own religious
attitudes toward one another in a similar way.[15]

Theologians test preformulated doctrines. By testing experiences
educators accept doctrines as theirs or modify them to conform to
their understanding of God. People are not the measure of theology.
Church theology is built over lengthy periods of time. It is definitive
because it rings true with Scripture and many people accept it as
truth. People are accountable to God for beliefs. Preformulated theology is only a set of statements until persons understand and begin
to relate them to specific events in life. Nelson states, "The educator
must help do the relating in order that theology illumines life and
death."[16]

Educators need an adequate theology to explain faith in God to
others. Having such a theology means they have enough confidence
to offer their faith to others. Educators' life-styles exhibit their
thoughts about faith and relate everything they are and believe.
They continue to learn, to read, to consult theologians, and to be
open to the leading of God's Spirit. Theology is partially mental but
its insights must be integrated to behavior. Nelson describes the
positive and negative aspects:

> Educators who are living examples of persons struggling for
> faith in order to find meaning in life are a great inspiration to
> their students. Educators who refuse to think about faith and
> simply retail preformulated statements about what people thought
> in former times are stunting the spiritual life of their students.[17]

Being conscious of the theological nature of life is not easy. Thus,
being or becoming theologians is not easy for educators. When they
think about religion, it requires knowledge about what others have
thought and what biblical writers say about doctrine. It also requires an effort to relate thought and life in an environment where
views are expressed, examined, and possibly even questioned. This
process takes time. It cannot be concluded in a short course but may
take months or even years. This can be realized through an all
age-graded discipleship training program. Educators sponsor some
forms of continuing discussion about theological issues and church
doctrines. This helps people develop the critical faith foundation
necessary to cope with life.

Christian education and Christian educators need to become more
theologically reflective. Browning describes its importance: "Christian
religious education should be understood as a process of practical
theology aimed at creating people capable of entering into a commu-

nity of practical theological reflection and participating in the action that would follow from it."[18] Seminarians learn theological reflection; it probably is best learned as it is modeled in their presence. If educators are to become theologians, what areas need theological reflection?

1. *Reflect on one's purpose as an individual believer and as part of the people of God, the church.* Aleshire notes:

> The nature of education and the nature of faith are joined in intricate ways when faithful people learn. They not only discover God's creative vision, they also come to know God. They not only learn of God, they also come to know each other. And when they know one another, they experience the gift of being known.[19]

Often educators feel successful if people actively participate in the church's educational ministries. Their goal is to encourage the development of Christian believers. Theologically, they must ask: What does it mean to believe? Aleshire observes:

> Christian believing is a combination of trust, thinking, feeling, and doing.
>
> *Trust* has to do with two ways of defining belief. We can "believe that" and that includes propositions, or we can "believe in" —and that is a fundamental investment of trust and confidence. A primary task, then, is to educate in ways that encourage the *possibility of trusting.*
>
> *Thinking*: The propositional content of our faith is important.... Content does make a difference. We must educate to encourage *the development of content.*
>
> *Feeling*: "And you shall love the Lord your God with all your heart, and with all your soul, and with all your might" (Deut. 6:5, NASB). Feelings—emotions—are a part of the believing experience, and they need to be educated and nurtured. Seventh graders need to learn what to do with their brand new, more adolescent versions, of emotions. Believers also need to learn what to do with their emotions.
>
> *Doing*: There is a behavioral aspect to our believing. There are ways that nurture/educate behavior that are different from ways that educate/nurture other aspects of the believing experience. An example is tithing.[20]

2. *Theological reflection takes place also in one's role as a Christian educator.* "Christian education is not a 'stand alone discipline.' It must be understood as a part of practical theology."[21] Theological disciplines are taught together. Practical theology includes the pas-

toral disciplines, pastoral care and preaching, and the educational disciplines, education and administration. Aleshire writes:

> Practice cannot be left to the pragmatic.... Theology cannot be left to thinking alone. The incarnated truth of Christian faith has to do with life, hope, love, passion, meaning. None of these is exclusively a phenomenon of thinking.... Truth—in Christian tradition—needs to be tested and tutored by life in the world. The teaching ministry of the church has no value apart from the teaching of the church. And the teaching of the church, its theology, cannot exist as a set of ideas apart from the pain, hurt, hope, need of the people whose lives are fashioned by that teaching.[22]

3. *Educational method is also a subject of theological reflection.* Aleshire notes:

> The educational approach is dictated by our understanding of canon, not just educational method. Some things are to be accepted. The Torah is what the Lord says. It is taught as catechism. There is the kerygma. Without this we do not know the thoughts of the gospels. There are those things to be experienced. Prophecy is the unsettling word of God that critiques us. It tells us who we are, what we are doing with the responsibility God has given us, and the grace God has entrusted to us. Some things are to be reflected upon. In the writings is where we reflect. This is seen not so much as "Thus saith the Lord," as it is "this seems wise." The educational method grows from an understanding of faith. This is the faith of individuals, not groups. The community of faith is not just a programmable institution.[23]

Some fear sponsoring theological inquiry because people may not come to the right theological answer. If uniformity is sought, the educator sponsors events that describe what the church has taught about a particular doctrine; this is conveying one's heritage. A carefully guided discussion over time will not necessarily produce more diversity, but it can alter shallow, superficial ideas and earlier impressions. People can come out with more adequate theological affirmation. Theological diversity is not something new. The New Testament affirms that Jesus is the Son of God. Yet the four Gospels each present Him in a different way. When people are seeking the truth about God and God's will for them, debate is an old and useful method for arriving at the truth.[24]

Asking Theological Questions

Many feel theological ethics is crucial for an understanding of Christian education. Two kinds of questions are asked. "Deonitic" questions focus on what one has to do. These questions relate to one's duty or moral obligation. "Aretaic" questions identify the nature of the good person, and the nature of morally proper character, motivation, and virtue.[25] This is the science of virtue. It is the art or means of attaining happiness. It deals with the idea of happiness as the proper end of conduct. Questions in the area of Christian education are: who should be taught, when, how much, and how often. More important,

> are the aretaic ethical questions about the nature of the good person and the nature of good character and virtue.... If a central goal of Christian religious education is to help create a Christian person, then clearly a Christian ethic dealing with aretaic questions is fundamental.[26]

Browning feels confusion about the educational task of the church comes from the failure to anchor Christian religious education in the key discipline of practical theology and its key subdiscipline of theological ethics. He points out, "A central goal of Christian education is to help create people who are themselves practical theological thinkers and actors."[27]

Browning identifies five levels or dimensions to practical moral thinking which lead to the asking of five fundamental questions having implications for the Christian educator as theologian:

> What kind of world do we live in? What should we do? What are the basic tendencies, needs, and values which humans, because of their nature, seek to satisfy? What is the present cultural, sociological, or ecological context, and what constraints does it place on our actions? and What should be the concrete rules and roles that we should follow?[28]

Relevance of Theological Ethics to Christian Education

A practical theology considers theological ethics and Christian education. Such a theology requires both the principles and character of theological ethics and Christian education. Discerning and internalizing the characterological effect of the Christian story is the task of Christian ethics and Christian education. Neither is primarily a matter of moral decision making; however, eventually they entail this. Christian ethics as a practical, theological discipline seeks to understand the implications of being a Christian to help develop Christian character. Christian education as a practical theological discipline deals with forming the character of people. This comes by helping them appropriate, within the context of a Christian community, the full significance of the Christian story.[29]

Relationship to Pastors

Some felt MEs training in theology would set up potential conflicts with pastors, yet the opposite is true. Furnish notes:

> For when directors [of religious education] began to have more of an understanding of theology and biblical literature, pastors seemed more willing to acknowledge their expertise in religious education as well and to trust them more with the general program of the church.[30]

Educational ministers attained more standing with pastors as they were perceived as more professionally trained.

Becoming Theologians

Being a theologian is not an option for MEs. By nature of their work, they encounter theological ideas regularly. Not only are they called upon to be theologians, they also train others to be theologians. As they help persons grow in their Christian faith, they function as theologians.

Many MEs have been theologians by default. It is time they became theologians by design and intentional ministry and realized their primary ministry and function within the church is theological in nature. Many will continue to act as theologians without a conscious effort to do so. As they continue to equip and enable the people of God to live competently in the world, they are theologians. Theology is not an added dimension of educational ministry; it is an integral, definitive element of it.

Notes

1. Marvin J. Taylor, ed. *Changing Patterns of Religious Education* (Nashville: Abingdon Press, 1984), 15-16.

2. Daniel Aleshire, "Minister of Education as Theologian," conference at the Southern Baptist Religious Education Association, San Antonio, Texas, June 13, 1988.

3. Harry C. Munro, *The Director of Religious Education* (Philadelphia: The Westminster Press, 1930), vii.

4. Dorothy Jean Furnish, *DRE/DCE—The History of a Profession* (Nashville: Christian Educators Fellowship, 1976), 84-85.

5. Ibid., 85.

6. Daniel Day Williams, "Current Theological Developments and Religious Education," *Religious Education: A Comprehensive Survey*, ed. Marvin J. Taylor (Nashville: Abingdon Press, 1960), 44.

7. Sara Little, "Theology and Religious Education," *Foundations for Christian Education in an Era of Change*, ed. Marvin J. Taylor (Nashville: Abingdon Press, 1976), 31-33.

8. Ibid., 32.

9. Ibid.

10. Ibid., 33.

11. Williams, "Current Theological Developments," 44.

12. C. Ellis Nelson, "Theological Foundations for Religious Nurture," *Changing Patterns of Religious Education*, ed., Marvin J. Taylor (Nashville: Abingdon Press, 1984), 15.

13. Ibid.

14. Ibid., 16.

15. Maria Harris, *The DRE Book: Questions and Strategies for Parish Personnel* (New York: Paulist Press, 1976), 186.

16. Nelson, "Theological Foundations for Religious Nurture," 16.

17. Ibid.

18. Don S. Browning, "Practical Theology and Religious Education," *Formation and Reflection: The Promise of Practical Theology*, ed. Lewis S. Mudge and James N. Poling (Philadelphia: Fortress Press, 1987), 79.

19. Aleshire, SBREA, June 13, 1988.

20. Ibid.

21. Daniel Aleshire, "Finding Eagles in the Turkeys' Nest: Pastoral Theology and Christian Education," *Review and Expositor* 85, 4 (Fall 1988): 702.

22. Ibid.

23. Aleshire, SBREA, June 13, 1988.

24. Nelson, "Theological Foundations for Religious Nurture," 17.

25. Browning, "Practical Theology and Religious Education," 81.

26. Ibid., 82.

27. Ibid.

28. Ibid., 89.

29. Ibid., 83.

30. Furnish, *DRE/DCE—The History of a Profession*, 86.

Part III

What Are the
ME's Relationships?

Part III examines the ME's relationships in three areas: spiritual, personal and family, and staff.

Chapter 16 looks at the ME's spiritual relationships. It explores the educational minister's active spiritual relationship to God. Ways are suggested to help them maintain a significant spiritual relationship. Only by sustaining a strong, personal, spiritual base can they help others have spiritual strength in their lives.

Personal and family relationships are the subject of chapter 17. They are next in importance to one's relationship to God. Establishing the self and the family as priorities actually empowers educators to be better educational ministers.

Chapter 18 describes how to have good staff relationships. A good relationship with the pastor is essential for MEs. Church staffs need to work together harmoniously; this requires personal discipline in each staff member and cooperative efforts among the group.

16

Spiritual Relationship

While I was attending a national educational meeting, the worship leader asked participants to share how God's presence had been felt in a recent experience. This request jolted me. I had to confess I was spiritually washed out. I was in a spiritually dry time. I could rationalize why this was true. Our home life had been stressful due to caring for an aging mother. My work load at the seminary had been particularly heavy. Many excuses could be given. The truth was I had not taken the time to tend to my spiritual life. Most ministers go through periods when their spiritual lives are not as fervent or alive as they should be.

Religious leaders face the danger of spending so much time supporting others in their spiritual lives that they neglect their own. Being busy doing spiritual things at the church and for others is not the same as taking care of one's own spiritual relationship to God. The minister may put priority upon the ministerial role, but the primary relationship for any minister is first to be a Christian person. Mosley put this in its proper place by using a concentric circle (see figure 4) to describe the priorities in ministry. The priorities in order of importance are: (1) Christian person, (2) married person (or single person), (3) parent person, (4) church member person, (5) employed person, and (6) community person.[1]

Four principles are present in this model. One, priorities are controlled or restrained from the inside out. The heart of ordering priorities is in the center circle, in the relationship to God as a Christian person. Moving outward, each circle influences the circle outside it. Behavior control flows from the inside to the outside. Mosley writes, "In much the same way that the heart pumps blood, distributing energy and cleaning the body, the central priority in

Figure 6

ministry supplies life, energy, support, and renewal to all the priorities outside it."[2] The relationship to Jesus Christ holds a minister's life and work together. When this relationship is neglected, all the attention focused on outer priorities will not cause them to achieve and maintain their potential. Good relationships and opportunities represented in the other circles' priorities are possible as they are held together from within.

The second principle is this: if an inside circle is weak, the potential in the circles outside it is limited. Mosley notes, "Since the inside circle serves as a base for the circle outside it, a person is foolish to allow an inside circle to receive inadequate attention."

The third principle is this: trouble may occur when an outside circle takes priority over an inside circle. Ministers may give priority to an outside circle and feel capable of doing it without loss of success in an area that has higher priority. However, the neglect of the inner circle will weaken the outer circles.

The fourth principle is greater satisfaction is experienced in ministers' lives if the order of priorities is maintained. They will also experience greater success in ministry.

> It is an attempt to balance the importance of who we are with the importance of what we do. External affirmation most often comes from what we do and may cause us to give too much time and energy to the work arenas that produce it. Internal affirmation comes from what we are and supports and encourages us when the things we do are not producing applause or encouragement of the public.[3]

This principle is particularly significant for educational ministers. Usually, since little public affirmation is bestowed upon them, the tendency is to devote more time and energy to areas that bring personal satisfaction. This is not the best or most effective use of time.

MEs experience growth and joy as a result of priority living by clarifying their values and ordering their priorities. Mosley states, "The feedback is growth and joy which enlarge the inner man and provide a better foundation for effectiveness in marriage, parenthood, church membership, employment, and responsible citizenship."[4]

Priority of Personal Spirituality

Many ministers make the church the top priority in their lives. O'Connor cautions ministers about the significance of spiritual relations. She writes:

> We are not called primarily to create new structures for the church in this age; we are not called primarily to a program of service, or to dream dreams or have visions. We are called first of all to belong to Jesus Christ as Savior and Lord, and to keep our lives warmed at the hearth of His life. It is there the fire will be lit which will create new structures and programs of service that will draw others into the circle to dream dreams and have visions.
>
> To understand this is to be thrown back upon those disciplines which are the only known gateways to the grace of God; for how do we fulfill the command to love, except that we learn it of God, and how do we learn it of God, except that we pray, and live under His word and perceive His world?[5]

MEs agree with her. Every minister of education knows this is an active struggle. This important relationship is established over days, weeks, months, even years. It requires constant work and attention. It is frightenly easy to get involved in doing the work of ministry and neglect their spiritual relationship with God. Recently a minister was forced to resign his church because of a morality problem. He acknowledged he had gotten too busy to pray as he was telling others how to have successful ministries. As his prayer life deteriorated, his home life also was neglected and eventually fell apart.

MacDonald has a book that helps ministers and Christians put order into their lives.[6] He perceives most people having the public dimension of their lives fairly well organized. He points out a need people feel when he observes, "It's this private part of life where we know ourselves best of all: this is where self-esteem is forged, where basic decisions about motives, values, and commitment are made, where we commune with our God."[7] Christ cannot dwell with and within except through personal invitation and commitment. This cannot happen unless MEs permit Christ to take control over every segment of life. MEs want God to dwell within their lives. How can this become a reality? If they find inner strength, it is actively sought. MacDonald proposes a five step process to begin to order our private world. These steps are: motivation, use of time, wisdom and knowledge, spiritual strength, and restoration. These are discussed here as they relate to MEs' spiritual lives.

Motivation

In this context, motivation describes that which causes MEs to do what they do. Somehow, living in a success-driven world where many fall into the trap of being successful regardless of the cost, God calls them to be the best they can be under His leadership and direction. A great barrier to MEs' communion with God is being busy doing the things of ministry. They are busy planning, getting ready for and attending meetings, preparing for teaching and other assignments, and they do not have time to spend with God in a personal, intimate, devotional way. They become so driven their ministry loses its joy and gratification. They become victims of burnout; they may cause co-workers and associates to experience burnout, too.

Instead of being driven by personal success, MEs can seek motivation and empowerment by Christ. MacDonald describes Paul, a driven person, and the change that came over him:

> Paul the apostle in his pre-Christian days was driven. As a driven man, he studied, he joined, he attained, he defended, and he was applauded. The pace at which he was operating shortly before his conversion was almost manic. He was driven toward some illusive goal, and, later, when he could look back at that life-style with all its compulsions, he would say, "It was all worthless."

> Paul was driven until Christ called him. One gets the feeling that when Paul fell to his knees before the Lord on the road to Damascus, there was an explosion of relief within his private world. What a change from the drivenness that had pushed him toward Damascus in an attempt to stamp out Christianity to that dramatic moment when, in complete submission, he asked Jesus Christ, "What shall I do, Lord?" A driven man was converted into a called one.[8]

MEs identify with Paul as a driven person. Called persons see themselves as Christ's stewards. They do not perceive themselves as masters of their purpose, role, or identity. Having a clear sense of call from God, the role of educational minister is a secondary though significant ministry of the church.

Religious educators have ego needs like others, but knowing who they are and their role in ministry keeps them from many pitfalls. The temptation to be driven is great as they live and function in a competitive world where achievement seems to be everything. It is easy to be driven to hold on, to protect, to dominate. MacDonald shares from his own experience:

> Having listened to God's call, I can know my mission. It may demand courage, and discipline, of course, but now the results are in the hands of the Caller. Whether I increase or decrease is His concern, not mine. To order my life according to his expectations of myself and others; and to value myself according to the opinions of others; these can play havoc with my inner world.

But to operate on the basis of God's call is to enjoy a great deal of order within.[9]

Proper Use of Time

Time management experts agree the proper way to use time is to establish priorities. Once priorities are determined, it is imperative to order life based on those priorities. A frequent excuse for neglecting one's spiritual life is the lack of time. MEs have many tasks to accomplish on a regular basis which take major chunks of time.

Faced with a multitude of tasks, how does one find time to develop and maintain a spiritual relationship with God? I schedule a devotional time. I literally make an appointment with God! This is the first appointment scheduled after I get to my office. Some have their daily quiet time early in the morning, others before going to bed. It should be a time when one is fresh and has plenty of energy regardless of the time of day, a time when communion with God is not hurried.

Protecting such valuable time is a nagging problem. MacDonald says of Jesus:

> Jesus was never to be caught short on time. Because he knew His sense of mission, because He was spiritually sharpened by moments alone with the Father, and because He knew who the men were that would perpetuate His mission long after He ascended into heaven, it was never difficult for Him to say a firm NO to invitations and demands which might have looked good or acceptable to us.[10]

If time is recaptured, MEs must learn their rhythms of maximum success. Some people are morning people—they do their best work early in the day; others are evening persons—they are more fresh, have more energy, are more productive in the evenings. Either type of person must give God time when they are fresh and highly energized. They must guard it, protect it! If one is not careful, God will be crowded out of the schedule entirely.

Growth in Wisdom and Knowledge

The importance of growth is illustrated in the life of Jesus: "And Jesus grew in wisdom and stature, and in favor with God and man" (Luke 2:52, NIV). Christian growth as a life-style requires commitment. MEs cannot authentically lead others into spiritual growth unless growth is taking place in their own lives. With the commitment to spiritual growth comes a reordering of their values and activities. Choices are made about how time and energy are expended.

As they spend time with God, their minds and intellects ought to expand. Trueblood describes it:

> No vital Christianity is possible unless at least three aspects of it are developed. These three are the inner life of devotion, the outer life of service, and the intellectual life of rationality. In short, the Christian is called, not to just one operation, but to three.[11]

Educational ministers must grow in wisdom and knowledge for their ministry—equipping and enabling the people of God to do the work of ministry—involves thought and study and planning. Making the Christian message and gospel relevant and applicable to the needs of modern society requires intellectual prowess and constant prayer for wisdom. People face unique moral and ethical issues today. How do they fit them into a Christian context? What does the Word of God have to say in these areas? This is the work of educational ministry.

MEs grow in wisdom and knowledge by accepting responsibility for their own mental growth. Listening is a way to grow mentally. MacDonald observes, "We grow through listening, aggressive listening: asking questions, watching intently what is happening around us, taking note of the good or ill consequences that befall people as a result of their choice making."[12] I profited greatly from two or three significant mentors in my life. They taught me a great deal, in formal settings and in the informality of conversation or observation of them working with groups or individuals.

Another way of mental growth is reading books, magazines, and periodicals other than those used to prepare for speaking or writing assignments. I was impressed with one of my professors who, when asked how many books he read a year, responded: "Two hundred to two hundred and fifty." This challenged me to spend more time reading.

Spiritual Strength

I like to jog. I try to do it at least four or five days a week. I do it for physical and mental health. There are times it has a spiritual element to it, allowing time for prayer, meditation, and enjoying the world God made. To stay in physical shape, I exercise several times a week. A two or three day lapse shows the next time I get out to jog. The same is true in the spiritual realm. Having a consistent quiet time with God requires constant attention. In working with a discipleship training program, one suggestion for establishing a regular quiet time is to do it for twenty-one consecutive days. The idea: with repetition, it becomes a part of the person.

Spiritual strength comes to those regularly spending time with God. Nothing is too insignificant to talk over with Him. MEs' strength comes in knowing God is leading and directing every aspect of their lives. They talk with Him as one friend to another. Through this relationship with God, they are not afraid to be alone and quiet before God. I used to go to a small college chapel when I felt inadequate, or had to make a difficult decision, or needed to pray for someone. Often I stayed there two or three hours before God gave me peace or a sense of direction. What made these times special was waiting for God to speak to me—to make His will known to me.

Renewal

There are times MEs need to break their patterns and routines. Sunday is such a day for most Christians. Yet, educational ministers find Sunday a busy and hectic day. Worship is part of the day, but it is often surrounded by meetings and other responsibilities. Sunday "feels" like another work day.

The Jewish idea of the sabbath was primarily one of rest. Another dimension of refreshing oneself is proposed by Moses in Exodus 31:17: "In six days the Lord made heaven and earth, but on the seventh day, He ceased from labor, and was refreshed" (RSV). MacDonald comments that the literal translation suggests the phrase "He refreshed Himself."[13] Lamm describes the Jewish understanding of *shevitah*, "the use of leisure to restore one's individuality in all its integrity, as a time when a person would cease from usual labors."[14] By getting a respite from routine activity it allowed a person to rediscover self by emerging from the workweek. He states:

> Overinvolved in and overwhelmed by his set pattern of work, a man's dignity is threatened. He begins to identify himself by the functions he performs in society or family and turns into an impersonal cipher.... By disengaging from his involvement with nature and society, with business, man is permitted self-expression. His real "self" comes to the fore.... By means of *shevitah* on his Sabbath day of "rest," he can start expressing the real self that lies within.[15]

The next step after *shevitah* is *nofesh* which is more than self-discovery. *Nofesh* uses leisure for self-transformation and requires a certain kind of personal, inner silence in which one becomes available for a higher expression. Lamm writes, "*Nofesh* means not to fulfill yourself but to go outside yourself, to rise beyond yourself; not to discover your identity, but rather to create a new and better identity."[16] It requires MEs to take their creative talents and turn them inward and create a new, real self. This is re-creation, not relaxation. These concepts of the sabbath provide incentives to enrich and refresh self by developing or creating the spiritual dimension.[17]

That God rested is important. MacDonald states, "The rest God instituted was meant first and foremost to cause us to interpret our work, to press meaning into it, to make sure we know to whom it is properly dedicated."[18] Rest also permits refreshing one's belief in and commitment to Christ.

MEs must use a day other than Sunday as a time for renewal and refreshment to take place. It is important if they are to maintain dynamic, spiritual lives.

Notes

1. Ernest E. Mosley, *Priorities in Ministry* (Nashville: Convention Press, 1978), 12.
2. Ibid., 13.
3. Ibid., 17.
4. Ibid., 18.
5. Elizabeth O'Connor, *Call to Commitment* (New York: Harper & Row, 1963), 94.
6. See Gordon MacDonald, *Ordering Your Private World* (Nashville: Oliver Nelson, 1985).
7. Ibid., 7-8.
8. Ibid., 48.
9. Ibid., 81.
10. Ibid., 72.
11. Elton Trueblood, *While It Is Yet Day* (New York: Harper & Row, 1974), 97-98.
12. MacDonald, *Ordering Your Private World*, 107.
13. Ibid., 163.
14. Norman Lamm, *Faith and Doubt* (New York: KTAV Publishing House, 1971), 203.
15. Ibid., 202-3.
16. Ibid., 204.
17. Ibid., 204.
18. MacDonald, *Ordering Your Private World*, 165.

17

Personal and
Family Relations

The second most significant relationship for educational ministers next to the relationship to God and the Christian experience is the family. I recognize that many educational ministers are single; however, this chapter primarily addresses the married ME.

The first relationship formed within the family is between husband and wife. When children are born, they often become the chief concerns of one or both parents, supplanting the primary marriage relationship. This chapter focuses on the importance of the relationship between husband and wife. Also the chapter examines parenting roles and responsibilities in the educational minister's home.

The Married Person

For the married ME, it is essential that marriage be healthy. Because of the closeness in the marital relationship, whatever happens in it and to it affects all other relationships. Mosley notes:

> Marriage provides the ideal laboratory for experiencing and expressing the fruit of the Spirit. All of the expressions—love, joy, peace, patience, kindness, generosity, faithfulness, tolerance, self-control—are constantly needed in the growing and nurturing process of the marriage relationship.[1]

A quality marriage does not just happen. To live together as husband and wife is an act of God's grace. Mosley observes, "It is a miracle in human relationships. Two persons have given themselves to being with each other, growing with each other, and helping each other to become what God designed them to be."[2] The primacy of the marital relationship is established in Genesis 2:24: "For this reason a man will leave his father and mother and be united to his wife, and they will become one flesh" (NIV). The apostle Paul likened the marital relationship to that between Christ and the church in Ephesians 5:21-33:

> Submit to one another out of reverence for Christ. Wives, submit to your husbands as to the Lord. For the husband is the head of the wife as Christ is the head of the church, his body, of which he is the Savior. Now as the church submits to Christ, so also wives should submit to their husbands in everything. Husbands, love your wives, just as Christ loved the church and gave himself up for her to make her holy, cleansing her by the washing with water through the word, and to present her to himself as a radiant church, without stain or wrinkle or any other blemish, but holy and blameless. In this same way, husbands ought to love their wives as their own bodies. He who loves his wife loves himself. After all, no one ever hated his own body, but he feeds and cares for it, just as Christ does the church—for we are members of his body. For this reason a man will leave his father and mother and be united to his wife, and the two will become one flesh. This is a profound mystery—but I am talking about Christ and the church. However, each one of you also must love his wife as he loves himself, and the wife must respect her husband (NIV).

There are mixtures of influences that help ministers maintain good marital relationships. Mosley lists several of these ingredients:

> They include the dogged determination to make marriage work and thus honor a commitment expressed when the marriage was formed, spiritual strength that comes from prayer and Bible study, fear of humiliation in the church and among peers in the denomination, desire for continuing ministry opportunities, and growing freedom for spouses to find fulfillment in occupations and relationships outside the home and the church.[3]

A key ingredient is the "dogged determination" to make it work. It is a Christian marriage and the partners receive strength from the Bible, prayer, and from each other.[4]

Establishing the Marital Priority

A great hindrance to quality ministerial marriages is the demand made upon a minister's time. Educational ministers have many pulls upon their lives. They are professional persons—ministers, married persons, possibly parent persons, community persons. Denominations put pressure on MEs to help with local, regional, and statewide meetings. All these roles and activities are good things demanding time and energy from educational ministers. The gifts of this minister benefit other churches and Christians in growth and spiritual maturation. How then does one schedule time for spouse and for self? One way is to schedule family and personal times on one's calendar, just as church, professional, and community commitments are scheduled. Couples need time that is just theirs, an occasional evening out or a special luncheon date. Mosley points out: "Couples who are creative in guarding and using their time together on a regular basis will find ways to maintain their togetherness."[5]

A Healthy Marriage

Healthy couples have shared power, mutual respect, open communication, capacity for intimacy, and highly satisfactory sex. Shared power means both husband and wife are competent and capable of providing the family with leadership. Areas of competence complement each other. There is little competition in the relationship. Each partner respects the viewpoint of the other and listens carefully. Problems are approached in ways that allow each family member to have his or her say. Each member's feelings and thoughts are important. In families with shared power, children find less to rebel against because they are treated as individuals and with respect. When a consensus cannot be reached, they are good at compromising. There is little difference in each person's power of influence. Neither partner is consistently dominant or submissive.[6]

Good communication is a sign of a healthy family. A genuine desire exists to share understandings, feelings, and dreams. Such open communication focuses on the worth of each person rather than on the position or role of each person. Mosley observes, "Experience in open communication between persons who know love, joy, and peace enables them to develop the ability to reject ideas without rejecting persons with their feelings and dreams."[7] Good communication creates emotional security, allowing room for expressed love and expressed anger. Married couples may express hope and also express fear. They may express trust and jealousy.[8] Lewis notes, "Empathy is extremely important in human relationships because it leaves the other person feeling deeply understood and encourages further sharing and psychological intimacy."[9]

Intimate Interaction

Healthy marriages require a capacity for intimacy and the presence of high levels of intimacy. There is the feeling of "being in love." Couples deeply care about each other. The relationship has a strong "charge" still in it.[10] Intimacy must be nurtured throughout the marriage. It grows as couples risk greater openness. Each partner becomes more honest with self. There is greater awareness of one's own faults. They do not blame others for times of conflict. Only as each person becomes more open can intimacy develop in the relationship. It means being a real person who does not put on an act. The Clinebells write, "Intimacy thus requires mutual openness and the willingness to risk genuine encounter or meeting in areas which are important to either partner."[11] Intimacy grows as couples become emotionally present to each other. Intimacy requires one to give his or her spouse all of one's attention some time. As couples develop a high degree of caring for each other, intimacy grows. They can feel deeply cared for and understood.

An essential ingredient in intimate relationships is affectionate concern for the partner's safety, well-being, and growth as a person. Growing intimacy depends on caring enough to make a continuing self-investment in the relationship and in meeting the needs of the other. A climate of trust based on commitment to fidelity and continuity help intimacy grow. A mark of genuine intimacy is the respect for the need of each partner for periods of aloneness. Too much "togetherness" may create the illusion of intimacy. The Clinebells observe, "If marital partners are too dependent upon each other for a sense of self-worth and even identity, there is a kind of compulsive togetherness which is not genuine intimacy."[12] Most people need both intimacy and autonomy because all have two sets of needs. One is the need for dependence, love, and nurturance; the other is the need for autonomy, self-fulfillment, achievement, and independence.

Intimacy, particularly in marriage, is often identified with sexual intercourse. Being intimate is more than something physical. It can be a nonverbal, non-physical, emotional, psychological, even spiritual experience. Greenfield notes, "When two human spirits are in communion with each other, they are at the intimacy level."[13] It is possible to have intimacy with persons other than one's spouse, though it should be easier with the spouse. Greenfield describes the oneness of intimacy as:

> Intimacy involves deep sharing of one's innermost experiences and feelings. Intimacy calls for transparency: total honesty couched in love. Intimacy involves the deepest possible trust, believing that the other person has your best interests at heart and would never think of violating that trust. Intimacy expresses itself in the deepest altruistic concern for the other. Empathy prevails throughout the relationship. Touching each other on this level is as natural as speaking.... On this level you can touch or look into each other's eyes and clearly communicate, never having spoken a word.

> The oneness of intimacy is much more than intellectual agreement or relational unity. Intimacy is possible with someone with whom you may disagree on certain opinions, beliefs, or convictions. Two people can continue to be unique and separate yet one in spirit. Such oneness involves total acceptance with no judgmental reservations or subtle plans to change the other.[14]

Within marriage there are several dimensions of intimacy. There are many opportunities to experience marital intimacy. The Clinebells identify several dimensions of intimacy. They compare it to playing several strings of musical instruments. The intimacy pattern varies at different times in the marriage. Couples discover the particular harmony and melody of intimacy they find most satisfying. Intimacy is not static but dynamic. There are times when intimacy is interrupted by disharmony or even silence.[15]

Each dimension of intimacy has the potential to draw couples closer together. By looking at intimacy in these different dimensions, it allows opportunities for couples to relate to each other significantly in an increasing number of areas. Intimacy has two particular meanings in marriage. It may describe a close moment or period of intense sharing, or it may depict an active quality of the relationship. This may be present even in times of some distance or conflict. This is the "we-ness" of a good marriage. An abiding sense of oneness is established through increasing moments and periods of intense closeness.[16]

A healthy family encourages the continued growth of each partner. The husband and wife in such a family should value the emotional closeness necessary to provide growth in intimacy.

Mutual Understanding of Ministry

MEs received a divine call from God for the ministry. A church also extended a call to serve. The spouse may not have felt that same call. Yet a mutual understanding must be developed about what this call means and how the spouse and family are involved in it. The ME cannot work a simple eight hour day and do the job properly. Sundays and Wednesdays are particularly long. There are times they have discretionary time. They can go to the barbershop and run errands during working hours. Some ministers take off early in the afternoon when they have a night meeting, others come in later the next day. Despite certain amounts of discretionary time during work hours, there are times when this ministry will require extra time, disrupting personal and family schedules. If the ME is not careful the family, particularly the spouse, can feel that the church has priority.

A Parent Person

Ministers as parents fit third in the order of priorities. It comes after being a Christian person and a married person. Mosley explains:

> One reason for this priority sequence is because God made us first for fellowship with him. Out of our intimate fellowship with God we are nurtured to the personal growth and productivity that are essential to abundant life. The priority relationship with God equips us for being good parents.
>
> A second reason why the priority relationship cannot be higher than this is because God made us for fellowship with a person in marriage. In the intimate marriage relationship we experience affirmation as persons and joy in a human relationship.... When the parent priority appears more valuable than the marriage priority a serious problem has surfaced. Without a strong marriage relationship base, parenting will be overloaded with difficulties.[17]

A key ingredient in good families relates to the husband. Husbands have a heavy investment in their work. It is important to have energy and emotion available and to be significantly involved with their wives and children. When my children were small and busy in community sports activities, I took their game dates and put them on my personal calendar. Often I turned down other opportunities because I had a previous appointment— watching Rob or Mason play baseball or football or watching Alice play T-ball or be a cheerleader.

Notes

1. Ernest E. Mosley, *Priorities in Ministry* (Nashville: Convention Press, 1978), 42-43.

2. Ibid., 44.

3. Ibid., 42.

4. Ibid., 42.

5. Ibid., 47.

6. Jerry M. Lewis, *How's Your Family?* (New York: Brunner/Mazel, 1978), 8-39, 53, 88.

7. Mosley, *Priorities in Ministry*, 50.

8. Lewis, *How's Your Family?*, 54.

9. Ibid., 50, 61-62.

10. Ibid., 29.

11. Howard J. Clinebell, Jr. and Charlotte H. Clinebell, *The Intimate Marriage* (New York: Harper & Row, 1970), 25.

12. Ibid., 27.

13. Guy Greenfield, *We Need Each Other* (Grand Rapids: Baker Book House, 1984), 29.

14. Ibid., 151-52.

15. Ibid., 156.

16. Clinebell and Clinebell, *The Intimate Marriage*, 34. The Clinebells have an excellent discussion of various levels of intimacy on pages 28-34.

17. Mosley, *Priorities in Ministry*, 64-65.

18

Staff Relationships

Good staff relationships are crucial for a church. Westing describes the role of the staff: "The pastoral staff should show how acceptance, forgiveness, sharing, supporting, encouraging and the accomplishment of common goals is practiced. The staff must be a microcosm of the body of Christ, a church in miniature."[1] Excellent staff relations are important to educational ministers. They want good relationships with pastors and other staff members. Staff members need the ability to work in close personal relationships. A church cannot move forward with a divided staff or one that cannot work together well. A pastor I know has a three-pronged approach to staff relations: be happy, be loyal, or be gone. It may sound crude but it is a good approach. If people are unhappy, it affects the way they relate to others. It also influences the quality of their work. Loyalty is essential for good staff relations. They are loyal to the pastor, other staff members, and to the total church program. Attempts to resolve the rough spots and issues must be sought.

Who comprises the church staff? Church staffs are composed of the professional ministers and the support persons. The professional clergy have professional training and a sense of calling to a particular ministry. Most are ordained or qualified for ordination. The church also may have a church administrator who is a part of the professional staff. Often the largest number of people on the church staff are support staff. These persons fit into one of three categories: those who do functional roles for the congregation, such as hostess or dietician; the secretarial staff which helps the professionals in fulfilling their responsibilities; and those who function in the upkeep and maintenance of the building and grounds.[2]

What is a church staff team? Brown defines it as:

> A group of Christian persons who in response to a divine and ecclesiastical calling willingly covenant with God, a local congregation, and one another to live out their vocational mission sharing responsibility and authority for enabling the church in its mission.[3]

Judy states it this way:

> The church staff is composed of a group of professional persons, presumably competent in their respective fields, who blend their services together to perform a ministry as a whole to the congregation. This leads to definite functional roles for persons on the church staff as the entire staff working together attempt to help the individual Christian fulfill his responsibility in worship, nurture, and work.[4]

Westing describes it thus: "a team is a group of God's people which utilizes to the ultimate the gifts God has given them and which works in beautiful fellowship connection within itself."[5]

Good church staff relations do not just happen. They are the result of deliberate actions by the staff and the church whom they serve. The church plays a significant role in good staff relations. Church members see the staff as competent persons with a ministry to do. They also try not to play one staff member against another.

Respect: An Essential Ingredient

Good staff relations depend upon respect for each other as professionals and as persons. The ME, the pastor, and other staff members who respect the professional competency of others feel persons can do the ministry for which the church called them. They function in ways that are professional and competent. This is essential for all staff members. I will examine this for the pastor and the educational minister, though it applies to all the professional ministerial staff.

The pastor or senior minister has competency to provide pastoral leadership for the congregation. The pastor leads in the achievement of the church's mission. This requires a good vision and grasp of the church's purpose and objectives. The senior minister encourages staff members and church members by providing leadership and energy for the various church activities and the church's planning processes. Among all the church staff, the pastor especially has a complete picture of what the church is and what the church is doing to realize its mission. The pastor is a leader of leaders. Whenever the pastor as chief administrator does not lead, the organization is in trouble. If no one assumes leadership, the church flounders and is weak in its ministry.

Pastoral ministry includes the responsibility to proclaim the gospel to believers and unbelievers through the church's pulpit ministry, plus much more. Proclamation is the communication of the gospel through teaching, discipleship training, missions education, and the church's outreach/visitation activities. The pastor has opportunities to proclaim the gospel from the pulpit and in various teaching situations. Staff members count on the pastor to provide spiritual nourishment and inspiration for them and the congregation. The pastor actively participates in the church's program of evangelism, often coordinated through the Sunday School program under the direction of the ME. The program is promoted and participation is encouraged by the pastor from the pulpit and in the church's publications. The pastor takes the lead in training others in evangelistic witnessing through one to one training or leading groups in witnessing skills. The pastor leads in the church's program and activities of proclamation.

Pastoral ministry work also includes providing care for the church's members and community persons. A church large enough to have an educational minister is too large for one minister to meet all the pastoral care needs. Most pastors share this responsibility with other staff members. As an ME, I expected to attend to the pastoral care needs of either leaders or members of the church's educational program. I informed the pastor what I was doing to meet those needs. This did not keep the pastor and other staff members from ministering to these persons, but I was the primary caregiver. For example, I once worked with a young adult who taught in the children's division. He became ill with a rare malignancy. The pastor and I discussed how his needs and his family's could best be met. Since I already had a close relationship to them, we decided I would provide the basic pastoral care. The pastor and other staff members visited him in the hospital, but it was my primary responsibility. While he was hospitalized, I visited him regularly. When he went home, I continued to maintain a relationship with him and his family. This personal ministry went on for more than two years. At times I asked the pastor to visit to maintain that important touch from him.

The educational minister provides pastoral care by visiting in hospitals, in homes at times of illness and death, and serves as counselor as needed for educational leaders, their families, and members of the educational programs. The same is true for the music minister, youth minister, and other age-group ministers who provide primary pastoral care for their leaders and members. This approach involves staff members in the lives of the total membership, not just those in their program. There are times when the pastor is primary in the pastoral care of a member or family. Just as the pastor cannot be all things to all people, the educational minister or other staff cannot do it all either. The pastor and staff have to learn how best to work together as a team. Difficulties may arise if this is the first time a pastor has worked with a staff or if the staff member lacks experience in this area.

Few pastors serving a multi-staff church began their ministries with an ME; most functioned as their own educational ministers in the early days of their ministry. In working with educational ministers, pastors must know what the church's educational ministry is. Without this knowledge they cannot provide adequate leadership. Pastors need an understanding of the educational program and its organizations and their tasks, objectives, and goals. This information comes from seminary training, personal reading, attending conferences and workshops, and keeping close working ties with the church's educational minister. Even more important, the pastor needs to express appreciation for the work of the organization, its volunteer leaders, and the ME.

While pastors need competency in providing pastoral leadership for the church, MEs need educational competency. Pastors utilize other ministers to support pastoral ministry; MEs provide leadership to the total educational program. Some churches have age group specialists who work directly with educational ministers.

Respecting each other as persons is equally as important as respecting each other as competent professionals. Mutual respect is a building block of trust. Respect comes from seeing lives illustrate the essence of the Christian gospel and display qualities of Christian character.

Pastoral Relationship

The ME's relationship to the pastor is crucial. They need compatibility in theology and in their understanding of how to do church. These areas are carefully examined before the educational minister goes to the church; much of this information is secured on the interview visit with the pastor. In considering a church, the ME wants to know as much about the pastor as about the church. Good relationships with the pastor take time and effort by both parties.

Relating to Other Staff Members

All staff members work under the supervision of the pastor or a staff administrator who enhances staff morale by treating all equally. Good staff relations are built on common ministry goals and dreams.

All staff relationships are important. MEs relating to other staff members as colleagues build relationships upon their common work. Authority and accountability are not the first nor most important qualifiers of healthy staff relations.

Relating to Staff Subordinates

In churches where there are educational associates, the educational minister supervises them as he or she wants to be supervised. MEs should treat these associates as they want the pastor to treat them. This can be a very delicate area since staff associates feel called to their specific ministries.

Genuine bonds of personal and spiritual strength can come from jointly praying about issues confronted and needs in the congregation. MEs can also ensure the staff associates receive recognition for quality work and their contribution to the total life of the church.

Relationship to the Support Staff

Significant relationships are formed with the church secretaries, custodians, and other support staff. Without these persons MEs' work becomes very difficult—if not almost impossible. These persons are colleagues in ministry to be treated with dignity and respect.

A brief note of appreciation for a job well done is always time well-spent. Some MEs acknowledge the work of the support staff, anniversaries of their service, or other important milestones by notes in the church paper or recognition in public gatherings.

These persons' attitudes reflect the church's approach to ministry. Some of them feel called of God to do the work they are doing in the church. It is not a job with them, but a ministry they render for God, the church, and the members.

Notes

1. Harold J. Westing, *Multiple Church Staff Handbook* (Grand Rapids: Kregal Publications, 1985), 11.

2. Marvin T. Judy, *The Multiple Staff Ministry* (Nashville: Abingdon, 1969), 37.

3. Jerry W. Brown, *Church Staff Teams That Win* (Nashville: Convention Press, 1979), 23.

4. Judy, *Multiple Staff Ministry*, 33.

5. Westing, *Multiple Church Staff Handbook*, 16. He describes five advantages of a team concept for the church on pages 21-22.

Part IV

How to Get Started
as an ME

Part IV offers practical ministry suggestions for the ME by exploring four concerns: how to get before a church; what happens when visiting a church; how to get started in a new church; and what to do when leaving a church.

Part IV is written specifically to the ME. The pronoun "you" is used as I want to converse with the educational minister.

Chapter 19 suggests ways a candidate can get before a church. It examines how to deal ethically with a church.

Visiting a potential church is the subject of chapter 20. How can this experience be positive for the candidate and the church? It presents lists of potential questions the candidate may be asked. It also identifies questions the candidate may have of the church.

Chapter 21 describes how to begin ministry in a new church. How one begins a new ministry influences future ministry in that church. This chapter describes some practical concerns.

Leaving a church is the topic of chapter 22. There are times when one is available to move; there are other times when a move would not be wise.

19

Getting Before a Church

This chapter addresses issues germane both to veteran MEs and persons making initial entry into this ministry. Each has unique problems and issues to consider. Standards and guidelines are offered to help educational ministers trying to secure a church. Getting before a prospective church can be a very hard task. Different denominations have their ways for candidates to get before a church. In those that place or assign ministers using denominational hierarchy, potential educational ministers must meet educational and church requirements for these positions. A bishop or district superintendent makes an assignment acceptable to the church and the candidate. The process is very easy once the candidate meets denominational criteria or standards. When the candidate is arbitrarily placed, many steps proposed for the ME candidate in this chapter are not relevant.

However, I come from a denomination that practices congregational polity, and it is harder for MEs to get their names before a prospective church. It has been considered unethical to send an application to a church though some churches now invite persons to send resumes. Getting before a church can be a lengthy process creating anxiety and various levels of frustration for both parties. Before discussing some ways to get before a church, I describe some ministerial ethical standards.

Ministerial Ethical Issues

Assuming both the candidate and the potential church act responsibly and with Christian ethics, below are some ethical principles or guidelines that should permeate the relationship between candidate and church:

● **MEs seeking ministry placement desire God's will for their lives.** They spend much time in prayer, being open to the leadership of the Holy Spirit about where God wants them to serve. Divine leadership is crucial to educational ministers wanting to find the place of service. A proper placement is more than deciding this is where God wants them, or the church saying this is the person they want. It involves God's leadership in bringing candidate and church together as they each search and act upon their perception of God's will.

● **Both the ME and the church deal with only one church or candidate at a time.** Students facing graduation are often confused about what to do when they know their name has been placed before more than one church. Unless the candidate is negotiating with a church, one is free to deal with any church that might make an approach. When either church or candidate decides they are no longer interested in the other, that decision is communicated so neither is operating with false hope or assumptions. If they are talking with a church, the second church is told they are not available now. If it is questionable whether they will accept the first church, they can request some additional time from the second church.

● **If an ME is not seriously considering the church, the church should not seriously consider them.** Some ministers have a need to be "courted" or "needed." They permit their names to be before several churches when they have no intention of making a move. If ministers expect churches to deal ethically and above board, they should conduct themselves in the same manner.

● **MEs may use any ethical and proper means to get their name and qualifications before a church.** Recommendations usually come from one's circle of friends, professional colleagues, educational institutions, and denominational placement offices.

● **MEs take their families into confidence when considering a move.** Depending upon the makeup of the family, the depth of involvement for various family members varies. If the educational minister is married, the spouse's feelings and how the potential move affects the rest of the family are considered. Though the ME is the person engaged in ministry, the family makes a significant contribution to the success of ministry and relationship to the total church life.

● **The ME's pastor is taken into confidence when seriously considering a move.** The pastor is asked to keep this information confidential and to pray for God's will about this decision. The pastor is advised about potential visits to the prospective church. It is not necessary to communicate every inquiry; this may create the feeling of desiring to move. Only when they have a definite leading to make a move to another church should the educational minister consult with the pastor.

• **MEs consider the welfare of the church presently served, their relationship to the congregation and staff, and how much investment the present church has in them.** The church may have aided them through a study leave, provided financial support for a graduate degree, or assisted them to purchase a home. The educational minister carefully and seriously analyzes and evaluates the present church in the following areas:

1. What is the quality of relationships with the pastor, staff, and congregation?
2. Is the church growing and making progress toward established goals?
3. What are the possibilities for the church both now and in the future?

The ME needs to answer this question: What effect will my leaving have on the church and the programs in process? In contemplating a move the educational minister should be patient, deliberate, and slow.

• **The ME is called by the church upon the recommendation of the appropriate committee.** The educational minister should not accept a position offered only by the pastor and a church committee. Being called by the congregation establishes one as a minister. One ought to know who else has been consulted and involved in the process. Have the program leaders of the educational organizations been consulted and given their approval? Have the pastor and church staff been involved in the process? Have the deacons and church council members been supportive of the personnel committee in their decision?

• **MEs avoid making recommendations about whom their successor might be.** The church needs the freedom to select the appropriate committee and to do its work without interference from former educational ministers. I have been asked by MEs to recommend them to a church I was leaving. I always declined, but advised them of the appropriate persons to contact. I did not want to be in the position of selecting my successor. It is ethical and appropriate to refer the church to persons and institutions where potential educational minister candidates are found.

• **MEs, when changing churches, should make the transition when the work is going well, not in a time of crisis.** It is better to work through problems, whether with programs or people, before moving to a new place of service. When it is not possible, especially when educational ministers have been asked to leave, they should leave quietly. During their ministry they attempted to strengthen and build up the church. Their leaving also should seek to help the church, not involve it in controversy or divisive movements.

• **MEs should not resign simply because the pastor does.** They are called by the congregation and have a ministry whether the church has a pastor or not. Educational ministers serve at the pleasure of the church, not the pastor. I never served a church after its pastor left, but I know that sometimes new pastors want to assemble their own staff. My approach with a new pastor would be as follows: "I feel we can work together; at the least, we should try to do so for six months to a year. If during that time, we are not able to work together, I am willing to leave. I would ask and expect you to give me a reasonable amount of time to relocate."

Matching the ME and the Church

The process of matching the ME and the church varies with each candidate depending on whether the candidate is now an educational minister or is a recent seminary graduate. Every ME should first prepare a resume describing his or her qualifications and experiences in Christian education. Figure 5 is a guide for preparing a resume. The resume is brief, preferably one page. It contains only information that qualifies them for the position they seek in Christian education. The resume should be attractive. Many persons never get contacted because the resume does not present a pleasing image. References are included so the prospective church can do some preliminary investigation without having to contact the candidate.

The person seeking the first position as an ME would be wise to work with the seminary's alumni placement office. It circulates names and resumes to churches seeking educational ministers. It is also appropriate to send your resume to influential pastors, other educational ministers, and denominational leaders in regional and state judicatories. These people are often asked to recommend potential staff people. Since they receive resumes from many candidates, send some additional information and data not contained in the resume to introduce yourself. Tell why you want to work in that particular location.

When the ME candidate knows about a potential church, a friend can send a resume accompanied by a personal recommendation. I have done this for many students and friends.

Many denominational agencies have offices for ministerial placements. These staff relations offices have two primary functions: one is to help match churches with potential ministers; the other is to help when a minister and a congregation are having problems. These offices have helpful knowledge about churches and ministerial candidates.

Sample Resume Form

NAME:
ADDRESS:
PHONE:
BIRTHPLACE:
MARITAL STATUS:
EDUCATION:

SECULAR WORK EXPERIENCE:

CHURCH WORK EXPERIENCE:

FAMILY:

CHRISTIAN EDUCATION EXPERIENCE:

PRESENT CHURCH MEMBERSHIP:
RELIGIOUS EXPERIENCE:

ORDAINED:
FOUR REFERENCES:
HEALTH:
DATE _____

Figure 7

All ethical means are used to get a candidate's name before a congregation. Once the resume is before a church, placement personnel and the candidate can only pray and wait. If as a candidate, you are not now serving on a church staff, volunteer to do something in the educational ministry in the church you attend.

One other method of helping the candidate and the church get together is for the candidate to attend meetings where pastors are present. This ranges from attending local ministerial meetings to attending regional, state, or national meetings.

A Personal Word

Every position I have ever had came through personal contacts and recommendations. Of course, candidates must have skills and abilities for the desired task. They should attain the necessary educational backgrounds and qualifications. However, this does not guarantee they will be called by a church. I have been recommended by former professors, colleagues, and friends. Sometimes I have initiated contact with these persons; at other times it was done without my knowledge. Suggestions for negotiating with a prospective church is the subject of the next chapter.

20

Visiting Potential
Place of Service

Both you and the prospective church act under the leading of the Holy Spirit. You both make this a matter of serious prayer that God's will be done. Before visiting a potential place of service, you and the church gather data about each other. You want as much data about the history and growth cycle of the church as possible. Because working with the pastor is so crucial, you want to investigate the pastor's attitude toward the ministry of education, the pattern of staff relations, theological position, how long the pastor has been at this church, and what his projected tenure is.

The initial visit to the prospective church is part of the negotiation process. This visit should not be undertaken if either party feels any hesitancy. Its purpose is to explore the possibility of working together. Due to distances and expenses, sometimes this visit is made as you complete the decision process. It is better, yet, if this visit is explorative as both seek to get to know each other better.

Before the Initial Interview

Before the initial interview, several steps are taken. The church receives and evaluates your resume. This includes checking out references, attitude and loyalty to the denomination, doctrinal position, and other pertinent information. The church examines your record if you are an experienced minister of education, or the potential as seen by professors, church leaders, or others who have observed you in ministry situations.

You need to receive information about the church, the pastor, the staff, and ideally, a written job description. You and your family need to know something about the new community, including information about schools, cultural and educational activities, and demographic information. You and the church need arrival information and how much time is available for the interview process. You both profit if a schedule of meetings and other activities planned is finalized prior to the visit.

A Pre-Visit Check List

Several things are considered before making the initial visit:

• **Deciding when to visit the prospective church.** Schedule the visit when it is least disruptive to your present church and personal schedule, and to the prospective church. Your visit to the potential church is confidential, although your pastor prays with you as you make this decision. The visit occurs when the prospective pastor is in town and has adequate time.

Once I visited a church in view of becoming the ME. We agreed on the time of my visit and arrival in the community. Much to my surprise, a church member met me at the airport and took me to the hotel. He took me to lunch where I met the pastor when he dropped by our table. After two hours in the hotel room, the pastor finally picked me up and spent about thirty minutes with me. He then left me at the church to make hospital rounds (not emergencies). I saw the Minister of Music and was able to ask about the church and the pastor. I never received a job description but was asked to write my own. I met only part of the personnel committee and none of the lay educational leadership. The initial interview was as far as it went. My feeling was that if the pastor lacked time for me while I was there for the interview, there wouldn't be time for me after I got there.

• **Allow enough time to deal adequately with the important issues.** Usually two days are ample. It is preferable they be over a weekend. Plan to go when your spouse can go also. Involve him or her in some interviews and some social times with the families of the pastor and other staff members.

• **Have an open mind.** If you have already decided this is not the place for you, do not make the initial visit. But if you are undecided and trying to get a feel for what the situation is like, the visit might reveal whether your abilities fit the particular position.

• **Be prepared with a devotional or a message should the church want to "see you in action."** This ought to be agreed on before arrival.

● **Clarify with the church when and how arrival will occur.**
Secure telephone numbers where emergency calls can be referred
should you need to be reached.

After Arrival

After arriving in the city, do several things before beginning the
interview process:

● **Take a quick tour of the city.** See how it is laid out and places of
interest, such as schools, shopping centers, and residential areas.
This should not take long, but needs to be comprehensive enough to
get a good perspective of the area.

● **Take a brief tour of the church campus.** Convey interest in
the buildings, grounds, and facilities. A brief walking tour helps
form a perception of the church and how it functions.

● **Spend time in the educational records.** Examine the records
for Sunday School, discipleship training, and the missions education
organizations. Compare what you find at the church with your
previous analysis of the church.

With Whom Should You Meet?

During this initial visit meet as many church leaders as possible.
Each person and group who interviews the potential ME wants to
feel they had sufficient time and have not been rushed in the process. Before encountering the persons and groups with whom the ME
will meet, there are four cautions to consider. They are:

1. **Dress appropriately.** Be careful neither to overdress or un-
derdress. Some ministerial candidates whose appearances give a
negative impression never get seriously considered.

2. **Be positive.** Be positive in your outlook and viewpoints. Do not
be critical either of the church or of decisions leaders in the church
have made. Your purpose is to get acquainted with the church and
its present leaders, not to offer criticisms or suggestions.

3. **Be relaxed.** Unfortunately, interview visits have been called
"trials." Remember both of you are looking at each other. You should
behave with as little self-consciousness as possible. Accept that you
probably are and should be nervous, and relax anyway! Consider
yourselves honored guests, not anxious ones.

4. **Do not oversell.** It is a mistake to try to oversell either yourself or your abilities. The church will see through this attempt easily

enough. Hopefully, the church is not looking for "Superperson," but is looking for an ME who has strengths and weaknesses.

Persons and groups with whom the ME should meet include the following:

• **The Personnel Committee.** An extensive interview with the personnel committee is crucial. They ask questions about items on the resume and clarify information they received from your references. They also may want to see how you handle yourself in such circumstances. This is a time for them to get to know you and your spouse in a very personal way. Areas to explore with this committee are Christian testimony, call to ministry, spiritual pilgrimage, personal and family backgrounds, and views of the church, particularly of the educational organizations. They may ask you what you see as your strengths and weaknesses. If married, the spouse is part of this interview and given an opportunity to share. The setting for this interview is in a relaxed environment and not under a tight time restraint. Both parties should feel free to ask questions with the expectation of receiving honest answers.

• **The pastor.** Time with the pastor may be more crucial than that spent with the personnel committee or any other person or group in the church. You will both want to discuss your philosophies of ministry and the church. You do not have to be in complete agreement, but your approaches need to be compatible so you can form a significant ministry team. You must know what the pastor expects of the ME as a person and a professional. This is the time to explore what goals the pastor wants you to reach and the time frame in which the expectations are to be finished. When I went to the church in Greenville, the pastor wanted me to do two things. One was to help move the church from one location to another. The second item was to pick up a declining Sunday School. Relocation was in the immediate future. He did not tell me how quickly he wanted the Sunday School turned around.

This also is the time to ask if expectations are renegotiated once these initial objectives are completed. There should be an openness between the pastor and you. Important to you is the pastor's tenure and plans to remain in this church because it directly influences your future success and ministry in this church. Time with the pastor may be more important than time touring the church. Ample time is allowed for this interview so each gets to know the other. Possibly more than one interview time should be arranged and planned.

• **Other staff members.** A meeting with all the staff can be helpful to see how the pastor and staff members function together. Then individual conferences with various staff members prove useful for hearing how the staff members perceive their work. Be sensitive to note how staff members feel about their work and their general attitude toward the church. In a private conference, the staff member feels more open to share honest feelings describing what it is like to work with the pastor and the congregation.

• **Educational organizations leadership.** You will want to meet with the heads of Sunday School, discipleship training, and missions education organizations. Probably a general meeting with these leaders would prove valuable. You can observe how well these organizations relate to each other and mesh with the goals and objectives of the church. During this time, the program leaders explore your feelings and ideas about how their organizations can strengthen and help the church fulfill its purpose. You answer any questions these leaders have and relate how you work with lay leaders. This is the time to discover their expectations of the ME and to share your expectations, to discuss established objectives and goals and what they foresee in the future. As a potential ME, you want to see how much of their planning is already in place and how much could be shaped as you seek to work with them in designing plans. The leaders' perception of the strengths and weaknesses of the present programs helps validate your impressions of the educational program. Much can be done in a large group meeting; again, there is merit also to having individual conferences with each leader. This allows persons to express ideas more completely than in a group setting. There are usually a few deep thinkers who will not express their feelings in a group.

• **Other church leaders.** Your work is primarily with the educational programs, but is not limited to them. Perhaps you will meet with other church leaders, such as deacons and committee chairpersons and members. The purpose is to become better acquainted with the church leadership and to learn more about the church as viewed by others. These meetings should consist of free interchanges of information and data. Questions are initiated both by church leaders and the ME.

• **Educational program workers.** You also want to meet the persons with whom and for whom you will work—the congregation. This can be done in a reception with the purpose being to meet as many people as possible, not to conduct in-depth interviews. If someone has questions that will take a significant amount of time, arrange for this sometime additionally during the extended visit.

• **Non-ministerial staff.** A good source of information about a church is its church secretaries, particularly if they have been at the church for any length of time. You also need to meet the support staff, including the secretarial and custodial staffs.

After the Interviews

Assuming the interview process went well and you each have good feelings about the other, what happens next? If both affirm pursuing the relationship, usually additional time elapses before the next meeting. It takes time for the church to work through its process before issuing a call. You have to return to present responsibilities. The following suggestions should prove beneficial:

• **Keep the present pastor informed.** Since the present pastor knows about the potential new ministry, you need to honestly share feelings about the potential church; but you do not need to offer a resignation until you are prepared to accept the call issued by the potential church.

• **Make no assumptions.** Both you and the prospective church make no assumptions about the future relationship. Do not assume the church will issue a call. The church, also, does not assume you are coming to the church. Both need time to pray about what each believes is God's will for this relationship.

• **Take adequate time.** Neither you nor the church should make an emotional decision. Both take time to pray about and think through a move before the visit, during the visit, and after the visit. Take sufficient time to be convinced of God's will.

• **Confide with family and friends.** The family also needs to pray about, think on, and discuss the potential move. You and your family should have a feeling of shared ministry, especially so between marriage partners. The impact this move has on your family now and in the future is considered. Older children are brought into the decision-making process. A move is interpreted in a positive way—not as a means of getting away from a bad or difficult predicament. You as the candidate consider a move because you feel God is calling to you; but the final decision is a family decision. Let God speak to the whole family.

• **Set reasonable time limits.** The decision-making process needs adequate time but should not be drawn out unnecessarily. If later visits are necessary to help make the decision, these are done when possible without disrupting your present position. A decision-making tool that helps is to take a sheet of paper and draw a line down the middle. Write the word "positive" on the left side and "negative" on the right side. List all the "positives" under the left heading. Then do the same for the "negatives" in the right column. Next, spend time evaluating the "positives" and the "negatives." See which dominates.

Several years ago I was invited to become ME while serving another church. I had positive feelings about the pastor and the church. When confronted with making a decision to permit my name to be submitted to the church, I did not have a firm feeling that I should do it, nor that I should not. I asked for some time and sought additional counsel and information. I used the decision-making tool mentioned above. This went on for about four weeks without a definite feeling this was what God wanted me to do. At that point, I advised the pastor that my answer had to be "no." It was not fair to the church or me to delay the decision any longer.

Potential Questions

During the initial interview, you and the church expect to ask questions. For example, you should investigate what freedoms and restraints would affect your work.[1] The purpose of this section is to suggest some questions each might be asked so both can be better prepared for the initial interview process. These questions are not intended to be extensive but to suggest issues of concern. Hopefully, you and the church could use these questions as a basis for framing specific questions about particular, relevant concerns.

Questions You Might Anticipate[2]

1. What experience have you had in the church and the business world?

2. Where were you born? Where did you grow up?

3. Are you ordained? Do you see yourself as a minister or as a layman?

4. What do you see as the primary work of the ME? If you were ME here, what would you expect to do?

5. What is the role of the ME in visitation? How much time should be spent and what types of visits would you make?

6. Should the ME be a counselor? How much counseling should be done and what kinds of counseling can you handle?

7. Should the ME maintain regular office hours? How much time is spent in the office?

8. Do you engage in personal witnessing with lost and unchurched persons?

9. How do you feel about age grading of adults? How strictly should the church policy be enforced? What are the reasons for age grading? How do you feel about the annual promotion date?

10. How much time should the ME spend in teaching, i.e., new church members, potential teachers, study courses, or other types of classes?

11. Should the ME work with and develop the standing and special committees of the church?

12. What are your feelings about the curricula provided by the denomination for the educational organizations?

13. How can the ME be a resource person for the total educational program?

14. What is your feeling about a church kindergarten? Weekday ministries? Church sponsored schools—kindergarten through high school?

15. Should the church have a weekly workers' meeting for Sunday School leaders? Why or why not?

16. Should *all* educational programs have a monthly council meeting? Why? Why not?

17. Should the ME enlist workers for the educational organizations?

18. How do you feel about starting new classes and departments for Sunday School and discipleship training?

19. Should the ME be involved in the church's stewardship emphasis? If so, how?

20. How should the ME relate to the pastor, other staff members, educational organizational leaders, the music ministry, Church Council, youth and their leaders, Vacation Bible School, church membership at large?

21. How should the ME be related to family life education and Christian Home Week?

22. What are your feelings about the church and the denomination's stewardship program? missions program?

23. How much time should an ME spend a year in personal continuing education activities?

24. Should educational workers participate in local, state, or national training conference?

25. Should Christians be involved in contemporary social and moral issues? What should be the stance of the church in such matters?

26. What religious education periodicals and journals do you read regularly?

27. What kind of materials would you use to train church leaders and workers? Why would you select these materials?

28. What are your ideas about a church-wide visitation program? How do the church educational programs fit into the visitation program?

29. How does your family feel about your being an ME? What activities do they enjoy in the church? In the community?

30. Does your family enjoy entertaining people in your home?

31. What are your feelings about the denomination?

32. What part should the ME have in the church worship services?

33. What role should the ME have in revivals, attendance and enlargement campaigns, social events, church-wide activities?

34. How involved should the ME be in the record keeping process of the church?

35. How do you feel about working with people?

36. Have you helped in the planning and building of new educational facilities?

37. What do you believe about the Bible? What does it mean in your daily life?

38. What uses do you envision for the church media library?

39. Which church organization do you feel should receive the greatest emphasis?

40. With which church committees do you most enjoy working?

41. What do you feel is the primary purpose of Christian education?

42. What do you feel is the basic purpose of the church?

43. If you become ME, how much salary would you expect?

44. If you were called, when could you come?

Questions You Might Ask the Church[3]

1. How does the church perceive the ME—administrator? coordinator? supervisor? publisher? educator? other?

2. What are your expectations of an ME?

3. How well does the church leadership support the educational ministry?

4. Is there a need to upgrade organizational and educational techniques? Would there be an openness to doing so?

5. What growth plans does the church have for buildings? expansion of existing programs? outreach?

6. What are your current programs for training leaders, and visitation of members and prospects?

7. How does the ME relate to the publicity ministry of the church?

8. Who are your previous MEs? How long did each serve here? Where did they go?

9. How long has the pastor served here? What are his plans for the immediate future?

10. How does the pastor feel toward the church and its members? How does the church feel toward him?

11. Is there a need for additional educational staff?

12. What secretarial staff does the church have? Who will handle the ME's clerical tasks? Who supervises the secretarial staff? Is there adequate secretarial help for the staff?

13. Does the ME serve at the pleasure of the pastor or the church? Do I resign if the pastor resigns?

14. Does the ME serve as director of the Sunday School and discipleship training programs?

15. Does the church provide for the ME's housing needs?

16. How do you feel that I could best serve as ME?

17. Who makes arrangements for the moving of church staff? Does the church pay all moving expenses? Does the church provide any post-moving expenses, i.e., costs related to moving into new housing?

Notes

1. Maria Harris, *The DRE Book: Questions and Strategies for Parish Personnel* (New York: Paulist Press, 1979), 50.

2. J. Ralph Hardee, *Church Staff Entrance and Exit: A Procedural Manual for the Minister of Education* (n.p., 1979), 10-14.

3. Ibid., 14-16.

21

Getting Started
on a New Field

Getting started in a new position brings many emotions. You feel great excitement, yet you know it will be difficult to make new friends, establish confidence, and get acquainted with new people. This experience requires patience on your part and by those with whom you work. Ideally you spend several weeks and months getting acquainted with the church, the membership, the educational leadership, and the programs. Your previous analysis of the church interview is beneficial in deciding the direction of your ministry. Your strategy depends on what is happening in the church. If things are going well, you go with what is already taking place, at least initially. If the church is having problems with its educational ministry or is not growing, you cannot be passive or hesitant about making strategic changes.

A church I served peaked ten years before I arrived as ME, and had been declining slightly since that period. The year I arrived on the field the denomination changed the entire age-grading criteria, teaching procedures in two major divisions, and revamped the entire Sunday School curricula. The only preparation this church made for the changes was ordering the new curriculum. I did not have time to wait. I had to get more than two hundred Sunday School workers ready to use new curricula and organized for the new grouping and grading plan. Often I wished for more time to prepare myself and the teaching staff to use the new curriculum and get the program organized.

If the church is growing, things are well organized, and the educational staff functions well, then devote significant time getting to know the church, the leadership, the educational workers, and the church staff. You may need to make some minor adjustments but have the advantage of building on your predecessor's work.

The ME on a new field should adopt the posture of eyes wide open, observing both people and programs; ears open, listening often and speaking little; and the heart open, seeking to identify with the people, building rapport and a team spirit through genuine interest. Patience is needed to acquire complete data about people and programs before making judgments or decisions.

This chapter seeks to help you adjust, establish relationships, and embark on a fruitful ministry on a new field of service and ministry.[1]

Preparing Yourself

Before physically moving to a new church community, prepare yourself for the move. The following suggestions prepare you mentally and spiritually for this experience:

• **Evaluate the quality of ministry at your previous church.** Spend a day or so analyzing what went well. Be critical about strengths and weaknesses; be as honest as possible. Take pride in what was accomplished. Acknowledge the contributions that pastor, staff, and educational workers made to the victories. Take this opportunity for a time of self-evaluation.

• **Make an open-ended time commitment to God and to this new church.** The church extended you an indefinite call; plan to have a long and fruitful ministry with this congregation. A church should not become a stepping-stone to a larger church or greater position. Both ministers and churches usually grow through a long-term ministry.

• **Enter the new position with a positive attitude.** God and this church present you an opportunity for ministry and service. Cultivate a humble spirit—because you are teachable by God, the Holy Spirit, and by other people. Your faith strongly affirms that this ministry is God's ministry. You believe all things are possible with God's help and guidance. You are not a blind optimist, but you do seek to discover ways things can be done rather than decide why they should not be tried.

• **Acknowledge your strengths and weaknesses.** There are some things you do well. There are also some things you do not do well. Build and develop your ministry around your strengths, knowing that weaknesses can be built into strengths.

• **Establish your family as a priority.** Starting over in a new church presents the opportunity to establish or reestablish your family as a top priority. Ministers tend to put family in a secondary role in terms of relationships and priorities. Without a strong, healthy, happy home base, you will not be effective.

Your Family and the Move

Probably family members feel more displacement with the move than you. You are the reason for the move. Usually, you find your place quickly as you immerse yourself in the challenge and excitement of work. Family members have to establish new relationships and find new friends. Hopefully, the new church gives you adequate time to help your family move into new living quarters and begin settling into the new community. Moving into a new house or apartment seems to create a million and one things to do—hanging drapes, servicing and connecting appliances, unpacking boxes, cleaning and filling shelves, arranging furniture. Church members and their families can smooth the transition process by introducing various family members to potential friends, schools, shopping centers, banks, and doctors. Help your family become functional in your new setting just as others are helping you learn to function in your new ministry.

Now the Church

After the family is settled, you are ready to begin the work at the church. First, settle into your new office, placing books on book shelves and making the desk and office functional. Enlist another staff member to orient you as to how the church functions; you need to know how to secure office supplies, how the purchasing system works, details of the sick leave policy. A staff manual is very valuable to read at leisure or to look for answers to questions as they arise. Once you are familiar with how the church functions, begin to build relationships with the pastor and staff.

Building Pastor/Staff Relationships

Spend quality time with the pastor. The pastor should initiate an orientation interview with you to ensure you know the various policies and how they affect you. Part of this briefing could be reviewing items in the staff manual. This conference helps begin a solid working relationship with the pastor and helps establish an honest, open, trusting relationship, too. The foundation for building good relationships is to respect each other as professional ministers and persons of integrity.

Getting acquainted with other staff members is of utmost importance. Seek to get to know them; encourage them to share about themselves, personally and professionally. Ask staff members to describe what they do on the staff and how this benefits the church. Find out how each staff member assesses the ME role and contribution to the church.

When older, more experienced staff persons are present, seek their counsel and advice. Their experiences have provided good knowledge about how the congregation functions and how it is likely to respond. They can be a valuable bridge to beginning your educational ministry in the congregation.

In beginning to build relationships with the pastor and church staff, show them you are a team person. Avoid any hint or appearance of competition; rather convey loyalty and dependability. Each member of the ministerial team is worthy of love, trust, and help.

Success in a church also depends on good relationships with the nonministerial staff. Take time getting to know these persons. They include the secretarial and custodial staffs, church hostess, and others described in chapter 18. These persons are in a support role, but are crucial to the success or failure of the church's ministry. They need to feel they are significant and important to the working of the church.

Educational Leadership Team

Much of the work of educational ministry is done through lay leadership. Spend sufficient time getting to know the educational leadership and each one's strengths and weaknesses. This is best done informally—by visiting in their homes, sharing coffee breaks, or hosting them in your home for food and fellowship. These leaders must see your philosophy and approach to ministry is that of "an equipper and an enabler" of them (Eph. 4:11-12) rather than only on you and your efforts. You must convince them you are a team player, devoted to helping each leader function effectively.

Get to know each leader and become well acquainted with their families. As a result, you will often be their minister in times of need. Nothing proves genuine interest in people more than knowing their family members' names and what is happening in each of their lives.

Building Congregational Relationships

Write a letter to the congregation and publish it in the church paper expressing your joy and pleasure being in this church. Express appreciation for the call from the church and for their confidence in your leadership.

Discuss with the pastor and staff ways to get better acquainted with the congregation. They might suggest participation in church worship services, greeting people after the worship services, or encouraging departmental leadership to invite you to their departments. During the first few weeks you may feel all you do is attend meetings, which may be true. Yet these small group meetings provide some of your best occasions for becoming better acquainted with the members. Do more listening at these meetings than sharing, and communicate your desire to be helpful in the success of church tasks.

Learning names in a new church is a difficult task. Encourage people to tell you their names each time they meet you. Frequent contact and interaction help in remembering a person's name. Let people know you are genuine and real and they will share themselves with you.

Identifying Key People[2]

You need to know who the leaders are in this church. The following questions need to be answered. Some answers are printed in information about the church; some can be answered by staff; some will require your careful observation.

- Who are the key leaders?
- Who has the power to approve or disapprove of programs?
- Where is the power in the church?
- Who will be my allies when anything different is tried?
- Who is likely to resist new ideas and programs?

Remember, the people you find may *not* be the elected leaders. You should not let these persons dictate what you can or cannot do. You should attempt to win over a potential adversary through conversation, discussion, and your desire for inclusiveness in the church's ministry. If you succeed in providing ministry leadership for this church, you must know who will serve as allies.

Create Bonds of Trust

Developing bonds of trust between yourself, the educational leadership, and the congregation takes time. Harris suggests some practical things to do:

The main contribution a DRE can make toward creating a bond of trust is to do the job for which he or she was hired. Listening to others, sharing their lives, presence, and hard work are noticeable qualities, and when DRE's involve themselves in parish life with obvious concern, they are contributing in the best possible way toward the creation of a bond of trust.[3]

Tips on Beginning Well[4]

You sense, no doubt, the importance of making a good beginning Here are several tips to help you begin well:

• **Keep a notebook with you for the first several weeks.** Inundations of information come as you begin your work. Do not rely on your memory. Make notes of things you need to remember, jot down questions you need to ask, record names of those you meet, the context of the meeting, and any personal facts you have gathered about them.

• **Pace yourself.** Usually the first few days and weeks in a new position are stressful—getting started in the new ministry, managing the move, myriad invitations to you and your family to welcome you to the new church. You need to conserve your energy and get plenty of rest.

Look energetic but do not overdo it. Many people start out a career or a job with such great energy and enthusiasm it cannot possibly be sustained. You may seem overeager at the beginning. The best progress is steady progress.

• **Ask the right kind of questions.** Some people are afraid they will be thought inadequate if they ask questions. When you do not understand something, ask questions until you do. Elwood N. Chapman notes:

> A right question is one you need to ask to be effective; a wrong question is one that does not apply to the task being explained. . . . In asking questions, keep in mind that you must listen to the answers with your eyes as well as your ears. . . . You will make a better impression on people if you form the habit of listening with your eyes as well as your ears.[5]

• **Work normal hours.** Beginning a new job, people are prone to work extra hours and days. Remember: this does not prove your worth to the church. If the church knows you plan to spend the rest of your ministry at this church, you have plenty of time. Chapman comments, "It is better to make full use of the time you spend on the job than to try to impress others with your willingness to work extra hours."[6]

● **Do not flaunt your education or previous experience.** Your educational background was disclosed to the congregation and staff during the interviewing and calling processes. It is not as important now as your ability to do the job. Make few references to your former place of service. Do not compare this church to your former one; this church may do things differently. Your way of doing things may be better; Chapman warns:

> But until you are sure, be safe and do it the way the people at the new job do it. Give your co-workers the satisfaction of explaining how they do things. You will have plenty of time later to make any changes that will be an improvement.[7]

● **Make friends, but do not make close friends too soon.** You may build one or two strong friendships at the expense of others. Welcome those who show you friendliness as you start at the church, but concentrate on building relationships with all the people rather than one or two.

● **Read the staff manual.** Becoming acquainted with the staff manual lets you understand policies and procedures.

● **Send out positive verbal and nonverbal signals.** Many verbal signals create a good first impression. Courteously greet others. A smile can be a friendly nonverbal signal. Chapman states:

> People who develop confidence in sending out such signals of friendship make excellent first impressions. They quickly increase their sphere of influences and build many lasting working and personal relationships. Have confidence in yourself and your ability to send such signals. Take the initiative. Send out your own brand of signals in your own style, and be an easier person to meet.[8]

Notes

1. J. Ralph Hardee, *Church Staff Entrance and Exit: A Procedural Manual for the Minister of Education* (n.p., 1979), 31.

2. Maria Harris, *The DRE Book: Questions and Strategies for Parish Personnel* (New York: Paulist Press, 1976), 89-90. She raises several questions related to a parish that are applicable to a church.

3. Ibid., 94.

4. Elwood N. Chapman, *Your Attitude Is Showing: A Primer of Human Relations* 5th rev. ed. (Chicago: SRA, 1987), 103-109. Though the book is written for persons entering the secular work world, the ideas are easily adapted to fit the church situation.

5. Ibid., 105.

6. Ibid., 106.

7. Ibid.

8. Ibid., 109.

22

Now That My Work
Is Done

Effective MEs have opportunities to move. Some invitations you will automatically decline—an opportunity to move shortly after making a move, when your moving would adversely affect your present church, when new programs are just getting underway and your leadership is crucial to their continuing success, or it is a bad time for your family to relocate. Other invitations you will contemplate, seeking to discern the will of God. There have been times I declined to consider a move when I could not give a reason for my decision; I simply sensed it was the proper thing to do.

Ministers have difficulty knowing when to leave one church and move to another. There are times the decision is made by someone else—by the pastor, the church personnel committee, or another church body. However, in this final chapter I make the assumption it is your decision to choose a voluntary move. The factors that may cause you to consider moving to another church are analyzed. The times when a move would be unwise are described.

Transitions are not easy, particularly when leaving a church where you had a good experience. You will have feelings of grief and loss leaving the church as a body and the staff with whom you worked closely. Friendships, security, and stability are relinquished in moving from one community to another. This has been your home.

Moving has frightening aspects to it. In essence you have to start over. In your previous church you were respected and credible. You paid your dues there. Now the process starts all over and you pay your dues again. Despite years of experience as an educational minister, this new church and these people do not know you.

The transition involves more than the ME. It involves your family. Some of your concerns will be: How will the family like the new church? Will they like the new community? Will the children be happy in the new schools? Will my spouse find a place of ministry in the new church and community? How well will we like the new house? Will the new house be an apartment, house, or condominium? Going into the unknown creates anxiety and concern for all.

To Move or Not to Move?

This very difficult question requires careful prayer to discern the will of God.

When Should You Consider Moving?

Every opportunity to move provides a time to consider whether you should move. One or more of the following elements are involved as you seek to interpret the call of God to a new place of ministry and to know God's will for your life. They are:

• **When you feel your work is finished.** This does not mean you have done all that can be done, for a church under God's leadership calls different persons to realize specific goals. It means you have done all you can do in this church except regular maintenance. The work that can be done is not completed, just your portion of it.[1] This was my feeling when I felt I should leave First Baptist Church, Greenville. I completed the two goals the pastor had for me.

Duke K. McCall wrote in *The Tie*[2] that after a minister has been in a church five to ten years, a covenant with the church leaders needs to be renegotiated. He feels the original goals have probably been realized after serving those numbers of years, and new goals need setting. This is good advice for every minister and church to practice. I tried to do this but was unsuccessful. I could continue to do what I was doing, but felt status quo was not as challenging as I desired or needed. Although there were other educational challenges and work to be done, I felt I had done what I would be permitted to do.

• **You are aware of overwhelming opposition.** You expect to encounter a degree of friction and opposition, but there are times when the opposition is so great it is unwise to continue. You do all within your power to deal constructively with the opposition, but sometimes it cannot be resolved. Leaving is not necessarily surrendering to the opposition but recognizing continued resistance will prove detrimental.

• **You feel the challenge of an inviting opportunity.** While you feel you can continue to be productive and helpful to the present church, you also feel the compelling opportunity of another place of service. Most ministers I know say it is best to move to another church while things are going well in your present church. The new opportunity may use your gifts and abilities more than the present place, and you may need a new challenge.

• **You have the conviction a move is in order.** You feel this is God's will for your life.[3] You experience an overwhelming sense of divine leadership.

• **When you have lost your place of leadership in the church, it may be time to move.** There are many reasons you may have lost leadership in the church. A mistake may have shaken the confidence of the people in your leadership ability. A portion of the church withdraws its support because of a decision you led the church to make. Without the trust of the church, your days of productivity are over. However, do not move without first honestly determining why you lost your place of leadership. Learn everything you can from such a painful experience. You do not want to repeat it.

• **You have an inner feeling of restlessness.** This is not the restlessness that prompts frequent moves for some ministers. They never have problems either with people or churches because they do not stay long enough for problems to develop; they move every two or three years. This restless feeling startles those who are usually content. It is a mixture of discontent and anticipation as you sense God preparing you for something new, for a new challenge in your ministry. This inner restlessness can be a sign it is time to consider making a move.[4]

When Not To Move

Ministers make serious mistakes when they move for the wrong reasons. Some signs that suggest a move is not wise at a particular time include:

• **When there are problems in the church.** This includes difficulties within the church staff. It could be that you and the pastor are having problems. If you stay in a church for any length of time, you will go through some trying times completely unrelated to your success as a spiritual leader. This may be a sign you should stay. There may be "problem" people with whom you work. Sometimes such people run off ministers before the church's problems are dealt with properly. Lowrie notes, "Usually such persons need loving confrontation—not fearful avoidance."[5] It seems problem people have clones in every church. If you change churches because of these problems, you are probably simply changing the names of the problems. Problems, whatever or whoever they are, are rarely a sure sign you should seek another church.[6]

• **Spiritual dryness is not a sure sign you should move.** You may call this "burnout," when you do not feel as good or as enthusiastic about your ministry. Perhaps things are not going well in the church or your family is in a particularly stressful time. Although you continue to work hard and pray, you see little progress personally or in your work and begin to feel that the "grass is greener on the other side." These are normal times to contemplate changes. Recognize your ministry will go through various cycles as will you and your family.

If you are in such a season of life, you need to address the cause of the dryness rather than look for a new place of ministry. You may need only to take a break—go on a vacation or take a few days off. I once took a dry spell as a sure sign I should move. I even went as far as visiting another church. After returning home I felt very uneasy about the whole situation. I visited a chaplain friend who helped me put it all in perspective. He suggested I read Donald Smith's *Clergy in the Crossfire*.[7] It changed my ministry and kept me from making a move that would have been a mistake.

• **An "open door" is not a definite sign you should move.** You will feel flattered when another church seeks you as a minister. If you are doing a good job, inquiries and even invitations from other churches will come. Speaking candidly, it certainly gets your attention if it is a larger church. These are not divine mandates to move. An open door does not comprise a reason for moving.[8]

• **Even a church with an obvious need for your services is not a sign you should move.** Lowrie offers good advice: You may find yourself confronted with a church that has great need and opportunity. If you move every time you are confronted with such need, you will get to know the men at the moving company better than you do your deacons. When you move it should be for the right reasons.[9]

Preparing for Your Departure

Terminating relationships is never easy. You will have mixed feelings leaving one church for another—sadness at the thought of severing relationships, excitement as you anticipate a time of beginnings and new work. How do you go about preparing both the people and the church for your departure? These suggestions may prove helpful.

• **Telling the pastor and staff.** The pastor has been informed about your negotiations with the other church. Once you have made your decision, the pastor should be the first to know. Then work out a time schedule for telling staff members, your secretary, and others employed by the church. They should hear it from you, not secondhand.

• **Share your decision with the educational leadership.** This involves the program directors and primary leaders with whom you've worked. I tried to see program leaders, sharing with each why I was leaving and what I was going to be doing. I attempted to interpret for them how my move fit what I felt was God's will for my life. The educational workers should not be told until you have officially resigned. One of the hardest tasks I have ever faced was telling educational workers I was leaving. I built strong ties of friendship and Christian fellowship with them as we worked together planning and executing programs.

• **Submitting a letter of resignation.** In congregational polity, you address this to the pastor and the personnel committee. In this letter, express appreciation and gratitude for the privilege of having served this church. Communicate the joy of working with the pastor, other staff members, and the educational leadership. Give information about the new position and how you feel it is God's will for your life. Give the dates when you will end your service including unused vacation time. This is not the time to be critical or attempt to correct problems in the church. Satchel Paige, the great baseball pitcher, had a worthy philosophy: "Don't look back, 'cause they may be gainin' on you." Take the forward look. Be an optimist. Use your departure as a time to strengthen the church and give a word of encouragement.

• **See that your work is in order.** In your last days, work as if you were just starting. Give attention to the details of your job. In most churches when the ME leaves, the successor is not called for several months. This means someone else picks up what you have been doing or it goes undone. If you have been a good equipper and enabler, members of the congregation can fill the gaps until another educational minister arrives. You will be tempted to slack off. You are busy saying good-bye, people are entertaining you and your family, and you are now thinking about the new work you are to begin. You have an important responsibility to see that the educational house is in order and continues to function effectively and efficiently after you leave.

• **Write down the things you do.** Ask yourself: "If I were coming in as ME what information would help me do the job?" List those routine tasks you do, but do more than just make lists. Identify the things you do on a daily, weekly, monthly, and annual basis. Identify the people with whom you worked to accomplish these tasks. It might be helpful to also note how much time is involved in each task and why you did them. Share these lists with the pastor and the personnel committee. Some of these tasks cannot be delayed until your successor arrives.

• **Interpret your decision to the people.** Your letter of resignation is not the place to interpret why you feel that this is God's will for your life. Laypersons struggle with how to discern God's will for their lives. You will have planning meetings with the educational organizations before leaving. Use these opportunities to share with the people how you arrived at this decision. Do not be afraid to let them know it was not easy. Describe your struggles. Let them know you prayed about it, and included your family as you sought to discern God's will. Even share with them those with whom you discussed the possible move and how they helped you. I also would use the church paper to interpret the move to the congregation at large. If the pastor gives a church service to you before leaving, use this opportunity to share about the new work God is calling you to do.

• **Accentuate the positive.** Your leaving is not a time to take potshots at problems within the church. If you have not been successful in dealing with them while you have served the church, chances are your leaving will not solve them either. I do not mean to imply you act dishonestly or unrealistically, but remember this is a time for affirmation. Your ministry sought to strengthen the church. Your departure has the same goal.

• **Bring closure to your ministry.** You had an effective educational ministry in this church. You helped people become Christians and join the church. You ministered to them significantly at times of illness and death. You counseled them when they experienced personal and family problems. Some people found Christ as Savior and Lord of life because of your personal witness. Others were discipled by you. Some church leaders are persons you enlisted for places of leadership—you trained them, encouraged them, challenged them to be good servants and ministers of Jesus Christ. You leave with many memories of God's blessings upon people's lives. You walked with some of them in the shadows of the valley of death. Your life has intersected with their lives. Some ministered to you and your family in times of personal need. You have built deep relationships with the people of this congregation.

How do you bring closure to these relationships? Your ministry closes when you cease to serve that church as a minister. You are no longer their minister but you are and can be their friend. The church's loyalty and support belong to the person the church calls as your successor. Some attempt to flatter you when they tempt you to minister from afar. Always refer them to their present ME or minister. Assure them of your prayers about their concerns so the friendship or relationship is not broken. You can always attempt to meet the needs of friends but not as their church's minister.[10]

• **Leave your office in good order.** Your personal belongings—books and other items—are removed from your office. Leave what belongs to the church. This may be building plans, equipment the church purchased for your use, books purchased by the church, or other significant resources. Information related to the church's educational programs and other areas of your responsibility are arranged so your successor can easily find them. Filing cabinets are cleaned out, but church information and data are left. If you feel you need particular items, make copies for yourself. Tell a secretary or the pastor what you are leaving in the office, and show them where it is.

Ministerial Ethics

MEs ought to practice good ministerial ethics in leaving as in going to a church.

• **Resign in such a way that you safeguard the work left.** Your resignation should not come as a surprise to the pastor. The timing of your resignation should ensure the educational work will continue in a healthy way until your successor arrives. As much as possible, prepare the way for your successor.

• **Leave in good graces with the church and community.** Your relationships in the church and the community should permit you to return to any former church to serve again. You can look everyone in the eye without any embarrassment. This means all financial matters are settled or specific arrangements are made to cover them. As you leave, people in the church should have a good feeling about you and your family because your conduct in the community has been one of responsibility and you have been a practitioner of good citizenship.

• **Be cautious in returning to former places of service.** If you or your family cannot stay away from the former church, you probably should not have left it. It is wise to allow adequate time to lapse before visiting your former church, exercising finesse, discretion, and judgment when you do so. Your return visits are as a friend, not as educational minister. The initial visit is better when you are responding to a special invitation. Do not plan to return too often. As a courtesy, let your successor know when you are returning.[11]

After the Move

After you move to the new church, it is good to follow up with several matters related to the former church. Write letters of appreciation to the former pastor, former staff members, and individual letters of appreciation to former key leaders. Letters of appreciation are also appropriate for secretaries and custodial staff who were helpful to you in your ministry.

Once your successor has been selected, you should write a letter of congratulations. This letter has two purposes. One is to offer congratulations and the second is to offer encouragement. Remember what you felt when you first began the job. Assure the new ME of your prayers and support in his or her new venture.

Notes

1. D. L. Lowrie, *A Glad Beginning—A Gracious Ending* (Nashville: Broadman Press, 1988), 70. Lowrie writes from the perspective of the pastor, yet his insights are applicable to the ME and other staff members.

2. Duke K. McCall, *The Tie.* This is the alumni paper published by the Southern Baptist Theological Seminary, Louisville, Kentucky.

3. J. Ralph Hardee, *Church Staff Entrance and Exit: A Procedural Manual for the Minister of Education* (n.p., 1979), 2-3.

4. Lowrie, *A Glad Beginning,* 70-71.

5. Ibid., 66.

6. Ibid., 65-66.

7. Donald Smith, *Clergy in the Crossfire* (Philadelphia: Westminster Press, 1974).

8. Lowrie, *A Glad Beginning,* 67-68.

9. Ibid., 69.

10. Robert E. Bingham and Ernest Loessner, *Serving with the Saints* (Nashville: Broadman Press, 1970), 27.

11. Hardee, *A Procedural Manual for the Minister of Education,* 4-5.

Name Index